Tales of Mama and Other Reminiscences

Tales of Mama and Other Reminiscences

Lillian Bressman

Writers Club Press
San Jose New York Lincoln Shanghai

Tales of Mama and Other Reminiscences

Writers Club Press
an imprint of iUniverse.com, Inc.

For information address:
iUniverse.com, Inc.
5220 S 16th, Ste. 200
Lincoln, NE 68512
www.iuniverse.com

ISBN: 0-595-15056-X

Printed in the United States of America

Dedicated to:
My wonderful Mama and Papa
My beloved Husband
My devoted Daughter and Family
My loving Son

CONTENTS

ACKNOWLEDGEMENTS

I would like to thank my dear husband for his help in so many ways. I appreciate his kind patience in never complaining that he could not see the top of our dining room table that was often covered by my manuscripts for months.

I am especially grateful to my dear friends Nessa and Jerry Ben-Asher, Molly Burack, Dr. and Mrs. Max Pusin and Natalie and Ron Tambor for their sound advice, helpful suggestions, infinite patience and constant encouragement.

INTRODUCTION

Dostoevsky wrote in *The Brothers Karamozov*, "My dear children, you must know that there is nothing higher and stronger and more wholesome and good for life in the future than some good memory, especially a memory of childhood, of home. If one carries many such memories into life, one is safe to the end of one's days."

Stories and memories shared in the home leave long and lasting impressions on children far beyond childhood and into adulthood. Children internalize these impressions and hand them down to their own children. I can recall the actual feeling of my mother's hand in mine as she firmly clasped it when we crossed the street. I can close my eyes and feel her gentle touch as she braided my hair. These sense memories are so strong that they arrest time and allow for unforgettable reminiscences.

My relationship with my mother was very special. She was truly beautiful in every way. She was bright, loving, and compassionate with a delectable sense of humor. Mama delighted in puncturing the pompous. She cared passionately that her children grow up to be real *menshen* (decent human beings), sensitive to the needs of the less fortunate, and that they strive in some measure to make this a better world.

My writing about her first began as an expression of love. After her death, I often wondered, "What am I to do with all this love? To whom do I give this love that was hers alone?" Every day I still celebrate the life from which mine had come. Repeatedly I summon her wisdom and love and wrap them close around me like a comforting shawl. Nature has a way of replenishing and directing this powerful love and it now flows in an endless stream into my children and grandchildren.

Neither my maternal nor paternal grandparents came to America. As children, my sister and I hungered for a *bubbeh* and *zayde* (grandmother and grandfather). My mother and father felt our need and filled our lives with endless tales of our grandparents. They told us about the world they lived in and how they lived. As a result we felt very connected to family.

Today, the press is replete with sad stories of abused children and broken homes. My life experience was with extraordinarily loving Jewish immigrant parents who inculcated in me a love for humanity and *Yiddishkeit*. Because my childhood was so enriched, I have deep feelings about the need for storytelling. It provides warmth and continuity to life. When I hear my daughter hand down our family stories to her children, I experience once more the closeness of my parents, linking the past and the present with the future and I feel complete.

My tender and vivid recollections found their way into a column I have written for the New Jersey Jewish News since 1969. A wide readership's enthusiastic responses to those pieces and the many requests for a collection in book form have motivated me to compile this volume in which the stories have been arranged thematically. I have been told repeatedly that my stories resonate in readers and remind them of their own families. The uniqueness of being an American is that we are all products of the immigrant journey.

In this book I hope to share with you a glimpse of the stories, memories, impressions and humor that surrounded me as I was growing up and have shaped my life. My earnest wish is for the reader to enjoy them and to sift them through their own experiences.

Author's note on the spelling of Yiddish words:
While writing this book I checked three sources for the spelling of the English transliteration of Yiddish words.
For example:
>   *mashiach*—as spelled by Leo Rosten
>   *meshiakh*—as spelled by *The Yiddish Dictionary Sourcebook*

mehsiekh—as spelled by Uriel Weinreich's *English-Yiddish Dictionary*

Again and again I came across three different spellings for the same word.

Leo Rosten wrote there is no "standard" or official way of spelling Yiddish words in English. In 1937, the YIVO Institute for Jewish Research established governing rules for orthography, but they are widely ignored by editors and writers who use Yiddish words in English.

Two dialects dominated the way Yiddish was spoken. Litvaks were Jews from Lithuania or neighboring regions. Galitzianers were Jews from Galicia, a province of Poland/Austria. They each had their own distinctive pronunciation.

I heard Leo Rosten lecture many years ago. He said the proper way to spell a Yiddish word in English is to simply write it as you hear it. In order to keep my sanity I have opted to use my Litvak ear.

STORIES FROM THE SHTETL

Love of *Bubbeh* and *Zayde* Is Far Reaching

I never knew my grandparents. They did not come to America. They remained in Europe. Perhaps that is why I was always interested in how they lived.

Papa's grandfather, an eminent rabbi and scholar, was called "Modreh Tzopkeh" in Polish, and was known in Yiddish as a man with an *offen-eh kup* (open-minded, brilliant, filled with wisdom). He spoke seven languages and his reputation as a sage was legendary. When papa's relatives immigrated to America and we gathered together, they would pat my sister's head and my head and exclaim, "What an honor it is for you to be the great-grandchildren of the famous Modre Tzopkeh." Secretly, we were very flattered to have such a distinguished great grandpa from afar, but we would have preferred even a plain ordinary one nearby.

Papa's father was a known scholar. He spent his life poring over books and giving Talmudic interpretations and counsel. People from far and wide came to him for an *aye-tz*eh (advice). Although he had the required educational qualifications to be a rabbi, he chose to be a *dayen*. He decided questions of ritual and cleanliness, and settled disputes and family problems. He found solutions to many questions by consulting the Talmud. These treasured books contained the answers to the most difficult problems put before him. In a way, he was a forerunner of the present day psychiatrist. Instead of Freud's text and teachings, he used the Talmud.

My father was nine years old when his mother died after a brief illness. She left 11 young children. Grandfather found solace by spending time engrossed in his books. It was an escape from his painful plight. An orthodox man was not allowed to be without a wife, so a short time after his wife died he married a local widow from Warsaw. She moved in with a horde of her own children and proved to be a mean, stingy woman, a real Cinderella stepmother.

While Papa's father closeted himself totally in his book-lined study dispensing wisdom and advice to others, he was unaware of the conditions in his own household. His second wife fed her own children the little food that was available and often let her stepchildren go hungry.

When my father and his sisters and brothers complained to their preoccupied father, he answered, "Don't worry, God will watch over you." While this explanation may have been comforting to the children's souls, it did not relieve the hunger pangs in their stomachs. Wise men are not always sages in their own families.

Anti-Semites killed my mother's father when my mother was two and one-half years old. Her beautiful young widowed mother, 29 years old, was left with nine children. She worked hard to raise her children and never remarried.

I asked my Mama, "How did your mother and father meet?"

Mama answered, "It was a prearranged *shiddach* (match). My mother, Ethel, was 13 years old and the groom, Theodore, was not quite 16."

Some of Ethel's girl friends were already married off to skinny, scrawny, pimply youths and she was worried and frightened that this sad fate would befall her too.

When the *shiddach* was being arranged by both sets of parents, she pleaded with her mother, "Mama, mama, please let me take one glimpse of my intended, just a peek from far away. I cannot bear the thought of spending my life with an ugly husband."

Her mother assured her not to worry. The future groom came from a refined, scholarly family. Poor Ethel was not reassured as she thought that a skinny, scrawny pimply youth could easily come from a refined, scholarly family.

Her anxiety grew each day and on the wedding day they wrapped her face with thick veiling. Her heart pounded as she wondered what she would see when the veil was unwrapped. Much to her relief she saw a tall handsome young man with laughing eyes and a dazzling smile. It was love at first sight for both of them. They never ceased to be grateful for their good fortune in their perfect match.

I often think how lucky children are to know and grow surrounded by grandparents, and to physically see and feel the continuity of family. Although I was never privileged to know any of my grandparents, all my life I have loved them in a very special tender way.

Mama Learns to Cope with Life and Yenta

Mama was two and one-half years old when her father's bruised, limp body was found in a nearby forest. On the way to Pinsk to transact some business he was suddenly attacked by a band of anti-Semitic hoodlums. He suffered for several weeks before he mercifully passed away at age 29.

Mama and her eight brothers and sisters were left orphaned. My grand-mother and the older children worked hard to maintain the little business, a general supply store, attached to their modest village house. Everyone was assigned chores, and even though Mama was the baby in the family, she acquired many jobs as soon as she could reach high enough, or was strong enough to do them. Weeks passed into months, months into years, and the hard struggle continued.

Every two weeks Mama's handsome older brother, Moishel, rode his buggy into Pinsk where he bought supplies and merchandise. It was on one of these trips that he met the daughter of a fine merchant. Her name was Yenta. Moishel was impressed by her city manners, and after a short courtship, announced that he was going to marry Yenta. Preparations for the small wedding were exciting, and as was the custom, another room was added to the little village house where the newly married couple would live. Mama was 12 years old at this point and enjoyed all the fuss and flurry.

Yenta's arrival was most dramatic. She came with fancy leather luggage, an elegant plumed hat sat fashionably on her head, and she wore thick heavy eyeglasses. She was extremely nearsighted and could barely see any-thing without them.

Everyone stared at the eyeglasses, for this was the first time they saw a person wearing this strange appliance. However, the whole *mish-poch-eh* warmly embraced her. Yenta stood rigid with her hands clasped tightly in her muff.

In the weeks to come, it was soon apparent that she was full of lofty mannerisms and was determined to cling to them. Her nose was always up in the air and the neighbors said she had *fliggin in nuz* (flies in her nose). This was a colorful expression used to describe an uppity person. She never helped with anything and often quoted an old Russian saying: "Work does not make you rich, only round-shouldered." Her days were spent preening in the mirror or taking a stroll under her special parasol.

Yenta found it most convenient to have her mother-in-law serve her meals and tend her clothes. In the beginning, everyone waited on her, eager to be polite and make her feel welcome. As time went on, Yenta became more and more demanding. It deeply hurt Mama to see her mother cater to the arrogant girl with her affected city ways.

Mama was desperate and decided to have a long talk with her brother Moishel as soon as he returned from his next business trip. He was away much of the time and was unaware of his wife's tyrannical behavior in his absence.

Yenta was taking her daily afternoon beauty nap when Mama heard the horse and buggy in the yard. She rushed out, and before he could dismount from the buggy, she told him all the grievances and injustices that his wife inflicted on his family.

Moishel was greatly surprised, and promised to straighten everything out. He gave Mama a pat on the head and told her to dry her tears.

It turned out that Mama's pleas were wasted. Yenta denied everything. She accused "that 12-year-old *bluffer-keh*" of spinning lies about her. Moishel warned Mama that it is fine for a child to have an imagination, but to create a conspiracy against an innocent victim like poor Yenta was unforgivable!

"And," he added, shaking his finger in Mama's face, "the next time you try to make up a story about my wife, I'll give you a *chmoll-yeh* (clout) you won't forget." Mama realized that honest confrontation was not the answer to her problem.

The more unreasonable Yenta became, the more determined Mama was to get even. Yenta broke her only pair of eyeglasses and Moishel took them to the city for repair. It would take two weeks before they were ready. Meanwhile, Yenta groped about and walked very gingerly.

She had a large box of heavily perfumed face powder that she kept on the dresser in her room. A soft powder puff rested on top of the powder. Several times a day she would retire to her room and generously powder her face.

Mama was intrigued by this ritual and watched with wonder as Yenta smugly powdered layer upon layer upon her pampered face. Suddenly, a lovely thought occurred to Mama. While Yenta was sitting outdoors fanning herself with a rare imported fan, Mama went into Yenta's room, carefully emptied the contents of the box of face powder into a bag, and refilled the box with ordinary flour.

She placed the powder puff on top and closed the lid. The box was highly perfumed and the smell permeated the flour. For two weeks Mama had the delicious satisfaction of watching Yenta powder layers of flour on her face as she squinted into the mirror sans glasses.

When Moishel returned with the repaired glasses, Mama knew the pleasures she derived from Yenta's flour face were ended.

Mama was plotting her next move and she focused on Yenta's favorite hat, a fancy peacock-feathered hat. While feeding the chickens in the coop, Mama noticed that the chickens liked to sit on the rafters instead of the cold floor. Since there are no bathrooms in chicken society and sanitary conditions are most primitive, their droppings fell off the rafters on to the floor.

After one particularly hard work-filled day cleaning the coops, Mama was infuriated to see Yenta sitting under a tree munching on fresh blueberries. Yenta was complaining, "There must be a more modern way to keep the coops clean." Mama silently agreed, and one evening she took Yenta's peacock-feathered hat and gently laid it upside down-under the rafters.

The next morning Yenta's favorite hat wasn't even fit for a chicken to wear. No one ever found out how that hat was mysteriously spirited to the coop. Meanwhile, Yenta was not to be consoled by the loss of her hat. Mama secretly *shepped nachas* (had pleasure).

Mama was driven by a need for revenge on her sister-in-law for all the thoughtless, selfish actions Yenta imposed on the family. This time, Mama thought, she must think of something that would have a more permanent and lasting effect on Yenta.

Yenta had a city dweller's dreadful fear of mice. Although she considered herself sophisticated, her greatest fear, even greater than that of mice, was of the *dybbuk* (an evil spirit or a demon that takes possession of someone). This happy combination of fears made Mama's head spin with plans.

Business demands kept Yenta's husband away for long periods of time. Perhaps this added to her frustrations for she was especially cruel to everyone. Her demands grow intolerable. She spoke to her mother-in-law in a gruff voice and my mother ached when she heard her dear mother addressed in this manner. Mama clearly saw the need for drastic action. The time was now.

Late one evening, when everyone was asleep, Mama quietly crept into the storeroom where the corn, flour, and oats were kept in barrels. She carried a sock in her hand. It was no problem at all to catch a field mouse in the sock.

She ran back to the house and tiptoed into Yenta's room where Yenta was asleep, snoring with her mouth open. Mama gently lifted the corner of the *peh-reh-neh* (feather quilt) and released the mouse out of the open end of the sock into Yenta's bed.

Then, Mama went quickly back to the bedroom she shared with her mother. Within a few minutes Yenta's shouts of "A *dybbuk, a dybbuk*" (a demon, a demon) came echoing through the night.

My grandmother half awakened from a deep sleep and Mama whispered to her, "Go back to sleep. I know just what is bothering Yenta. I'll help her. Go back to sleep." After a heavy day's work, my grandmother was glad to drowsily slump back to sleep.

Meanwhile, Mama dashed into Yenta's room and heard her say in a choked frightened voice, "A *dybbuk*, a *dybbuk* has come to possess me. Help me. Save, me from *a schvartz yor* (black year). I'll do anything to make the *dybbuk* go away." Yenta's eyes were popping out of her head. She was almost in a state of shock.

Mama savored the scene. "Yenta," she said, very slowly, "you have mistreated us all and the *dybbuk* has come to show his displeasure."

"*Oy vay iz mir* (oh, woe is me)," Yenta moaned each time she felt the lively, active mouse, "I feel the evil spirits. Help, help, please help!"

It was the first time Mama heard Yenta say the word 'please.' Mama spoke with all the authority she could muster. "I happen to know a lot about the *dybbuk* and his ways. In order for him to leave your soul at rest, you must promise to always show respect for my mother and not abuse her. You must never again be bossy and mean."

"I promise, I promise," cried Yenta.

"And," Mama continued, "You must always keep your promise or the *dybbuk* will promptly return as soon as the promise is broken."

"I'll be good, I'll be a *mensh*" Yenta wailed, almost relieved that she was at last held accountable for her deplorable misdeeds.

In order to catch the mouse, Mama crept under the *peh-reh-neh* that covered Yenta. Yenta interpreted this as a comforting gesture and gave Mama a soulful thankful look. Mama's experience in catching field mice came in handy. Within a few minutes she held the little mouse firmly in her hand. Yenta knew nothing except for the fact that this child performed a miracle. Her little sister-in-law had exorcised the *dybbuk*. Tears of gratitude poured down Yenta's face.

After that night she exerted every effort to make life more pleasant for all. Occasionally Yenta's memory lapsed, and she would start to revert to her old *shticklach* (tricks), but the thought of the *dybbuk's* strict rules regarding broken promises was so strong that she was always on guard to correct her conduct. It worked like an effective post-hypnotic suggestion.

Yenta eventually turned out to be nicer than anyone dared hope. I cannot help but be proud of Mama. She was truly a pioneer in the annals of medical research. Long before scientific tools for behavioral modification were named, she used mice, hypnotism, and shock therapy to help solve a behavioral problem successfully!

A Baby—Lost and Found

Mama had a bad fall and broke her wrist and thumb. She recuperated in our home. When a friend asked, "Where did it happen?" Mama answered, "On the way to the store."

My friend replied, "What a dull way to break a wrist." Mama said, "So if I say I broke it playing tennis, it will heal quicker?"

All her life Mama has been very creative with her hands. She sewed beautifully and crocheted like a craftsman, or is it now called "craftswoman"?

Having her arm in a cast was particularly difficult for her normally busy hands. I tried to make the time pass by as pleasantly as possible.

Mama was like Scheherazade and "The Arabian Nights." She told me a thousand and one tales about her life in Russia. The original stories of The Arabian Nights were spun in Persian, Indian and Arabic. Mama's stories were handed down to me in Yiddish.

One day, as we were sitting under a tree I asked Mama, "As long as I can remember, our cousin Rosie was always referred to as *a ge-fun-en-eh kind* (a found child). Why was this so?" Soon Mama was unfolding an incredible tale.

Mama's older sister Mollkeh was a beautiful woman. She had a pale, delicate face with perfect features. Mollkeh was married to Meyer in Russia and they loved each other dearly. Within a year they were blessed with a handsome baby boy, Theodore.

Meyer decided to seek his fortune in America, promising to send for his beloved Mollkeh and their son as soon as he had earned enough money for their passage. Meyer came to America and worked long and hard as a presser of men's vests. He almost had the necessary money saved to bring his family over when he received a shattering letter from Mollkeh telling him that their precious son had died of scarlet fever.

Mollkeh was inconsolable. She was young and frightened and her husband was thousands of miles away. Meyer immediately took his hard-earned savings and spent it on his own fare back to Russia in order to be with his bereaved wife.

One year later, with the financial help of relatives, Meyer set out for America again, leaving a pregnant Mollkeh behind and trusting to God that this time fate would be kinder. Once more he worked in the sweat-shops, saving every penny until the happy day when he mailed a *shif's carte* (ship's passage) to Mollkeh and their three-month old baby girl, Rosie.

Some relatives and a few *landsleit* (people from the same town) were making the journey at the same time. At the appointed hour, they all met and were instructed to walk quietly together to a designated point where they planned to *ibber gon-ven-en dem greh-nehts* (steal across the border).

The travel agent would bribe the border inspectors to look the other way when the scheduled group of travelers would illegally cross the border without proper papers. The truth of the matter is that even if a Jew pre-sented himself with all the proper papers and his passport in perfect order, the border inspector would invariably find some minor technicality to reject him. The inspectors were poorly paid and supplemented their incomes by accepting bribes. There was always the risk of a last minute change in inspectors, and if the replacement inspector was not bribed beforehand there was sure to be trouble.

The travelers were warned to walk in silence. Mothers were given strict orders to place a pacifier, sprinkled with sugar, in the mouth of a baby. If a baby cried out, it could ruin the chances of the whole group if the cries attracted the attention of an unbribed inspector.

Mollkeh wrapped her few belongings in a straw suitcase, carried another bundle stuffed with diapers and sundry baby needs, then *vickelled* (rolled) the baby in a blanket and tucked the baby under one arm. She clutched the straw suitcase and the other bundle in her hands, and set forth with the group. As previously instructed, they trudged very quietly through the fields on the way to the border. Mollkeh, laden with packages, suddenly realized that the baby had slipped out from under her arm.

She whispered to her sister-in–law Fay-gel, who whispered to the others. Without a moment's hesitation, they all turned back to look for the baby. Soon they discovered little baby Rosie sound asleep in the field of grass. With grateful thanks to God, they all started to walk back towards the border once more.

Mama explained, "Now you understand why Rosie was always called *a ge-fun-en-eh kind* (a found child).

I was deeply touched and told Mama, "We can all learn a lesson from this story. What a beautiful spirit of selflessness they demonstrated when they all risked their futures by turning back to look for the lost baby."

Mama replied, "It only proves a saying in the Talmud. 'Righteous people say little but do much.'"

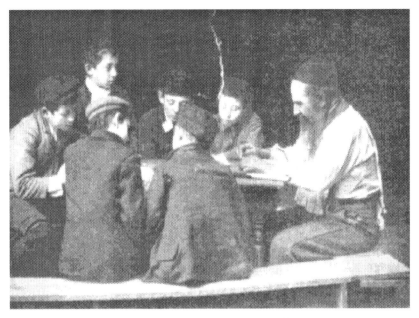

Cheder Bochers and *a Melamed*

A Beard in the Hand Is Worth Almost Anything

I was reading some thought-provoking newspaper articles recently on the state of our present educational system. They wrote of so many methods of teaching, from traditionally strict disciplinarian techniques to progressive, unstructured, open classrooms. Mama sat nearby knitting.

I read aloud. "Several students in a Bronx school splashed tar all over a very strict teacher. He could not get the tar out of his hair and the teacher had to have his head shaved." I asked Mama, "What is this world coming to?"

"That's nothing new," she answered, without losing the rhythm of her knitting needles. She saw the puzzled look on my face and told me her story.

Mama grew up in the small *dorf* (village) of Kritishen near the *shtetl* of Yoniveh. All Jewish boys attended *cheder* (Hebrew School). They had to learn to *dahven* (pray) and to say *kaddish* (a mourner's prayer). The *cheder* curriculum was limited and the pedagogical methods primitive. But it had a steady rhythm of drills, repetition, and firm *chmoll-yehs* (clouts) with a ruler across the knuckles or hands for the slightest infraction of any rule.

A young *melamed* (Hebrew teacher) was hired by the few Jewish families. Lessons were held at each home for three months. The teacher boarded at the home in which he taught and every three months he rotated to the next home. His pupils followed.

One room would be set aside as a schoolroom and the father of the house would hammer together a long wooden table and low wooden benches for the *cheder bochers* (students). The children called the teacher Rebbe and he occupied a chair at the head of the table where he could keep a watchful eye on all.

Girls were discouraged from going to *cheder*. They were expected to stay home with their mothers and learn how to cook, bake, sew and keep house. Mama's two brothers were attending *cheder* and she wasn't about to let them get smarter than she was. She was a liberated little girl and no amount of dissuasion could keep her away from learning. Every day she tagged along until she became a permanent member of the class.

The *melamed* was given lunch by the mother in whose home the class was held. A typical noon menu served by the *bol-eh-busteh* (homemaker) consisted of thick lentil soup, baked potatos, sauerkraut, sour pickles, home-made pumpernickle, lots of freshly churned butter and several galsses of tea poured straight from the samovar. The warmth of the coal stove permeated the room. After putting away this hearty lunch, Nacham, the teacher, could not keep his eyes open. He told the children to fold their arms on the table, cradle their heads in their arms and "take a rest."

He had barely finished barking his instructions when he laid his head on the table and started to snore loudly.

The young instructor had a disposition that could curdle vinegar and he had little patience for lively, prankish youngsters. When discipline was a problem, he pulled out his special ruler and hit hard, but only on the palm of the left hand. Mama's cousin Kalman pleaded to be hit on the right hand because previous hits by the teacher had swollen his left hand. Nacham was furious. "Never do I plant the ruler on the right hand! That would excuse you from doing your written homework, and you need your right hand to write." Of course, if the pupil was left handed, Nacham made an exception to the rule and reversed the procedure.

The atmosphere in the classroom was strained and the children banded together to fix Nacham once and for all. Cousin Kalman was the leader of the gang and his slogan was, "We'll make from Nacham, *nuch-im* (deceased or past tense)." Wild fantasies flowed forth.

Little Laibel thought it would be great to wait until after lunch when Nacham was sound asleep, then throw a sack over him and cart him away and lock him up in the chicken coop and let the chickens "pick on him like he picks on us." Kalman vetoed this idea.

"I know exactly what we are going to do," he said with a devilish gleam in his eye. "I have a scheme all worked out. Tomorrow I'll put gloves on my hands, wipe off the black axle grease from the wagon wheels with a rag, mix it with a little flour and water to make it more sticky, and the rest will be history." Kalman continued, relishing every moment of his importance, "Watch me, trust me, and tomorrow we will have full revenge."

The following day Nacham was particularly cross with the children and the ruler did not get a chance to cool off as he struck one palm after another. There was electricity in the air. Mama was the only girl in the class and she was warned not to make a false move.

Right after lunch Nacham put his head on the table for the daily rest period and in a few seconds his snores rang out loud and clear. The *melamed* who sported a long carefully cultivated goatee, had been nicknamed Goat's Beard by the children. Kalman quickly put on his gloves, tip-toed over to Nacham, took out the rag with the sticky axle grease and very gently lifted Nacham's goatee. With the dexterity of a safecracker, he generously spread the tar-like substance on the underpart of the goatee and carefully pressed it down on the table. The children were wild with joy and had to cover their mouths with their hands to suppress squeals of excitement. They watched Kalman dispose of the evidence, the rag and the gloves, like a professional.

Ten minutes later Nacham woke from his deep sleep and found his beard stuck tightly to the table. He could not lift his head and demanded that someone should fetch a pair of scissors and cut him loose. Kalman graciously volunteered and enjoyed every snip and slip. By the time he was pried loose, poor Nacham looked like a featherless chicken. He was seething mad and demanded that everyone hold out their hands. There was no doubt in his mind that he would find the tar on the hands of the culprit.

Kalman's foresight in wearing gloves while performing his *schtik* saved him from the slightest suspicion and he gained the awe and respect of all his classmates. That night Nacham left the *cheder*, never to return, leaving his ruler behind.

Mama slowly wound some wool around her forefinger, looked at me with a smile, and asked. "So nu, what's really new in the paper today?"

Mama Searches Pumpkin Patch for New Baby

Mama was the last of nine children. Anti-Semites killed her father when Mama was two-and-a-half years old. By the time Mama reached the age of five she noticed that most of her playmates had little sisters and brothers. She longed for a baby sister or brother of her own and she pleaded with her widowed mother to "please get a baby". Then she asked, "Where do babies come from?"

Her mother thought for a moment and replied, "Babies grow inside of *kir-bes* (pumpkins)."

A few days later when her mother took a driver and horse and buggy to town to buy supplies for the general store they owned, Mama thought it was a good opportunity to investigate the large pumpkin patch.

She climbed on a chair and took down a big kitchen knife and went outside to the garden. With all her strength she plunged the knife into one pumpkin after another looking for a baby inside.

When her mother returned she found Mama sitting dejectedly in the pumpkin patch still hoping to find a baby. Immediately Mama's mother saw that the whole pumpkin crop was completely ruined, but she hugged Mama closely, dried her tears and coaxed her back into the house. Later, Mama found out how babies were born by witnessing the birth of a calf.

Many years later Mama was settled in America, married, and with a family of her own. I was not quite five years old. She always took me along with her to pick up my sister Pearl at school at 3 P.M. To this day I remember the Russian folk songs Mama taught me as we walked and sang together. Usually we arrived early and waited for school to be let out. Almost every day a distinguished looking man passed by carrying a doctor's bag.

He always smiled and said hello to Mama, spoke to her briefly in Yiddish, and winked at me when he was close to us. Mama was filled with awe and admiration and pointed him out to me. "That's Dr. Newmann," she whispered, "he delivered you — he brought you into this world."

From then on I looked for him every day. Mama never told me this, but in my childish mind I figured it out. If Dr. Newmann brought me into this world, it was only logical that he brought me in his doctor's bag:

I eagerly watched for him to walk by. One day as I saw him approaching, I ran towards him, tugged on his coat and said in Yiddish, "Dr. Newmann, Dr. Newmann, *ich vill eich eppes zuggin.*" (Dr. Newmann, Dr. Newmann, I want to tell you something.)

He was surprised and amused at my intensity. He looked down and asked, "What is it?"

I continued, "*Ich vill eich b'dahn-kehn. Ir zine-t a goot-er un klug-er ducter.*" (I want to thank you. You are a good and wise doctor.)

Dr. Newmann was obviously pleased and flattered. He teased, "And what makes me such a good and wise doctor?"

I answered with great feeling, "*Ir zine-t klug vile ir hut mir ge-brocht tzu mine zee-seh mom-meh, tzu mine aye-gen-eh tire-eh mom-meh—un nit tzu kine frem-deh mom-meh. A-donk*, Dr. Newmann!" (You are wise because you brought me to my sweet mother—my very own dear mother — and not to a strange mother. Thanks, Dr, Newmann.)

Mama came to New Jersey and spent several weeks with us. We were busy almost every day. We went to the doctor, dentist and chiropodist in addition to attending to many of her other needs. One afternoon we returned late and I made some tea. We were sitting at the kitchen table when Mama reached over and tenderly put her hand on mine and in a voice filled with love said, "Yes, Dr. Newmann was a good and wise man. I'm so glad he brought you to me."

Stories of Greenhorns

All's Fare in Love, War and Trolley Riding

This story could never be written now that we have turnstiles and even exact change fare on buses. Shortly after coming to America, Mama spent a few days with her sister Mollkeh and family consisting of six children. It was slack season and Mollkeh's husband, Mayer, was temporarily out of work. As a matter of fact, with Mayer it was usually more slack than season!

Mama was registered in night citizenship school, and she was delighted when a cousin offered to get her a job in a dress shop "all the way uptown on 23rd Street."

She awakened early and dressed carefully, for this was to be her first day as a worker in America, the land of golden opportunities. Her sister Mollkeh was so hurried and harried attending to her brood of children that she forgot to give Mama two nickels for carefare. Mama simply did not have the heart to ask her. She knew only too well how her sister and family were struggling to make ends meet.

However, Mama was undaunted, and with all the great optimism and enthusiasm of youth, she was sure she would somehow get to her job.

Mama carefully read the detailed directions her cousin gave her and waited on the right corner for the trolley car to take her "uptown to 23rd Street." She hopped on the trolley and took the only remaining seat, the back seat.

Years ago in New York there were always two men to run the trolley. One was the driver and the other was the conductor. The conductor would go to the seated passengers, collect the fare, make change and give transfers. He would frequently know many of his daily passengers and inquire about their health and families.

All this transpired while the trolley was en route. When the conductor finally reached Mama in back of the trolley she didn't have the fare. She politely said, "excuse me," two brand new words in her English vocabulary, and she quietly got off the trolley.

Meanwhile she was about twelve blocks closer to her destination. She then waited for the next trolley and repeated the same procedure (always making sure to sit in the back) until she reached 23rd Street.

Later in the day, Mollkeh remembered that she had neglected to give Mama the 10-cent fare. She was gravely worried. "Such an innocent child — surely she is lost and wandering the streets of this strange land."

She was greatly relieved to see Mama back at 6 P.M. "Oy my poor *schvester* (sister)," Mollkeh cried, hugging and kissing Mama.

"How could I let you roam about without fare? I ruined your day's work. Where were you? What did you do"?

"Don't worry," Mama smiled reassuringly. In America they let you sample the trolley free for about twelve blocks. If you don't like it you can get off and try another. I 'sampled' going both ways!"

Di Green-eh Kuzeen-eh

The common name for a newly arrived immigrant was "green-eh" (shortened from greenhorn), green meaning fresh, new and unripe. A song that enjoyed enormous popularity in the early 1900s was "*Di Green-eh Kuzeen-eh*" (The Green Cousin). Due to the fact that the song has a lively tempo and a lilting melody, few people are aware of the plaintive lyrics. After humming the melody for years, I carefully listened to the lyrics and was surprised to hear the words convey a sad social comment;

Mama felt "*Di Green-eh Kuzeen-eh*" was so popular in its day because it accurately reflected the plight of countless eager young girls, newly arrived in this country with dreams and hopes of finding the streets paved with gold. Their high hopes for a promising life were never realized. Their future was devoured by the long harsh hours in sweatshops.

Loosely translated, the song tells of a pretty cousin who came to America with her cheeks like red oranges and her feet begging to dance. Her words were like music and she was happy and gay. Soon she found work in America and was enslaved at her job. After many years of toil, she was totally worn out from her hard labor. Gradually her cheeks lost their rosy glow and turned a sallow green. Beneath her pretty blue eyes, dark black lines were etched. Today when she is asked "How are you, *green-eh?*" She sadly answers, "May the blazes take Columbus' land."

While many immigrants were caught in this unfortunate web, there were also many success stories. They were repeated endlessly to feed hope to the others. Numerous immigrants were dynamic individuals blessed with nimble intelligence and indestructible optimism. They managed to subsist on their wits. They possessed a special sense of humor reflecting their joy and anguish, their aspirations and discouragements. The ability to laugh at theirselves was instrumental in their survival and gave them the strength to face the uncertainties of life in a strange land.

Mama had a collection of humorous "greenhorn" stories she loved to tell. Mama and Papa both liked this one. A husband and wife emigrated from Europe and immediately registered in night school. They spent their afternoons in a nearby park. Soon it was apparent to them that many of the Americans were reading a big newspaper,"The New York Times." In order to try to look American and appear educated, they brought a copy of "The New York Times" to the park although neither could yet read a word of English. They found a bench, sat down, opened the newspaper, and pretended to read.

"Moishe," whispered the wife to her husband, "turn your newspaper around, you're holding it upside down!"

"How do you know?" her husband whispered back indignantly. "You can't read English either."

She pointed to an advertisement, "See the picture of that man—by you he's walking on the ceiling!"

Papa's loved to tell this story. Bessie came to America from a little town near Pinsk, Russia and was met by her rich and pretentious son, Philip. "Mama," he said," I'll see to it that you have the best of everything in this land of plenty." He reserved a suite for his mother at the Plaza Hotel in New York and filled it with beautiful flowers. As an added surprise he arranged to have a bottle of the finest champagne and a tin of the most expensive caviar sent to her room.

The next day he called and asked his mother if she slept well. "And by the way," he inquired, "did you enjoy the gifts I sent to the room?"

His mother answered, "To tell the truth, my son, the flowers were lovely and the soda tasted fine, but the little huckleberries in the tin smelled from herring!"

Mama's favorite "greenhorn" story follows. Sam and Moe came to America as two penniless immigrants. They were fierce competitors and in a few years Sam made a fortune while Moe plodded along and struggled to make ends meet. One day they met and Sam could not refrain from boasting, "I'm taking a month's vacation, I'm going to Hawaii. I just love to visit the islands!"

"A waste of good money," replied Moe with a touch of envy in his voice. He continued, "Believe me, I know. I already saw all the interesting ones."

"What are you talking about?" asked the surprised Sam in disbelief, knowing full well Moe's financial straits.

Moe took a deep breath and answered in a ringing voice, "What islands did I visit? You really want to know. I'll tell you; Manhattan, Staten, Long and Coney, not to mention Ellis!"

Papa
Notice the gold watch chain in his pocket and the pin in his lapel.

With Right Photographer, a Picture's Worth a Thousand Words

My husband and I recently returned from Los Angeles where we spent a week at the Uiniversity of Judaism. We found our courses of study enriching and exciting.

One of the highlights of our stay was our visit to the Skirball Cultural Center and Museum in Los Angeles. Moshe Safdie, the Haifa-born architect brilliantly blended the traditional and contemporary into an edifice of breathtaking beauty. The exhibits on Jewish history, holidays, ceremonial objects, customs and rituals were handsomely mounted and visually delightful.

One exhibition, "Becoming American Women," that showed young immigrant ladies coming to these shores, was of particular interest to me. Soon after their arrival, relatives or social workers from the settlement houses took the young women in hand. They physically transformed the newcomers from greenhorns to fashionable Americans. Off came the babushkas, peasant dirndl skirts and embroidered blouses. Long, thick braids were cut and hair was styled in the latest bob. Heavy, sensible shoes were replaced by pointed, high-button shoes.

A placard at this display described the plight of a young greenhorn who was frightened when she saw the shoes and assumed that American women were born with pointy toes. "I'll never be able to squeeze my wide Russian feet into these shoes," she lamented. "I guess I'll look like a greenhorn forever."

I felt deeply drawn and closely connected to the immigrant experience portrayed by the tableaus. They hauntingly brought me back to Mama's and Papa's long journey and difficult transition from small *shtetl* to America.

What came to my mind was a particular custom that was prevalent at the time. It was de rigueur for relatives to take the greenhorn to a photography studio to sit for a professional photograph. Home cameras were non-existent. Mama's sister, Lena, took her to Gus' Photography Studio located on Rivington St. on New York's Lower East Side. Gus was not exactly an Alfred Stieglitz. Just as a Bachrach portrait was the status symbol of high society, Gus was the photographer of the immigrant.

Gus kept several costumes in a back room for customers to wear during their picture-taking sessions. Mama chose a riding habit and Gus gave her a riding crop to hold. Mama thought this was a thoroughly American style of dress. She had not yet cut her thick hair. Gus asked her to undo her braids and arranged her hair to fall over her shoulder. This treasured photograph sits on my piano. Right next to it, I placed a photograph of myself taken when I was a little more than a year old. I was sitting on a pony. The picture was snapped by an itinerant photographer who earned a meager living by roaming from street to street with an old box camera and a tired pony. He set up his studio wherever he saw a mother who was willing to pay 10 cents for a picture of her child seated on the pony. When he was ready to snap the photo, his head disappeared under a black cloth so he could see the image in the ground glass. This was the first and last time I sat on a horse.

When my daughter Beth was in fifth grade, she invited a classmate to our house. The friend, Holly, lived in Short Hills and had been taking horseback-riding lessons for several years. When Holly noticed the two photographs on the piano, she asked my daughter, "Who is the little girl on the pony?"

"My mom," Beth replied.

Holly then asked, "And who is that young lady wearing an old-fashioned riding habit and holding the crop?"

"My grandmother," Beth answered.

Holly, clearly impressed, exclaimed, "Gosh I never knew you came from a long line of horsewomen! Did they own their own stables?"

It took Beth almost an hour to fully explain our connection to the sport.

When Papa came to America, he too, was taken to a local photographer to sit for his portrait. Years later after Papa passed away, Mama give me a portrait of him taken soon after he came to America. I looked at it closely for the first time. "I know how poor Papa was," I said to Mama, "but I see in the photograph that Papa is wearing a gold watch chain. Is it attached to a gold watch? He also had a stickpin in his tie and a pin in his jacket lapel. How could he afford all this jewelry if he had no money?"

Mama explained, "Papa never owned a gold watch or a watch chain. This was a prop that Gus the photographer put on Papa for the picture and took it off right after he snapped it." Mama continued, "And the stickpin in the tie and the pin in the lapel were painted in. Gus was noted for making every *kobtzen* (poor man) look like Baron de Rothschild."

When I viewed the Skirball Museum exhibition of some of the bejeweled, affluent-looking immigrants, I couldn't help but wonder if Gus had a hand in their appearance.

This proves, after all, that a picture is worth a thousand words and with the right photographer, much more!

Bintel Briefs Recalled

In 1971, a glowing review of "A *Bintel* Brief" compiled and edited by Isaac Metzker appeared in the New York Times book section. The book was a collection of letters to the editor of the Jewish Daily Forward that provided a sensitive and nostalgic record of the personal and economic problems faced by the Jewish immigrant.

The advice to the lovelorn and the Ann Landers column probably stemmed from the Bintel Brief.

Another outstanding and compelling publication is "Portal to America, The Lower East Side, 1870-1925," edited by Allon Schoener. This book is based on the exhibition that was presented at the Jewish Museum in 1966 and contains many brilliant and haunting photographs of that era. A memorable part of the museum presentation was Zero Mostel reading the heart tugging "Bintel Briefs" on closed circuit TV.

"Troubles, Big Troubles and Terrible Troubles" were the recurrent themes in this human symphony.

Here are examples of two "Bintel Briefs."

1. Year 1908:
   Dear Editor,
   I ask you to give me some advice in my situation.
   I am a young man of twenty-five, sixteen years in America, and recently met a fine girl. She has a flaw, however, that keeps me from marrying her. The fault is that she has a dimple in her chin, and it is said that people who have this lose their first husband or wife.
   At first I laughed at the idea, but later it began to bother me. I began to observe people with dimpled chins and found out that their first husbands or wives really had died prematurely. I got so interested in this that whenever I see someone with this defect I ask about it immediately, and I find

out that some of the men have lost their first wives, and some of the women's first husbands are dead.

This upset me so that I don't know what to do. I can't leave my sweetheart. I love her very much. But I'm afraid to marry her lest I die because of the dimple. I've questioned many people. Some say it's true, others laugh at the idea.

Perhaps you, too, will laugh at me for being such a fool and believing such nonsense, but I cannot rest until I hear your opinion about it. I want to add that my sweetheart knows nothing about this.

Respectfully,
The Unhappy Fool

Answer:

The tragedy is not that the girl has a dimple in her chin but that some people have a screw loose in their heads! One would need the knowledge of a genius to explain how a dimple in the chin could drive a husband or a wife to the grave. Does the angel of death sit hiding in a dimple? It seems to us that it is a beauty spot, and we never imagined it could house the Devil!

It's tragic humor to find such superstition in the world today. It's truly shameful that a young man who was brought up in America should ask such questions. To calm him, we wish to tell him we know many people with such dimples who have not lost their first husbands or wives, but live out their years together in great happiness.

2. Year 1955

Worthy Friendly Editor,

My husband and I have been happily married for six years. This is a second marriage for both of us. We each have children, all who are now independent. I have a big problem facing me, and I beg you, earnestly, to give me advice.

When my husband's first wife died, he was very grieved and had a double headstone placed on her grave because he didn't think he would marry again. As time passed, however, and his wound began to heal, he realized it is not good to be alone. After that, the following occurred:

My present husband and I are *landsleit* (from the same town or area) and have been good friends since our youth. We also belong to the same society and we often met at the meetings. When he lost his wife I was already a widow, and as time went on, we poured out our loneliness to each other and he suggested that we should marry. I accepted his suggestion and we were married. We adjusted well and we are both happy.

At times we have occasion to go to the cemetery of our *landsleit*, where my first husband, my brother, relatives and my present husband's first wife are buried. Each time I pass her grave and see the double headstone with his name, I feel so bad that I get sick. This is always on my mind because I would like my present husband to lie near me, after a hundred and twenty years, and our graves should not be far apart. So I ask you what can be done about it?

With thanks and respect,
A.D.

Answer:

Since you and your husband belong to the same society, you must have known about the double headstone before you married him, and you said nothing to him about it. Then you must now make no demands of him. You must understand it is no minor task for your husband to remove the headstone from their double grave. Just for the sake of his children and members of the society, it is difficult for him to do this.

You married your second husband, not to have a piece of ground together, but because you wanted a friend for life, and since you have achieved that, you should be satisfied. Why should you destroy your happiness with thoughts of what will happen in the future?

Before quoting the two Bintel Briefs, I called the office of the author, Isaac Metzker. He was still working at the Forward Building, then located on East Broadway, on the Lower East Side of New York. I needed permission to quote several Bintel Briefs for this story. I dialed the number and his secretary answered. I told her why I was calling. She spoke with a heavy Yiddish accent. "From vair are you callink?" she asked.

"New Jersey," I replied."

"*Oy*" she said, "Mr. Metzker is not by his desk. Right now he is autographing his book in de book department by Macy's. I'm sorry you hed to vaste a lung distance cull all de vay fuhn New Joisey. Please cull him tomorrow munnink." I promised I would.

The next morning I called and his secretary answered. She immediately recognized my voice. "*Oy vay*," she said in an apologetic voice, " I kent kip up mit him. Today he is also not by his desk. Right now he is signing his book by Bloomingdales. I'm so sorry you hed to vaste annuder lung distance call all de vay fuhn New Joisey. Since his book got such good rewiews by de New Yuck Times, he tinks he is Villiam Shakespeare. But tomorrow, for sure, he vill be here."

The next morning I called and his friendly secretary greeted me like an old friend. She put Mr. Metzker on the telephone. His voice sounded like an old man. Actually, he wrote the Bintel Brief column from 1906 until 1971, 65 years. Assuming he was 25 years old when he started writing it led to the conclusion that he was approximately 90 years old.

I told him I was calling to ask permission to quote from his book. He asked me if I had read the raves the press was showering on him. I told him I did. "Lady", he said, "you are now speaking to a literary giant." He paused for a little while and then told me, "All right, I give you permission to quote only two Bintel Briefs. I'm not one to give away free samples. Tell your readers to buy the book!"

When Fate Takes a Hand

Mama often remarked, "A human being is no more than a human being." This was her way of explaining the need to respect the strong whims of fate that shape our lives more than we care to admit. The most carefully mapped paths are frequently rerouted, and strange, mystical powers appear to be in the driver's seat. At times we try to chart our destiny, meddle and change the course of fate, only to find that intervention can lead to disaster. Mama quoted from the sages. "Even a wise man does not know when to accept *ba-shert* (predestiny) without question."

Perhaps there is a moral to the following stories.

When I was a little girl. Mr. and Mrs. Kramer and their only daughter, Ruth, lived on the third floor. The Kramers were quiet, scholarly people who were wholly engrossed in culture and learning. Daughter Ruth (first in her class) graduated from college and became a high school teacher. Her parents were very proud of her accomplishments and introduced her with the phrase; "This is our daughter Ruth, our *teacherkeh*!"

One day Ruth went to a piano recital and a polite, serious young man sat in the next seat. They spoke during intermission and he asked for permission to take her home. His name was Sam. Pretty soon Sam was ardently courting Ruth. He always brought her a gardenia corsage. Sam was nice looking, neatly dressed, and courteous, even to the little urchins playing on the stoop (I was one of them). He always stopped to ask about our games as he gingerly stepped around us to enter the hall leading to the apartments. Sometimes he would pause, pat my head and say, "You have curls just like my little sister." All the kids on the stoop liked him. Normally, adults paid little attention to us except to shoo us away.

It was obvious (even to me, a child of ten) that Sam and Ruth were madly in Love. Mr. and Mrs. Kramer were alarmed and implored, "Ruth dear, how can you waste your time on Sam, an uneducated man, a trolley car conductor yet, and you a *teacher-keh*! He is simply not up to your standards. He will never make a living. You will struggle all your life."

Ruth defended him. "Sam is not an uneducated man. He is a trolley car conductor temporarily and he is saving his money to go into business in the future. He is as well read as I am and is self-educated. Also, he attends City College at night and one day he will graduate and get his degree. What do you expect?"

"Expect!" retorted the Kramers. "We expect a young man worthy of you. Everything you say about him is 'He's going-to-be', or 'One day he will' or 'In the future.' But right now he is a nothing, absolutely a nothing!"

Sam tried hard to be especially nice to the Kramers. It was a losing battle. His every gesture was misinterpreted, for they viewed him with jaundiced eyes. Poor Ruth was torn. She was very close to her parents. They were relentless and they hammered away endlessly, "You'll be throwing your life away, you must stop seeing that worthless Sam." They finally wore her down and with a heavy heart Ruth told Sam she would no longer see him. He cajoled, pleaded and begged her parents to give him a chance to prove himself, all to no avail. With a smug smile the Kramers shut the door. "Good riddance," they sighed with relief.

Ruth was heartsick. She lost weight, grew wan and pale and never regained the sparkle in her eyes. Also, much to her parents' dismay, she never accepted another date and remained a spinster the rest of her life.

As for Sam, he worked hard, continued in night school, married and opened a business that became known as S.Klein Department Store (On the Square in New York). As Mama always said, "When fate beckons, sometimes it is wise not to mix in"

Tessie, our other neighbor on the third floor, had a rich cousin. She talked about her cousin constantly. No matter what topic was being discussed, Tessle managed to weave her rich cousin Henrietta into the conversation with intimate details of Henrietta's life style, clothes and bank account. It gave Tessie a sense of wealth by association. According to

Tessie, there was only one problem. Henrietta was so busy leading the life of a "debutante," she never got around to finding the right man to marry. Now that she was almost 40 years old, she was ready to settle down.

Henrietta exhausted all her rich contacts with nary a marriage proposal in sight. In a low moment, she condescended to allow her poor cousin Tessie to look around for a suitable prospect or a reasonable facsimile. Most of the men Tessie knew were poor *shnooks*.

One day, Mama's single cousin, Hershel, came to visit. Tessie spied him in the hall and was impressed by his appearance. He wore a beret and an ascot. Hershel was a struggling writer whose career up to that point was three-quarters struggle and one-quarter unpublished writing. He was desperately looking for a sponsor. Tessie was hot on the scent and followed him into our apartment. Within two minutes she geared the conversation around to her wealthy "available" cousin Henrietta. Hershel was wildly enthusiastic about meeting her.

Mama listened to the arrangements with a wry smile. She once met the legendary "Rich Henrietta" and remembered her as being vain and spoiled, a *tchotchkeleh* (plaything).

Mama tried to warn her cousin Hershel, "Don't sell your soul, it's a high price."

Hershel, who five minutes earlier was a *farbrenteh* (hot) liberal, tried to rationalize his eagerness to meet this prospective patron. "This merger, if it comes to pass," he explained, "will help me to enlighten the impoverished masses in this world."

Mama didn't swallow this declaration. "Remember Hershel," Mama cautioned, "Gifts make slaves. So try to keep your feet warm and your head cool."

Hershel did not heed Mama's advice. Tessie introduced him to Henrietta who immediately overlooked Hershel's insolvency by projecting herself as the wife of an eminent literary figure. Hershel now answered to the name Henri. He continued to write and continued to be unpublished.

She tried hard to be civil for the first few months of their marriage. But her true character surfaced soon after she realized that his pile of unpublished work was growing and her dream of being the wife of a literary lion was reduced to being with a literary *gornisht* (nothing). They moved to a fancy Park Avenue apartment and invited some friends to the housewarming. The bloom was off their marriage and Henrietta was in a dark mood. In front of their friends, she could not help boasting. "If not for my money, we would never pay such exhorbitant rent and we wouldn't be here. And if not for my money we would never own such beautiful imported furniture and these magnificent antiques."

Hershel was normally a mannerly, sensitive man. But he could not restrain himself and surprised everyone by saying, "Henrietta, my wife, I think you have the right to know that if not for your money, I wouldn't be here!"

Ah, the Fickle Finger of Fate.

STORIES OF WORK AND POVERTY

A Model Greenhorn

Mama sat watching the TV commercial. I started to say something and she put her fingers to her lips and motioned me to "shush."

I looked at the commercial and saw a lovely young girl combing her long, thick beautiful hair. In the background, an announcer was heard describing her luxurious, shiny tresses. Then he lowered his voice dramatically and said in a most sincere tone, "Confidentially, this young lady had thin, limp, unattractive hair just six months ago when she started to use Simone's Sensuous Shampoo every day."

The commercial made clear (in a subliminal way) that the shampoo not only enriched her hair, but apparently enriched her mode of living. The end of the commercial showed her stepping into a Rolls Royce escorted by a handsome young man with a full shock of gleaming hair.

I could not imagine why Mama found this segment so intriguing. "Mama," I asked, "Why are you glued to the set watching this junk?"

She smiled and said, "Because it proves to me that over the years, the more things change, the more they are the same."

Mama explained that when she was a young girl, not quite seventeen years old and newly arrived in this country, her cousin Kalman helped her get a job in a dress factory. The hours were long, the work boring and the salary was three dollars a week. She immediately enrolled in Americanization courses that were given at night. The teacher, Mr.

Epstein was a jolly middle-aged man. He was kind and tried to be helpful to his students who were all full-fledged greenhorns fresh off the boat.

One evening, Mama wearily told a fellow student that she could barely keep her eyes open in class after putting in a 10-hour working day. Mr. Epstein probably overheard her remarks and the following week he asked her to stay after class. She thought, for sure she spelled the words wrong on the spelling test. When the class was dismissed, the teacher told her he had a friend who was looking for a young lady to fill a special job in the drug store he owned.

Epstein gave Mama the address of the drug store and urged her to go to see his friend, Mr. Cohen, the pharmacist. She put on her best and only good dress for the interview and borrowed her sister's *yontif* (holiday) hat. She anchored the hat with a large pin and set out to seek the new job. In the front entrance window to the pharmacy stood two large apothecary jars filled with colored water, one light blue and, the other light rose. Mama was very impressed by the fancy display.

She found Mr. Cohen busy filling prescriptions. She waited patiently until he was free and told him that her night-school teacher, Mr. Epstein, suggested she see him about a special job he had open. Mr. Cohen looked at Mama approvingly, then asked her to remove her hat. She was a little suspicious as she took out the large hatpin and placed the hat on the counter.

He then explained to Mama that the position was for a hair model and he requested her to take the pins out of her tightly coiled bun and let her hair loose. Mama was puzzled and she started to take out her hairpins vowing to herself that this was positively the last thing she would remove. When all the pins were out, her long thick hair fell gracefully to her waist. Mr. Cohen was delighted.

He kept repeating, "You're perfect — just perfect for this job. You are a gorgeous greenhorn, exactly the person I was looking for!" Mama felt embarrassed although she appreciated the compliment and asked for more specific details regarding the job. Cohen said, "I'll start you at fifteen dollars a week."

Mama couldn't believe her ears. Imagine progressing from three dollars to fifteen dollars a week. It was really true. America is the land of golden opportunity for all. Her future boss showed her the corner window setting consisting of a Victorian rattan vanity desk and chair. On the desk stood a brush, comb and oval mirror in an antique stand and a large jar of Cohen's Magic Hair Cream prominently displayed. Again Mama asked exactly what her job entailed.

Cohen explained, "Just sit in the chair in the window and be yourself. Let your hair fall loose. Every now and then pick up the brush and brush your hair gently and slowly. In between, you can sit gracefully and read a book." Mama was overjoyed. It did sound like a strange job. Perhaps this was an old American custom. Besides, she loved to read, and getting paid to read was something she never envisioned in her wildest dreams.

The first day she was self-conscious of the many people who stopped to look in the window. Some friendly folks waved, she timidly waved back. After work, she went to the Seward Park library with her brand new library card (another American miracle) and took out as many poetry books as was allowed. She floated home, her arms filled with the books, her heart filled with joy.

That night she also washed her hair before going to bed with the only hair-care treatment she used in America, a bar of Fels Naptha brown soap. Mama found it hard to fall asleep, her mind was awake figuring out how to best put to use her enormous salary. She decided that five dollars would go to her mother in Russia, five dollars to her sister Mollkeh to help buy food for her children, three dollars Mama would keep, and two dollars she would put into the bank to start a savings account.

Mama worked in the window for several weeks. She hungrily read Yiddish novels and poetry and was a steady customer at the library. Mr. Cohen was delighted. Business was boomng. While in her enclosure, Mama could not see or hear the customers in the store. Everything went smoothly until one day Mr. Cohen summoned Mama to leave the window and come into the store.

Mama walked inside and up to the counter and saw a towering, heavyset woman arguing with Mr. Cohen. He motioned Mama to come closer and said in a weary, exasperated voice, "This is Yetta Ginsburg, a very big customer (the description fit in more ways than one) and a very skeptical customer. She doesn't believe a word I'm telling her about your hair."

Yetta waved Cohen aside with one motion of her enormous arm and directed her comments to Mama. "Tell me, young lady, I want to hear it from you own lips. Exactly what do you use on your hair?"

Mama promptly answered, "I use only Fels Naptha soap to wash it, nothing else." Mr. Cohen looked like he was ready to jump into the colored water in one of his huge apothecary jars. Yetta glared at Cohen, poked a finger at him and screamed, "Faker, Faker!" as she strode out of the store.

Mama was suddenly struck by the realization of her part in the scheme. She was now totally aware of how she was being used to deceive customers. Mr. Cohen was willing to forgive her for being too honest, begged her to stay and requested that she be more tactful in the future. Mama politely told him that although she needed the job, she could not be a part of his scheme.

Mama gathered up her books, slowly put her hair up in tight coil, fastened it with hairpins and put an end to her modeling career.

He's an Uncashed Check

When I was a little girl, Fanny Finkel and her husband lived next door to our apartment on the second floor. They had a turbulent relationship and their loud quarrels (on every issue) echoed all the way up to the fifth floor.

Yussel Finkel was a hard working man, an ironworker by trade. He was employed in a factory making heavy iron fire escapes. Each morning at 7 A.M. as he was about to leave for work with his lunch pail, Fanny screamed after him, "Be careful, watch yourself. Don't get hurt with that heavy iron. Your life is in your hands.

"*Oy Gottenyu* (oh God)," she implored, wringing her hands, "guard him from harm." At night when he returned weary from work, she would greet him on the stoop with a tirade of complaints.

It was not a matter of eavesdropping, but her piercing voice bounced along the halls and penetrated right through our door. Mama and Papa felt that despite their constant bickering, Fanny really loved him and showed great concern for his health and safety.

Yussel was basically a modest man and tried to conceal his embarrassment by telling the neighbors, "When we were engaged, I did all the talking and Fanny did all the listening. After we were married a short time, she did all the talking and I did all the listening. Now we both do the talking and arguing and the neighbors do all the listening."

Fanny's rantings were interspersed with deep mournful sighs. One morning we heard her wailing, "Anybody who is envious of me is crazy. You work at such a dangerous job. If something happened to you at the shop, what would I do? And what would be the fate of your four little children? We don't have a penny to our name. You must take out an insurance policy to protect us. I found out you can take out a policy for a premium of 50 cents a week.

Fanny nagged and hounded poor Yussel until he agreed. The day he applied for a life insurance policy was cause for great jubilation. Fanny's strong voice resounded on every floor, from the janitor in the basement to the boys flying pigeons on the rooftop.

Meanwhile the insurance agent explained that the policy would not become effective for two or three weeks, taking into account that Yussel had to pass a physical examination in addition to the time it took for routine processing.

Fanny was tense and found it difficult to wait until the policy came through. Every morning we heard the same refrain, "Yussel, watch yourself, be very careful, remember your life is in your hands." As soon as the insurance company notified them that the policy was in effect, Fanny abruptly changed her tune.

We were shocked and couldn't believe our ears. "Yussel, do me a favor," she hollered. *"Ver geh-har-get* (get killed or drop dead). With my luck you'll never even get a splinter in your finger. How can I ever hope or expect a heavy iron to fall on your head?

"All we do is argue and fight, we're like oil and water. Look at me," she cried. "See how shabbily I'm dressed. A stranger would think I'm the hired cook."

Yussel was quick to retort, "Not if they tasted your cooking." He tried to ease the tension and joked, "Do you know there are three companies after me?"

Now it was Fanny's turn to snap back. "Yes I know, the gas company, the electric company and the finance company! Oy, I'm so tired of being at poverty's doorstep. Now with your insurance policy—to me you are a walking check I can't cash while you are alive. So please do me a favor and *ver geh-har-get* so I can live decently. Figure it out, the insurance benefits are worth more than you are."

This went on year after year. Apparently her husband turned a deaf ear. Fanny and Yussel celebrated their 50th wedding anniversary. He is still walking around—uncashed.

Pangs of Honesty Bear Fruit for Shaindel

Cousin Esther remained a *koptzen* (poor woman) all her life. Each new day was a financial struggle for her and her large family. Mendel, her husband, was a relaxed man who was often unemployed.

Gallantly he let his wife worry about tomorrow and such matters as food, heat, rent, etc. He laughingly quoted, "Poverty is no disgrace, which is the only good thing you can say about it."

Esther answered, "Mendel, you're laughing with tears in your eyes as she added more water to the soup to stretch a meal. The rent was two months overdue and Mrs. Cohen, the landlady, was not known for her empathy.

Esther and Mendel were blessed with six wonderful children. Shaindel, their eldest daughter, was 15 years old, beautiful, sensitive and responsible. She was so mature and careful with money that the owners of the fruit and vegetable store where she often marketed for her mother, offered her a job after school. She eagerly accepted, knowing that the $2 per week salary would be a great help to her family.

After a few days, Shaindel proved to be a valuable asset to the store. She took care of customers, gave accurate change, and swept up. It was apparent to the owners, Mr. Ludwig and his wife, Tzippeh, that they had a treasure in their new worker.

As Shaindel was preparing to leave one evening, Tzippeh approached her with a large brown paper bag filled to the top. In a syrupy sweet voice she said, "Here, take home some leftover fruits and vegetables to your family."

Shaindel thanked her and hurried home as fast as she could. The bag grew heavier with each step. Her family had not eaten fresh fruits and vegetables in months, and she was happy to be bringing home this special treat. When her mother emptied the contents of the bag on the kitchen table before the hungry, eager eyes of her family, they could not believe what they saw.

Wrapped in tissue paper were rotten apples, pears, black bananas, over-ripe grapes and withered scallions. A foul smell matched the sickening feeling in the room.

Their faces fell and stomachs growled. Shaindel was humiliated, she could not be consoled. Her mother advised her to say nothing to her boss, Tzippeh, for fear that she might lose her job. Knowing how much her salary was needed, Shaindel continued to work diligently.

Tzippeh often expressed her personal attitude towards money by say-ing, "It's a disease I'd like to catch, but not to spread." She asked Shaindel if there were anything she would like to take home from the store.

Shaindel painfully remembered the other incident and warily asked, "May I have the wooden crates in which the fruit comes packed? My mother could use it for kindling for the stove." Tzippeh agreed and also volunteered the tissue paper in which the fruit was wrapped.

"Take as many tissues as you like," she said. "They can also be used for toilet paper. Just stuff them in the wooden boxes and carry home as many as you can."

True, the family had more wood for the stove, and they had a surplus of fruit wrappings for the toilet, but food was still scarce.

Shaindel watched customers buy fresh fruit and vegetables and ached for her own family to enjoy them. One evening, while she was gathering the wooden boxes and wrappings to take home, Mr. Ludwig and Tzippeh were having supper in the back room. Shaindel suddenly found herself in the grip of a powerful urge she could not control and began to pack some wrapped fresh fruit into the boxes. She carried the heavy crate home and did not feel any pangs of regret as she watched her family devour the "fruit" of her labor.

Esther, her mother, was very Orthodox and she immediately saw God's hand in this blessing of food. She told Shaindel that she was going to the store the very next day to personally thank Tzippeh for the *mitzvah*. Shaindel turned white and her knees trembled.

"*Oy-gevalt!*" she thought, then suddenly she took hold of herself and heard herself telling her mother in a calm voice, "Oh, no, Mama, Tzippeh doesn't want you to thank her, it is a much greater *mitzvah* when one doesn't receive thanks for a good deed." Esther believed her daughter and promised not to spoil Tzippeh's *mitzvah*.

All night long Shaindel could hardly sleep. She thrashed about and woke with a start, drenched with perspiration. Not only did she steal, but she also lied to her trusting mother. Early in the morning, Shaindel tearfully confessed to her mother. Esther was deeply touched and enfolded Shaindel in her arms, dried her daughter's tears and softly told her that they would go to the rabbi for an *aye-tzeh* (advice).

They put on their best clothes and walked several blocks to Henry Street. A handsome young boy answered their knock on the door and ushered them into the rabbi's dimly lit, book laden study.

The air smelled of old leather and bindings. Shaindel could not stop the flow of words and tears, she told the rabbi everything. The learned rabbi listened intently, heaved a heavy sigh and slowly said, "My dear child, there is nothing *ge-schribben* (written) that can absolve one of stealing. You must never do it again. However, considering that your motivation was so pure in heart, to help your hungry family, I'm sure that somehow God will show his kindness in this special case."

The rebbitzin invited them to stay for tea and mondelbread. The handsome young boy joined them. His eyes were riveted on Shaindel since her beauty overwhelmed him. Somehow her sadness added a touching dimension to her perfect features.

Yes, God was merciful, and in His strange way showed his forgiveness. Shaindel and the rabbi's son fell in love and were married. They have five wonderful children and every holiday they all distribute fresh fruit to needy families!

Special 'Exercise' Program

Some time ago, while reading The New York Times Book Review Best Seller List, I found it interesting to note that out of 15 leading titles, four books pertained to diet and exercise. Obviously, in the eyes of Americans, "slim is beautiful."

In Mama's generation, the opposite held true. Being thin was considered a social stigma attached to a person who was undernourished and unable to afford plenty of food. Even an-experienced *shadchen* had a problem fixing up a skinny, gaunt girl. A young lady with a round, softly curved figure was attractive and desirable. People would go to the mountains on vacation to "fix" themselves. A vacation was not successful unless one put on a few pounds.

Anyone with ample body flesh was thought to have more strength. A skinny baby was a poor reflection upon the mother and a young mother worked hard to fatten her infant by *shtupping* (stuffing) food into the baby each time it opened its mouth.

More was better and *zoftig* (plump) was preferred. With this in mind I smiled when I viewed an old New York Times Best Seller List.

(1)   The Beverly Hills Diet
(2)   Never Say Diet
(3)   Jane Brody's Nutrition Book
Dr. Atkins Nutrition Breakthrough

Corresponding to the above titles, I could clearly envision the best seller list in the Jewish Daily Forward 50 years ago.

The Mostly Minsk *Meichels*
Always Say *Fress*
Gertie Goldberg's Gourmet *Gribbeness*
Dr. Kronkite's Chicken Fat and *Kishka* Breakthrough

There is no doubt that we have all been indoctrinated to exercise. The media grind out glowing reports on the benefits gained by keeping a regular regimen. Doctors agree that exercise is healthful and life prolonging. We have become a nation of physical "fitnicks." Men with big biceps and small hips are everywhere jogging and lifting weights.

Women are working-out with the help of health spas and special machines and equipment. Early in the morning, they are running, swimming, stretching, tightening, toning, flexing, limbering, strenghtening and firming their muscles and figures.

In Mama's day, the women also started to work out early. Every morning at 6 A.M., Mama piled wood into our coal stove to start the fire. The stove was used for heating the house and for cooking. Cold water tenements did not have hot running water. Mama boiled the family wash in special large vats on top of the stove and the steam from the boiling water provided a morning facial for her skin. After scrubbing the clothes on a hand washboard and rinsing them (developing hand muscle strength and endurance), Mama would wring the wash out by hand (tightening her pectoral area).

The next step was cramming the wash into a huge basket and carrying it up four flights of stairs to the roof. That accelerated the pulse rate and got the heart pumping more than aerobic dancing. Reaching high to hang the clothes on the rooftop line stretched and slimmed the upper body and waist while at the same time providing an opportunity to inhale fresh air thus expanding the lungs. Running down the stairs firmed the leg, calf and thigh muscles.

Mama prepared and served a hot and hearty breakfast for all of us and packed a lunch box for Papa to take to the shop. After she walked the children safely to school, the real day's work began. Dishes were washed, beds were aired and mattresses turned (great for limbering the shoulders). She then scrubbed the floors with a stiff hand brush (increased range in lower and upper arm and strengthened the knees).

Mama often cleaned the windows with Bon Ami Powder on Sunday when I was home from school and could help her. It was my job to clean the windows from the inside. Mama would lift the double-hung window and sit halfway out on the sill to clean the outside of the window. I always feared that Mama would lean back too far and fall out. From the inside I held on tightly and pressed down on her knees to firmly secure her on the sill. I loved to see her beautiful face appear through the windowpane, as she wiped off the opaque Bon Ami in graceful circular motions. I was relieved when she lifted the window to safely ease back into the house.

Of course, emptying the *schissel* (pan of water) under the wooden icebox was a daily chore (increasing flexibility of the back). I must also include marketing, cooking and baking (the kneading of the dough enhancing finger and hand coordination). These activities were all part of the regular routine.

Instead of lifting weights, Mama lifted the heavy iron she used to press the pile of laundry (tightening the abdomen). Mama sewed all our clothes on her Singer Sewing machine with the heavy black-iron foot treadle (toning her ankles).

In essence Mama was practicing physical fitness long before it was in fashion. Looking back, I marvel at the fact that although Papa was not a rich man, he did provide Mama with the equivalent of her own private spa, though admittedly the "equipment" was primitive!

Not to mention that in between she managed to run to classes and concerts at the Settlement House. And most important, with her busy schedule, Mama found time to volunteer her help to the Home for the Aged. She spent hours feeding the residents who could no longer feed themselves. Her face lit up as she explained, "This exercise is good for the soul!"

Mama's Sweatshop

The Power of Words

Mama was born in Russia in a *dorf* (little village) called Yonaveh. Her early years were spent in this rural setting filled with clean fresh country air. She was one of nine children. Two of her sisters and one brother immigrated to America. The rest of the family remained in Yonaveh.

After he lived in this country a few years, her brother-Itzhak sent Mama a *shiff's carte* (steam-ship passage) and she sailed for America, the *goldeneh medina* (the Golden Land). Mama was almost 17 years old.

Relatives still recall her glowing beauty and perfect cameo features framed by two long, thick, lustrous braids. She had warm bright brown eyes, natural rosy cheeks and a flawless complexion. Heads turned to admire her lovely, graceful figure.

When she arrived in America, Mama went to live with her sister Mollkeh and her family on the Lower East Side of New York. Mollkeh's husband, Mayer, was a sweet man who was frequently unemployed. He barely eked out a living for his wife, five daughters and a son. Their tiny cold water tenement had two bedrooms. Mollkeh and Mayer slept with the two youngest babies, and Mama slept on a folding cot squeezed into the second bedroom she shared with the other four children.

It did not take long for Mama to realize that America was not exactly the golden land she envisioned. She longed for her mother and family in Russia and she was homesick for the wide-open spaces, the fruit orchards and the clean fresh country air. However, she did not complain, and the excitement of being in a new country was stronger than her growing doubts. Immediately, she registered in night school and was wildly enthusiastic about her Americanization courses.

At the end of the first week in America, a cousin, Kalman Goldstein, came to Mollkeh's home bursting with the wonderful news. By a stroke of good luck; he found a job for Mama in a sweatshop on 23rd Street between Sixth and Seventh Avenues, and he made arrangements for Mama to meet Mr. Laibovitz, the shop foreman.

Mama was elated. She had no idea what a sweatshop meant. Laibovitz approved of Mama and sat her down at a sewing machine. He showed her what was expected, piecework on ladies' garments. He was pleased to see that she was a quick learner. Mama sat next to a row of pressers, and the fumes from their gas irons made her nauseous. After a few weeks, her sister Mollkeh sadly and silently noticed that Mama's rosy cheeks were gradually turning pale pink. At this point Mama would have gladly given a whole week's learner's salary for a breath of fresh air from the old country. However, she was young and optimistic and remained convinced that this was merely a start towards a better life in America.

In order to continue the shamefully low wages, the bosses kept the learners at apprentice pay, (three dollars a week) for as long as they could. After a few weeks, Mama mastered all the required skills, basting, pulling, cutting, finishing and buttonhole making. She spoke to the foreman, "Mr. Laibovitz, there is nothing left to learn. When can I be put on the regular payroll and earn five dollars a week minimum?" He said he would have to take it up with the "higher-ups."

This was simply a stalling technique and for weeks Mama's salary remained a learner's three dollars a week even though she was now teaching newcomers in the shop. Mama and the other girls in the shop sat with their young bodies bent over the machines. Laibovitz walked back and forth, back and forth, prodding them on in a commanding voice, "Hurry up. This order must go out today." Every day the order had to go out "today."

Mama's pay continued at three dollars a week. Some of the older workers took her aside and urged her to join the union or she would never see a five-dollar weekly minimum paycheck. Also they pointed out that she was now entitled to regular piecework rates as she was no longer an apprentice.

Mama attended all the union meetings. Soon she was elected to assist the union shop steward. Two months later she was made a delegate to help organize special committees when the workers voted to strike. Mama did not like to picket because the scabs the boss hired to try to break the strike frightened her. But she fulfilled her picketing assignments and worked with the union for a peaceful and fair settlement.

Far from her serene existence in Russia, Mama's life suddenly became very busy. Every minute was filled with activity. In spite of the long dreary working hours, she was dedicated to the union, participated in rallies in Union Square, attended night school and helped her sister Mollkeh with the children and chores. Mama also found the time to attend lectures and poetry readings at Cooper Union every Sunday and to go to the Yiddish theater.

She had an insatiable thirst for knowledge and culture and soon found herself part of an intellectual group of young people. Exciting discussions on philosophy and politics usually ended as lively debates.

Russian novelists were most popular, and Yiddish poets and their poetry reflected the feelings of the workers' souls. The most revered of the sweatshop poets was Morris Rosenfeld. The following poem was a special favorite of many workers and one they committed to memory:

> *"I work, and I work, without rhyme, without reason*
> *Produce, and produce, and produce without end.*
> *For what? and for whom? I don't know, I don't wonder*
> *Since when can a whirling machine comprehend?*
>
> *"No feelings, no thoughts, not the least understanding,*
> *This bitter, this murderous drudgery drains*
> *The finest, the best and the richest,*
> *The deepest, the highest that living contains.*
>
> *Away rush the seconds, the minutes and hours*
> *Each day and each night like a wind-driven sail*
> *I drive the machine, as though eager to catch them*
> *I drive without reason—no hope, no avail."*

With the union's help, Mama finally did get her deserved raise. Every week she handed her salary to Mollkeh to help feed the children and pay the rent, deducting only her carfare and a small amount for absolute essentials.

There were several young girls from Mama's *shtetl,* who, by the same stroke of good fortune were lucky enough to find jobs in the same sweatshop. They sat together at work, doing piecework under the piercing eye of Mr. Laibovitz, who constantly rushed them. This speed-up system existed in all shops and a slower worker soon found himself dropped from the payroll and out of a job.

The girls sat together, and because the work was so tedious, they told jokes to offset the grim long hours at the machines. They could work while they talked without missing a beat. At times, the jokes were a little off-color. It helped make the day pass. Sitting nearby and not part of Mama's Litvak group, was a young girl, a Galitzianer. She was a first cousin to the Big Boss and her name was Jennie Kolodney. However, she Americanized her name from Jennie to Joanie and assumed lofty airs. She repeatedly told everyone she was a superior person and came from a distinguished family. Actually, she was a rigid uptight snob. Mama could never understand why she was so snooty and made such a fuss over her heritage. The truth was (and everyone knew this) her father was an ordinary wagon driver.

The Litvak girls privately called her "Phony Joanie Baloney." She complained to Laibovitz that inasmuch as she was a genteel lady of high moral character, it was degrading to her to sit next to those Litvak shop girls and hear their off-color jokes. She demanded that Laibovitz stop the Litvaks from telling those corrupting jokes or else she threatened to take her complaint right to her cousin, the Big Boss.

Laibovitz, ever mindful of his job, told Mama and her fellow Litvaks they must cease telling these stories and must respect and be sensitive to a fellow worker's exceptionally high ethical and moral standards. The Litvak girls followed his instructions. They had to watch and censor every word and nuance and the jokes turned sour. The days seemed grim and endless again. Jennie was smug in her victory and never lost an opportunity to flaunt her refinement.

A few months later, Jennie suddenly quit her job and left the shop. She was married within a very short time, in December. Six months later, in June, Jennie gave birth to a bouncing nine-pound baby boy.

Laibovitz, the foreman, was astonished. He was in a state of shock. The Litvak shop girls insisted that it was their off-color jokes that demoralized Jennie and led to the loose behavior that caused her pregnancy. Mama had her own theory. With a straight face and a twinkle in her eye she carefully explained to a bewildered Laibovitz, "Jennie was so pure, so sheltered, so naive, she didn't even know it took nine months to have a baby. In her great innocence, she thought it took only six months!"

Mama often told us this true story. Many of her stories carried a subliminal message accompanied by an appropriate proverb or two. At the conclusion of this tale she would pause, then say, "Which only proves, never judge a book by its cover," or "Still water runs deep," or better yet, "Never underestimate the power of words!"

Champion's Cue Stick Handmade by Papa

My father died many years ago. I think of him often and whenever I think of him, I am filled with special warmth.

Papa was a crafter, an artisan wood carver and turner. He created beautiful wood sculptures and made frames for art museums in Europe. When he came to America, he found that due to the industrial revolution, hand crafting was virtually obsolete. Papa had a hard time finding work. Eventually he landed a job with M. Katz and Company in a shop that manufactured cue sticks. Papa found it difficult to adjust to mass production. Somehow he managed to put a special individual stamp on his work and Mr. Katz, the boss, was quick to notice this. Katz contacted Willie Hoppe, who was then the billiard champion of the world, and told him that he was mailing Hoppe a hand-turned sample cue stick made by a European crafter. After that, Papa custom made all of Mr. Hoppe's cue sticks. The sticks came in different weights and Papa made them with exactly the weight and balance that the champ requested.

Hoppe's career began at age six. In 1906 he defeated the international French champion and retained his title for 13 years. He traveled a great deal and gave exhibitions throughout the United States and abroad. According to an agreement with Mr. Katz, Hoppe's staff prominently displayed a placard at each exhibition. In bold letters the placard read "Mr. Hoppe's cue sticks made exclusively by M. Katz and Company." Naturally this was good for business and Mr. Katz basked in the attention and prestige added to him and to his company. But he didn't bask enough to raise Papa's $12-a-week salary.

Papa's artistic talent found expression in designing and embellishing Mr. Hoppe's sticks with hand-inlaid figures interlaced with mother-of-pearl. Mr. Katz showed Papa a letter he received from Mr. Hoppe saying that he had never seen such beautiful crafting in his whole career. He wrote that on his many world tours and exhibitions, countless people remarked that his cue sticks were truly works of art. Katz told Papa that he was very moved by the letter. But apparently not moved enough to offer a raise in salary.

Mr. Katz was a tyrant and squeezed every ounce of work out of his employees. He never had a kind word and constantly threatened his workers: "With a snap of my fingers I can fire you." The employees got together and decided to ask for a dollar-a-week raise per worker. Katz was furious and shouted he would rather close the shop than grant this "unreasonable" request for a raise. The men decided to join the union and go on strike. An enraged Katz told them, "Over my dead body will I allow a union shop!"

Papa came home and told us he was going to carry a placard the next day and picket the shop. It was bitter cold and all day I worried along with Mama and my sister Pearl that Papa would be freezing. Pearl and I came home from school and huddled around the kitchen table right next to the warm coal stove. We tried to concentrate on our homework, but our eyes kept looking at the kitchen clock.

About four o'clock in the afternoon Papa came home. I rushed to open the door and found him standing with one side of his face covered with blood. Somehow Mama kept calm and she quickly chopped some ice off the block in the icebox. Pearl dashed to get the ice bag. I found some clean rags. It seemed like a long time before the bleeding stopped.

I still remember the weary and defeated look on Papa's face. He explained that he arrived at the shop and joined the other employees who were picketing peacefully. Mr. Katz hired some scabs to cross the picket line and throw bricks at the strikers. He wanted to scare them off and break the strike. Papa was hit with a brick on the side of his face. His scars healed, but left a permanent impression on all of us. Mr. Katz won the strike. The workers went back to work without a raise.

Many years later I read in *The New York Times* obituary column, "M. Katz, philanthropist and leading manufacturer of billiard cues, died." He left $2 million to a hospital and a wing was dedicated in his memory.

Although my father and the other employees were not mentioned in the dedication, they rightfully should have had their names engraved on the wing.

The obituary continued, "Mr. Katz was noted for being the exclusive manufacturer of cue sticks for Willie Hoppe, the most famous billiard champion of the world."

When I finished reading the sentence, I actually said out loud, "Made by Benny Bernstein."

A few days later I showed the obituary column to Mama. She read it, paused for a long while, and said, "I guess Mr. Katz didn't know that charity begins at home. I feel sorry for him." She explained that in his greed to make a fortune, he was not generous enough to share some of it with the people whose toil, sweat and blood helped him acquire his wealth.

Mama repeated, "I really feel sorry for him—he never knew the joy of giving while living."

Pearl and I tried, but could not feel sorry for Mr. Katz. We were not as philosophical as Mama was.

Papa said, "Katz knew the price of everything, but the value of nothing."

Papa died at age sixty-seven. He worked hard all his life and was never driven to be a financial success. The love he gave to his family enriched his life and our deep love and respect surrounded him. His other love was classical music. Papa knew what was really important in life.

STORIES OF GUESTS AND RELATIVES

Entertaining, Then and Now

All through my early years our little apartment in New York was filled with a constant stream of immigrant families. The reputation of my parents' warm hospitality spread like wildfire throughout the Russian *shtetl*.

So, quite naturally, we frequently welcomed new arrivals to our house straight from Ellis Island. They came with wicker luggage, and a few *land-sleit* (people from the same area) brought knapsacks secured by tight knots.

Unexpected dinner guests never posed a problem. Mama simply opened another "box" of salmon, sliced some fresh pumpernickel and *tsi-bel-ehs* (onions) with vinegar, and the table was set. Conversation was the most exciting course of the meal.

Invariably someone needed a place to sleep over, and in order to stretch the walls of our tiny apartment, I was assigned to sleep in the kitchen. Mama would set up three kitchen chairs, and in lieu of a mattress, she would place a plump feather pillow on top of the bare chairs. Then she would gently put a heavenly soft *peh-reh-neh* (feather quilt) on top of me.

As I grew taller, the chairs were spaced farther apart. I really did not mind being dispossessed as I enjoyed sleeping near the cozy warm kitchen coal stove.

I loved to hear the interesting conversation drifting in from the next room. Many times my eyes grew misty as I raptly listened to the heart-rending tales of their struggles and hardships. I particularly enjoyed the descriptive names given to friends and relatives.

"What news do you bring from *Yussel der shainer?*" (handsome Joseph) or "How is *Far-bissen-eh Fay-galleh?*" (bitter stubborn Fay) were routine questions.

My mind would conjure up pictures of these people, and when they came to America and to our house, it was fun to see how accurately I envisioned them. Astonishingly enough, *Far-bissen-eh Fay-galleh* looked exactly as I imagined her.

One day I ran to answer a sharp knock on the door and I warmly welcomed *Fay-galleh* although I never set eyes on her before. She was flattered and amazed that I recognized her although I had never seen her. Little did she know that her grim set face and tight scowl were as accurate as identifying fingerprints.

Having company was the natural rhythm of our bustling household. In juxtaposition, entertaining today has grown to ridiculous proportions. Having guests sleep over is a traumatic experience for some hostesses.

Shortly after I was married, my husband had to be out of town for a week. When he mentioned this to a friend and his wife, they insisted that I spend the week with them. I arrived with my toothbrush, shorts and bathing suit for what I thought would be an informal, relaxed stay. My hostess announced that she had invited a small group of people to a cocktail party in my honor. The intimate welcoming party of twelve people lasted until 2 A.M. By this time I felt warmly welcomed and thoroughly sleepy.

At last I was alone in the guestroom. My hostess had thoughtfully provided fresh flowers on the night table next to several of the latest best sellers. Carefully placed across the bed was a glamorous nightgown hemmed with ostrich feathers. I looked around, half expecting to see Jean Harlow emerge from a cloud. Soft stereo music was wafting through the room. The stereo set was so cleverly hidden that my frantic search could not find the knob to shut the darn thing off. I wearily got into bed only to find that the sheets and pillowcases were perfumed. I started to sneeze without a stop. I also discovered that ostrich feathers tickle.

As I covered my head with the perfumed sheet to shut out the irritating stereo, I thought, in between the sneezes and tickles, how wonderful it would be to spend the night on the cozy kitchen chairs.

Tante Lena's Secret of Youth

Tante (Aunt) Lena and Mama were sisters but they were as unlike as day and night. Mama was a natural beauty while Lena was a firm believer in assisting nature. She frequently went to the beauty parlor where she had her hair waved and dyed a flamboyant reddish-blonde. Mama was prematurely gray, and it took me a long time to understand why Lena never had a gray hair on her head.

While Mama was busy taking night school courses, Lena was fast becoming a fashion plate. She avidly studied all the ladies' magazines and assumed the latest postures, poses and gestures in her desire to become thoroughly *modrin*.

When Mama saved enough money to buy a dress, Lena the *mayvin* would accompany her to the dress store. Sometimes the saleswoman remarked, "Now, that's a smart dress."

Mama did not like that expression. "So what's smart about a dress, a *schmattah*, it graduated from college maybe? It hangs like a rag on a hanger and suddenly it becomes smart?" I was always very careful to say a dress is made well, the material is soft as butter, the style is becoming; but smart, never!

Tante Lena was married to Uncle Joe, the owner of a lady's coat and suit store on Division Street in New York. They were married 30 years when Uncle Joe died. A year later Lena married Ben. Although Lena was eight years older than Mama (the youngest in the family) Lena lopped 10 years off her age, and was suddenly the baby in the family. At least that's what she told Ben, and Mama went along with it so she wouldn't spoil the *shiddach*.

Lena and Ben learned all the latest ballroom dances. They even did the *tvist* (twist) and won several dance trophies. They ran from one contest to the next. Papa was never fond of Lena and her frivolous ways; a light head was how he described her. After reading a particularly disturbing headline in the newspaper, Papa looked at Mama and he could barely control the tremor in his voice as he said, "The world burns and they prance and dance." My sister Pearl nicknamed them Ginger Rogers and Fred Astaire, and the nicknames stuck in the secret confines of our house.

Ben died after they were married 14 years. Twelve months later Lena was going steady with Jake. She called Mama to tell her she wanted Mama to look him over and give an opinion. "And you wouldn't believe it," she excitedly added on the phone, "he dances 'dewinely'." Mama's heart fell. She still had visions of poor Ben dancing himself into the grave, where unsuspecting Jake would probably follow. Still, she shook these thoughts from her head and told Lena she would be delighted to meet Jake.

They came for dinner the next week. Lena made a dash for the bedroom to dab on some more rouge and powder and Jake looked closely at Mama.

"Mrs. Bernstein," he asked, "although your hair is gray, you have such a young face. Tell me, are you Lena's younger sister?"

Mama didn't know what *Bubbeh-myseh* (tall tale) Lena had given Jake. Who knows, she thought, maybe Lena decided to tell the truth this time? Mama was really afraid to answer when suddenly Lena's voice called out loud and clear from the near-by bedroom. "Jake, vot a foolish qvestion to esk. Der is only vun enser — vee are tvins!"

Mama Meets a *Landstman, Vuss Machst Du, You All?*

Mama was sitting in her kitchen reading the *Jewish Daily Forward* when the doorbell rang. When you live alone in New York, you have to be cautious. Mama called out, "Who's there?"

"Kalmon Goldstein," answered the voice behind the door. Mama sat frozen in her chair. "But Kalmon Goldstein was my second cousin and he died 20 years ago — and I don't believe in ghosts," she said."

"I know, I know," answered the voice. "I was the departed Kalmon Goldstein's cousin, too. We were named after the same grandfather, and I knew your whole family in Russia. So open the door already. Let's not *funfer* (double talk) around any more. I'm 78 years old and time is running short. I came all the way from Texas, and it is easier to get into *Gan-aidn*, (paradise) than by you-all in the house."

Mama read so much about clever ruses used by robbers to get into apartments that she decided to play detective. "If you really knew my family, then what was my mother's name, and what was my brother's name?"

"Ethel and Moishel," the voice answered. Mama decided it was safe to let him in. After all, how many thieves would have this information?

She started to unlock all three locks and double locks and made a rattling noise as she unhooked the two separate chain latches. With all the security precautions, he probably thought he was entering Tiffany's. Goldstein proved to be a fine, charming old gentleman who spoke English with an interesting Russian-Yiddish-Texas accent. He spent hours with Mama recalling their youth. The following week Mama arranged for a reunion with four of their childhood friends and they all had a nostalgic, mellow time.

Mama kept me informed about these exciting events. I asked her, "How come Mr. Goldstein settled in Texas?" She explained that he came straight from Ellis Island to the Lower East Side and was advised by relatives to go to Texas to seek his fortune. After living in Texas 58 years, his wife passed away. It was then that he decided to turn his prosperous business over to his sons and come east to find whatever remaining *mishpocheh* and *landsleit* he could locate.

'Mama, what kind of business did he have in Texas?" I asked. *Eppes* the *chine-ick* and *ges rench* business, I think," she replied.

"I'm not positively, 100% sure," she continued, "but what else could it be? He said he was in the kettle and rench business. A kettle is a *chine-ick* no? And a rench, by me is a ges rench."

It took me a while to realize that Goldstein was a Texas cattle rancher.

A Tender Reunion for Mama

The wave of Jewish immigration in the late 19th Century and early years of the 20th century changed the history of this country. Many wonderful ingredients were added to the melting pot by the newcomers. Anthropologists feel that the more we know about the aspirations and struggles of our immigrant ancestors, the more we enhance the understanding of ourselves.

This true account of Mama's voyage to America is a recollection of a long journey filled with promise and hope. The story concludes with a tender reunion that ocurred many years later.

When Mama left Russia 80 years ago, it took six long weeks to travel by boat to America. She traveled steerage class. Her first cousin Ida Kalodney and Ida's little three-and a half year-old son Beryl boarded the ship with Mama. They were grateful to be together and eagerly looked forward to the exciting journey ahead.

Most of the passengers became seasick as soon as the boat started to move into turbulent waters. The ocean was unusually rough the entire trip. Mama's cousin Ida was deathly ill and could not lift her head off her pillow. Any physical movement made her violently nauseous. She was unable to eat and lay motionless in her crowded steerage quarters. Almost all the other passengers were similarly afflicted.

Mama felt perfectly fine and did not experience a tinge of seasickness. Her appetite was hearty and her spirits were high. Because her cousin Ida felt so wretched and helpless, the complete charge of little Beryl fell upon Mama who was not yet 17 years old.

The steerage passengers were huddled together like a herd of cattle. Mama never saw such crowds and she trembled lest little Beryl, who was a bright, curious and active child, would get lost in the milling multitude of strange people. The only safe solution was for Mama to tightly hold

Beryl's little hand in hers. They were practically glued together for the six weeks. Mama lost her heart to the precious little boy.

Beryl Kalodney and his family settled in Brooklyn and Ida and her husband were blessed with three more sons and one daughter. Beryl and one other brother became pharmacists. One went into business and the other brother became a doctor.

The Kalodneys were known for their warmth and hospitality. Our family took the Pitkin Avenue trolley and crossed the bridge to Brooklyn almost every week to visit them. There the whole *mishpocheh*, Yankees and greenhorns would gather and have a wonderful time.

We always enjoyed our visits. Ida insisted on giving us her home-baked cookies to take home, and my sister and I would munch on them while waiting for the trolley back to New York.

Years later, after Ida and her husband passed away, the house in Brooklyn was sold. Their children married and moved to distant points. Somehow the family drifted away geographically and we did not keep in close touch.

As Mama grew older, her fond memories of the long voyage to America grew sharper. She spoke longingly of her sense of closeness to little Beryl and often repeated, "I can still feel his little hand curled tight in mine. Every day for six weeks we were *tzu-geh-tchepp-it* (glued) together, and all the years that have passed cannot unglue that closeness."

David Kalodney, the youngest brother, married and moved to Fair Lawn, N.J. I called and spoke with David on the phone and told him about Mama's frequent recollections of her long journey to America and her special feeling for his eldest brother, Beryl. Beryl was now living in Queens, NY. I asked David to try to bring Beryl and Mama together and he promised he would try. Unfortunately, Beryl's wife was seriously ill and passed away. Beryl himself had a long bout with illness and his recovery took time. I felt the sands of time slipping away but never gave up hope that somehow this belated reunion would come about.

One day I received a call from David Kalodney. He too felt a sense of urgency and excitedly told me that he and his wife had arranged to pick up his brother Beryl in Queens and they would be coming to visit Mama on Tuesday. I immediately called my sister and brother-in-law in New York. They said they would not miss this special reunion and would join us so that we would all be together for the eventful meeting.

When we arrived to visit Mama, I was a little concerned lest it be too much of a shock for her. I tried to break the news gently. "Mama, I said, you always speak about your trip to America with the little boy constantly by your side."

Without a moment's hesitation she replied, "You mean little Beryl?"

"Yes," I answered, as I pointed and said, "Here is Beryl!"

They embraced and talked. They were in a world of their own. Beryl, now a distinguished man in his eighties, sat down next to Mama. They kept their hands locked all afternoon. He told Mama that he too went through life remembering the warmth and comfort of his hand in her's and that he often repeated the story of that voyage to his grandchildren. Tears welled in his eyes as they spoke of friends and family they had known and loved.

Eighty years had flown by and Mama and her beloved Beryl sat side by side with her hand firmly and lovingly enfolded in his.

About Furs, Wealth and Library Cards

In the 1930's we were in the midst of the Great Depression. In our society, anyone who held a steady job and had enough money to buy ample coal for the stove was lucky. And a family who could pay their electric bill every month so that the Consolidated Edison Company did not turn off the electricity was considered financially stable. In fact, anyone who was debt free and sufficiently solvent to pay the monthly rent and not be evicted was automatically thought to be "doing well." No one felt deprived. We didn't even realize we were poor because everyone we knew was in the same boat.

One thing remained a constant. Jewish parents conscientiously tried to raise their children with high moral standards. They worked hard to set a good example, stressed the importance of a good education, close family ties, and emphasized the virtues of honesty and clean living.

I must have been 11 years old when Mama heard that several girls in my class were smoking. She was concerned lest her children *zoll Gott up hitten* (God forbid) pick up this bad habit. Mama did not preach, lecture or sermonize. Instead, one frosty winter morning, she called me to come quickly to the front window.

The milkman's horse and cart stood directly across the street. A woman was walking by, puffing on a cigarette and exhaling the smoke through her nose. Mama told me to closely observe the horse breathing out the cold air through its nostrils. She continued, "Now look, at the woman blowing the smoke out. Doesn't she look just like the *fehrd* (horse)? Only the *fehrd* has more *say-khel* (sense). He is blowing out used up air; she is blowing out poison." Mama was convinced that smoking was a bad habit and harmful to one's health long before subsequent research proved it was so.

It was a strong visual lesson. I never smoked, and to this very day I can conjure a horse whenever I see someone exhale cigarette smoke.

Over the years our front window had many lessons to offer. Mama found it just the spot to help her explain her attitiude towards promiscuous sex.

Again, early one winter morning she called me to the window. It had snowed heavily overnight and the street and park benches were covered with glistening white snow.

Mama gathered the curtain to one side of the window and spoke softly, "Do you see the people leaving their apartments to go to work?"

I nodded.

She continued, "Watch carefully and you will notice that each person likes to make his own footprint and path on clean untrampled snow. It is the same when you fall in love and marry. It is especially beautiful to have a clean, untrampled past for your truly beloved."

The lesson at the window was suddenly interrupted by a loud knock on the door. It turned out to be our gad-about cousin Kalman. The whole *mish-poch-eh* affectionately nicknamed him *"Kalman der-Koch-leffel"*. A *koch-leffel* is a busybody who stirs things up. The name suited him perfectly. Before entering, he brushed the snow from his boots and could hardly wait to blurt out, "News, news, do I come with news for you!"

Papa took his coat and said, "Kalman, catch your breath. Sit down and have something hot to drink." My sister Pearl and I immediately sensed we were in the midst of something very important.

We all sat around the kitchen table listening raptly as Kalman unfolded his news. It seems Kalman had a *shtickel* (small) part-time job on Wall Street. And by some stroke of fortune he bumped into wealthy cousin Max. "Would you believe," Kalman, told us, "Max seemed so happy to see me. Me, Kalman *der Koptzin* (poor man)."

The rich cousin confided in Kalman that his two young daughters were attending an exclusive private school and their teacher in progressive education felt it would be healthy for their sheltered psyches to learn more about their origins by visiting "family". This would give them deeper roots and a stronger identity. Max asked Kalman to recommend someone in the family to visit who would fulfill these needs. Kalman was drunk with flattery. Imagine Max the millionaire asking him for advice.

After careful consideration, Kalman told Max that we would be the ideal family to visit. He said our family was fine, warm and loving with two little girls the same age as his daughters. Kalman guaranteed Max that we would set a good example.

To tell the truth, we were genuinely touched to be chosen as Exhibit A. Never ever did we dream we would see these legendary "billionaires" with our own eyes.

"When are they coming?" Mama asked, as she absently shined a spot on the coal stove.

"I don't know," Kalman replied, "but be prepared."

A few weeks passed. We were worn out from "being prepared." Papa was the only one who kept his cool. He wore an amused smile and announced, "I'm ready for the royal visit."

Mama said, "In a way I feel sorry for our rich cousins. They need instructions from their children's teacher to visit their own family."

"Don't feel sorry," countered papa. "If the rich could hire others to die for them, the poor could make a nice living!"

Mama laughed and replied with a sobering remark. "No one knows whose tomorrow it will be."

Pearl added, "The saying goes: 'Some people are chained to silver and gold!'" She started to giggle and said, "One thing for sure, there are no chains around here."

Papa teased back, "To have money is not so *ai-yi-yi* but not to have it is *oy-oy-oy*!

"Enough already with the proverbs," Papa said as he turned on the radio to listen to the New York Philharmonic. "Instead of the rich cousins, we are welcoming Fritz Kreisler to our home. He is the soloist this afternoon."

Pearl heard a buzz of voices in the street and she went to the window to look out. She excitedly motioned us to join her. The most beautiful car was parked in front of our apartment house.

Mama said, "Such a magnificent machine."

The neighbors gathered about to gape. Before we knew what was happening, we heard a knock on the door. I ran to open it, and there stood our rich cousins Max and Bryna and their two splendidly dressed daughters.

We welcomed them. They apologized for not calling in advance. Bryna said, "Somehow we weren't able to find you in the phone book." Papa answered good-naturedly, "You couldn't find us in the phone book for a very good reason. We don't have a phone." We weren't part of the unlisted elite. Technically we could have claimed to be listed under "Candy Store, Mrs.Glass, proprietor."

My sister Pearl and I were overwhelmed by the visit from these cousins. They seemed to come from another planet. At first they intended to stay for a little while, but soon decided to stay for supper. Mama was busy opening 'boxes' of salmon and seeing to it that her guests felt warmly welcome.

Max was a contributing patron to the New York Philharmonic and was surprised to find Papa so knowledgeable and interested in good music.

Bryna relaxed and soon was asking for some of the recipes from Mama's Nutritional Guide Book.

The girls had a good time. They had never seen a coal stove or a bathtub on legs in a kitchen. We played checkers and jacks and ball. It was most pleasant. Soon it was time for them to leave and we bid them a fond farewell.

They promised to get together soon for another "enriching" visit. I wondered, "How rich can they get?"

As soon as they left and were off in their fancy machine, my sister Pearl started to cry uncontrollably.

Mama ran to her, "What's the matter?" she asked, enfolding Pearl's sobbing body in her arms.

Pearl cried out, "Didn't you see the elegant black velvet coats and white fur collar and cuffs and fur muffs the girls wore? I never saw such fancy clothes. I suddenly felt so poor."

Mama's beautiful face was filled with compassion. She told Pearl she understood how she felt and suggested, for the moment, that she blow her nose and dry her tears. "Tomorrow I'll meet you after school," Mama said.

The next day Mama met us after school and we walked to the Seward Park Library. We talked about the visit the day before. She told us that fortunes are made and sometimes lost. We entered the library. As she handed our library cards to us, she said in carefully measured words, "This card is your greatest treasure. It is more valuable than any possessions, more valuable than any velvet coat and fur muff. This card means you are the owner of every book in this library. As long as you own this card, in prosperity or depression, you will always be rich."[1]

---

[1] In his book *The Joys of Yiddish,* Leo Rosten quotes Mr. Harvey Swados. "Of all the public libraries in New York City, the largest circulation of the classics was found in the Seward Park Branch; and the Metropolitan Museum of art finally opened its doors on Sundays because of a persistent campaign born in, and championed by residents of the Lower East Side. To me, one of the noblest images of human history is that of the newly arrived immigrant mother, unable to speak a word of English, who hastened to her branch library and held up one, two, three fingers—the numbers signaling the number of children for whom she wanted library cards."

Matches and Weddings

Honeymoon, No Time For Kissing Disease

It is most unusual for a bride to spend her honeymoon in the hospital, but that is where I spent the first ten days of my married life. We had reservations for a honeymoon trip to Bermuda. Instead, I took a trip to the Newark Beth Israel Medical Center

For a week before the wedding I was running a fever of 101 degrees. I felt tired and draggy and unlike my usual self. Mama insisted I call a doctor. Sweet old Dr. Solomon was away on vacation. On Tuesday, I called a former boyfriend who had a fresh diploma from medical school.

He said I had an extremely red throat, promptly gave me a shot of penicillin and promised I would be fine for my wedding which was scheduled for Sunday afternoon. The days passed, but my temperature remained the same. I shook and shook the thermometer down, but it kept rising to the same 101 degrees.

Mama was very perturbed. "Don't worry," I assured her, "I'm a healthy girl and my throat will clear up from that shot of penicillin."

"That's just what I'm worried about," Mama said. "By me the whole situation *klept soch vee arbis tzu der vont* (is as illogical as peas sticking to a wall). It seems *meshugge* to me to call a former boyfriend who may still care for you and ask him to make you all better to marry someone else. God only knows what he put into that penicillin! Meanwhile you are not getting better."

"Oh Mama," I answered, "how can you be so suspicious? I'm surprised at you."

"Surprise, schmerprise," she replied. "I brought you up to be a trusting human being, but this is too much."

Not relying on penicillin entirely, she swabbed my throat with Argyrol and hoped for the best. My condition remained the same. On Saturday my throat seemed to be closing, but I tried to convince myself that I would be fine for the wedding the next day. Saturday night I took a bath, combed out my hair, and polished my nails. Mama kept a careful and worried eye on me.

"Let's not do things *moishe-kapoyr* (backwards), let's be reasonable," she appealed. "If your temperature is still not down tomorrow morning, you should postpone the wedding until you are better."

Now, what bride-to-be is reasonable? I awoke early Sunday morning and again the thermometer registered 101. I heard Mama stirring. Quickly I took some ice water from the icebox and held it in my mouth. I repeated this several times with the ice cold water. Then I stuck the thermometer in my mouth for a very short time, took it out and showed it to Mama.

"Normal at last" she said gleefully.

My brother-in-law picked us up and drove us to the Essex House in Newark for the wedding.

My future husband's handsome friend, Dr. George, was a guest at the wedding and he knew I was not feeling well. He came over to me, offered his congratulations and whispered in my ear: "Follow me to the kitchen." I did as I was told.

He picked up a spoon and used it as tongue depressor. The caterer glared at him. Dr. George told me, "Your throat is very inflamed and I think I better speak to the groom."

At this point I felt more like a leper than a bride should. The rabbi commented that it was a longtime since he had seen a bride with such glowing red cheeks. Little did he know it was due to a fever!

After the wedding ceremony Dr. George took us aside and convinced us to cancel our honeymoon trip. He suggested that we stay overnight at the Essex House in Newark while he gave the case some careful thought. Apparently he called a consultant and the next morning at 6:30 there was a knock on the door. It was Dr. Lester who came to take my blood. He said very little and promised we would have a report as soon as the lab tests were completed. Late the next day the phone rang and I was advised to check in at Beth Israel. I had a severe case of mononucleosis.

My room at the hospital became the bridal chamber and it seemed that every one of the staff found some excuse to take a peek at the bride. Dr. George jokingly said, "Don't worry, I've got the groom packed in ice in the blood bank."

On the third day I found I could not swallow and Dr. Frank, a throat specialist was called in. He was a charming man and we exchanged some Yiddish stories. He assured me that nothing much could be done and the inflammation and swelling would go down in due time.

Meanwhile, Mama knew nothing about this course of events. I could see no reason to mar her happiness. It gave me pleasure to let her think I was in Bermuda on a beautiful honeymoon.

When I got out of the hospital 10 days later (exactly the length of time we were to be away), I called Mama and told her I was back. Technically, I was telling the truth. I was back from the hospital. I told her Bermuda was lovely, also the truth!

I was a happy bride and it did not take long for me to forget the whole incident.

When my daughter Beth was five years old, the pediatrician suggested I take her to Dr. Frank to decide whether she should have her tonsils removed. Just as we were about to leave for the doctor, Mama paid us a surprise visit from New York. I told her where we were going and asked her to come along. The waiting room was filled with noisy, squirming kids. After a long wait, the nurse directed us to one of the many little examination rooms. The doctor came in, took one look at me and asked, "Aren't you the bride who spent her honeymoon at the Beth Israel?"

I felt my cheeks turn red. My carefully guarded secret was exposed right in front of Mama. I smiled wanly and could not think of an answer.

At that very moment the nurse ran into the room and asked Dr. Frank to pick up the phone for the important long distance call he was expecting. It was a long and serious conversation. He never pursued his question to me.

On the way home Mama inquired what the doctor meant by asking me if I spent my honeymoon at the Beth Israel. In my heart I felt that once she knew I deceived her she would never trust me again and would worry over every real or imagined absence.

I thought for a moment and decided it was much kinder to say, "Mama, you saw how busy the doctor is. He sees hundreds of people. He made a mistake and thought I was someone else. I didn't want to embarrass him by correcting him."

"That's understandable" she replied. "We're all human. Just the same, let's hope he doesn't make a mistake with Beth's tonsils."

Silently I was still seeking justification when I thought of an old proverb. "One must not say a lie, yet some truths you should never tell."

From *Shadchens* to Computers and Classifieds

Mama was an amateur *shadchen* (matchmaker). She never lost an oppurtunity to arrange a *shiddach* (match). "It is a real *mitzvah* (good deed) to introduce two people who are meant for each other," she told me. I inherited this trait and have made several successful introductions. Today, there have been drastic changes in this time-honored profession.

In years past there were many professional, semi-professional, and amateur matchmakers. "Do I have a girl (or boy) for you!" was a salutation used like *shalom* upon greeting and bidding farewell to any single, eligible girl or bachelor.

Years ago a *shadchen* would arrange for a couple to meet and relate to each a few salient facts about the other, "a regular beauty she is, her father is in cloaks." Her beauty usually proved a little irregular and her father was a tailor. Nevertheless, many successful marriages were arranged in this manner.

Then came the resorts, and the social directors took over many of the matchmaker's functions. "Mingle, mingle, singles mingle!" cried Itchy, the social director in "Having a Wonderful Time." Simon Sez, cocktail hours and rotating guests at the tables in the dining room are some of the devices still used to bring singles together.

A few months ago I glanced through the resort section of "The New York Times" and read that a Catskill hotel is now having Encounter weekends for singles. My first thought was, "Who will lead them; the Simon Sez *tummler?* Will he say, 'Simon Sez go to the Encounter Group.'" It wasn't hard to visualize a middle-aged man meeting a middle-aged lady in the lobby and saying, "Hello sweetie. Let's not dilly-dally. Come join me in an encounter group and we will bare our souls." No more pursuit, in *drerd* the courtship, now it's encounter.

The computer, E-Mail and classified ads in the newspapers and magazines have taken over the *shadchen's* role. A friend recently sent me a list of actual Jewish singles personals and match ads that appeared in Israeli papers. Here are some samples.

Attractive Jewish woman, 35, college graduate, seeks successful Prince Charming to get me out of my parent's house.

Shul Gabbai, 36, I take out the Torah Saturday morning. Would like to take you out Saturday night. Please write.

Couch potato *latke* in search of the right applesauce. Let's try it for eight days. Who knows?

Orthodox woman with *Get* seeks a man who got *Get* or can get *Get,* got it? I'll show you mine if you show me yours.

Yeshiva *bochur*, Torah scholar, long beard, *payos*. Seeks same in woman.

Worried about in-law meddling? I'm an orphan.

Nice Jewish guy, 38, no skeletons, no baggage, no personality.

Are you the girl I spoke to at the *Kiddush* after *shul* last week? You excused yourself to get more horseradish for your *gefilte* fish, but you never returned. How can I contact you again? I was the one with the *cholent* stain on my tie.

Female graduate student, studying Kabbalah, Zohar, Exorcism of dybbuks, seeks *mensh,* no weirdos, please.

Jewish businessman, 49, manufactures Sabbath candles, Chanukah candles, *Yahrzeit* candles. Seeks non-smoker.

80 year-old Bubbeh, no assets, seeks handsome, virile Jewish male under 35. Object matrimony. I can dream, can't I?

Jewish male, 34, very successful, smart, independent, self-made. Looking for a girl whose father will hire me.

The stock market is going up, the economy is booming and jobs are plentiful. The poor *shadchen* has fallen on hard times and is being squeezed out and totally extinguished by the computer, cyber space dating, E-Mail and the classifieds. Alas, another catastrophic casualty of modern times.

Sharing the Past at the Lower East Side Tenement Museum

My husband and I recently spent a day with our daughter and grand-daughters at the Lower East Side Tenement Museum in New York City.

We saw an excellent slide presentation on the great mass of immigrant settlement during the 19th and 20th centuries. A fine video, narrated by Vic Miles, describes the area's physical and social growth during that period. Prof. James Shenton acted as commentator and interviewer.

With great interest, we viewed scenes of the long arduous journey to America by boat in steerage class, and the hoards of immigrants of Jewish, Italian, Irish, German and other ethnic backgrounds squeezed into the crowded tenements after their arrival. It was truly a melting pot with the pot overflowing.

After the slide show, we were escorted to the museum's 1863 tenement at 97 Orchard Street. The actual museum is housed at 90 Orchard Street. It was the first tenement to be designated a National Historic Landmark.

Our enthusiastic and knowledgeable guide in the tenement detailed the extensive research undertaken by the museum in order to locate the families who had lived there. Our guide made these families come alive. This was particularly meaningful to me because my family had lived in a Lower East Side Tenement.

My 14 year-old granddaughter, Annie, was truly moved when she saw the difficult and primitive living conditions endured by the tenement dwellers. Her seven-year-old sister, Rebecca, found it hard to imagine so many people crowded into such tiny rooms.

Rebecca was eager to see everything including the neighborhood candy store where I had bought penny candy. Suddenly, Rebecca tugged at my sleeve, *"Bubbeh, Bubbeh,* are we going to see the park and play-ground where you won the New York City jacks-and-ball contest?" I hated to disappoint her, but these two landmarks had been torn down to make way for a housing development overlooking the East River.

As we walked through the tenement's narrow, dimly lit hallways, the guide explained that one toilet had served the floor's four families, each of which often included six or seven children.

Rebecca asked if my family had its own toilet. I told her we did and that it was the size of a telephone booth. I added that when my mother came to America, she lived with her sister Mollkeh, her husband and six children in a tiny four-room tenement. My father immigrated to this country and lived with his cousins Yussel and Esther in the same building on the same floor.

One Sunday, when my father went to the hall toilet, he found it occupied. So he waited patiently in the hall. My mother came out and went to her sister's apartment. When my father returned to Yussel's apartment, he said, "I saw the most gorgeous young girl coming out from the toilet, a *shaynkeit* (beauty). I must meet her."

Yussel replied, *"Holt zich eine* (hold your horses), calm down. I know the young lady. You are right she is a beauty. She is a greenhorn, but not for long. She is going to evening classes every night and is always reading and studying. I will talk to her sister Mollkeh and you will meet her."

That is how my father met my mother.

I asked my granddaughters, "Can you think of a more romantic setting to meet a mate?"

After the tenement visit and lunch at Ratner's Restaurant, we returned to the museum for a guided tour of the neighborhood. We walked along Orchard Street where the old pushcarts are now replaced by stores and sidewalk vendors.

We had a great day. For me it was a sentimental journey sharing my family's past with its future.

This Was a Wedding to Remember!

Last winter we received an invitation to a very special wedding. Papa's niece's daughter was being married. Knowing the background of this young girl, we felt a lump rising in our throats as we read the invitation.

A large number of Papa's family perished in the concentration camps. His niece Pearl (Per-el) was an inmate at a camp where she lost her mother, father and younger sister.

Her present husband, Lazer, witnessed the slaughter of his first wife and six little children by the Nazis. His life was spared because he was a tall strong man and the Germans put him to work in a slave labor camp. Ten months later he was transferred to another camp where he met Papa's niece Per-el. When the Americans liberated the survivors, Per-el and Lazer were married and subsequently had two little beautiful girls, Pesha and Mindel.

They came to America to build a new life. Through all their hardships, they remained observant Orthodox Jews.

When we received the invitation to Mindel's wedding we considered it an honor to share in the *simcha*. The wedding was scheduled to be in Long Island at the end of January and some of the most Orthodox rabbis were invited to take part in the ceremony.

It was just our luck that there was a severe snowstorm on the wedding day. The radio and television forecast treacherous driving conditions. Over and over the news bulletins blared, "Slippery roads, don't drive tonight unless there is an extreme emergency."

The snow came down in swift, heavy clumps, and the temperature was steadily dropping. I asked my husband, "Wouldn't it be foolhardy to risk the long drive to Long Island?

Mama stood nearby looking out of the window. My husband asked Mama what she thought.

Mama replied, "The circumstances are special. These people lived through such *tzuris* that we should take a risk and drive to the wedding to be with them in their *simcha*. We must remember we are the only remaining living relatives they have on Papa's side."

Mama made the decision, my husband checked the tires, we bundled up and we were on our way to New York to pick up my sister and her husband. As soon as they were safely seated in the car, the snow turned to heavy sleet. The windshield wipers could not keep pace with the pounding sleet. My husband said he needed radar to help direct him because he could barely see out of the window.

At long last we arrived at the Jewish Center in Long Island. By the time we got out of the car and into the Center we looked like five snowmen. Papa's niece was truly concerned and she greeted us, saying, "All the way from New Jersey you came in this storm. We prayed for your safe arrival and God was guiding your way."

My husband smiled and said, "Better than radar!" We shook the snow from our clothes, checked our coats and thawed out. Many of the guests were traveling from a distance and would be arriving late.

The caterer hovered about worrying about the delay. Finally the lights flickered, signaling us to file into the chapel for the ceremony.

Mama whispered to me "Where is the ladies room?" I inquired and was told that the ladies room was located two steep stories down. Wishing to spare Mama all the steps, I asked the caterer if there was another ladies room on the same level.

He was most cooperative and led us through the chapel to a door leading from the chapel to the Center. He instructed us to knock on the Center door and ask anyone in the Center corridor to unlock the door.

The busy caterer hurriedly exited through the heavy chapel door. I heard it click and shut tight behind us and I immediately sensed disaster. I tried the chapel door and it was locked. Mama read my mind. "I hope we can get back in," she said.

I feigned confidence and tried to sound cheerful as I said, "Meanwhile, we haven't gotten into the Center yet. Let's worry about one door at a time." Mama agreed.

The Center door had a small glass panel and we could see a few teenage boys dressed in basketball gear. I knocked on the Center door trying to gain their attention. They totally ignored the frantic knocks. Finally, I caught the eye of one boy and shouted through the door asking him to please unlock it. He promised he would go to the office for the key and would be right back. Apparently he had a long walk or a short memory. He never came back.

I spotted a steep staircase and asked Mama if she thought we should go down to look for a ladies room. She was game and we carefully climbed down the darkened stairs. I asked Mama to stand still while I groped about the walls looking for a light switch. I finally found one that turned on a small naked bulb and we wound our way around until we came to a welcome sign reading "Ladies Room and Lockers."

The one dim bulb threw an eerie light in a shadowy pattern on the walls. It felt as though we were in a labyrinth of winding pipes. We soon came upon an enormous indoor swimming pool. Mama asked, "Do you think this is a deluxe modern *mikva* (ritual bath)?" Not being a *mikva mayvin*, I had no answer.

Mama's ever-present sense of humor saved the moment. She was trying to ease the tension and said, "if we only knew we would land here, we would have brought our bathing suits."

Suddenly the one light bulb went out. I grabbed Mama's hand. Mama said in a calm voice, "Aha, do you know what it means that the light bulb went out? It is an important *simmin* (sign)."

At this point I was ready to accept any *simmin*, or omen, even if it came from a gypsy. "Mama, what does it signify?" I eagerly asked, clutching her hand.

She continued, "Yes, this is definitely a *simmin* that the light bulb burned out and we are completely in the *finster* (dark)."

I found myself laughing. Mama's voice took a serious tone, "Wouldn't it be terrible, if after braving the snowstorm, we would miss the ceremony by being stuck in this dark cellar?"

Meanwhile, my husband and brother-in-law did not miss us since they were sitting on the men's side in the chapel. My sister thought we had returned from the laidies room after most people were seated and she assumed we took seats in the back of the chapel. So even our rescue squad was unaware of our disappearance.

Mama held on to me and I held on to her, and we inched our way to the stairs and climbed up. We felt totally isolated.

I began to knock on the thick chapel door; then I started to kick the door. Suddenly a tiny lady with a big *sheitel* (wig) opened the door a little. She put her fingers to her lips and said, "*Sha, sha*, go away, why are you intruding and making such a *tummult*, *Sha sha*, stop disturbing us, a wedding is about to begin."

I quickly wedged my foot in the door and begged her, "Let us in, Please let us in. We are guests from the bride's *mishpochah*."

She looked at us as if we came from outer space. Actually we came from under space.

We gratefully sat down, and a second later the radiant *kalleh* (bride) marched down the aisle escorted by Papa's niece, Per-el, and her husband Lazer. There wasn't a dry eye. We cried too, for sheer happiness, and for simply being there!

MUSIC AND ART

Lillian and Her Violin

Papa Listened to the Beat of a Different Eardrum

Papa had a deep love and appreciation of classical music. It was his avenue of escape from the hard workaday world in the shop. When I think back, I still marvel at Papa's accurate and sensitive musical ear. I could turn on the radio in the middle of a selection. Papa would listen intently, and in a minute or two identify the piece, composer and the movement.

Then he would add, "That's the Philadelphia Symphony," or "the Boston Symphony Orchestra." He was always right. I was impressed and, wondering, asked, "Papa, how can you tell one orchestra from another?"

"It's like recognizing the voice of an old friend. Each orchestra has its own unique sound," he explained. "The Philadelphia Orchestra has the sweetest strings and the Boston Symphony has a distinct blending of the brass section. Really, it's easy to tell them apart if you listen often enough."

I tried hard but could rarely pick up the subtle nuances that Papa heard so clearly.

Papa's favorite instrument was the violin, and Jascha Heifetz and Mischa Elman were familiar names in our household. We were not permitted to listen to "junk," and Papa had us almost convinced that we would ruin the sound of our precious Bosch radio if we allowed popular music through the delicate speaker. Once in a while my sister Pearl would sneak in the serial, "Myrt and Marge," but Papa thought it was a waste of time and electricity.

We owned an old handcranked Victrola, and although the budget was tight, somehow records of Jascha and Mischa and Fritz Kreisler found their way into our home.

Pearl had a boyfriend who loved swing music. Papa distrusted this young man immediately and justified his feelings by saying, "Any boy who knows all about Harry James and Benny Goodman and nothing about Bach and Beethoven, what kind of a prospect can he be?" He judged a man by the musical company he kept.

Tante Lena gave me a violin when her son Teddy flatly refused to play another note on it. She presented it to me with these encouraging words: "I'm giving this violin to you to keep myself from breaking it over Teddy's head. For two years I wasted money on his lessons, better I should have sent the *gelt* to poor relatives in Europe."

It was a proud day for Mama and Papa when I was chosen as a violin scholarship student at the Henry Street Settlement School of Music. I secretly yearned for a piano but I was realistic enough to know that we could not afford one. And even if we had been able to afford one, it was physically impossible to squeeze a piano into our tiny apartment unless we all moved out.

The Henry Street Settlement School of Music was one of the finest schools in New York and I plunged into the musical program. The eminent American composer, Aaron Copland, was my theory and harmony instructor. I was the smallest, skinniest member of the children's chorus in one of Copland's earliest operas, "The Second Hurricane."

We were directed by a dynamic young genius who yelled and screamed as if he were already famous. He demanded perfection at every rehearsal and performance. Perhaps he was practicing for the day he would become famous. His name was Orson Welles.

The music school filled my life. Scholarship students were given free tickets to concerts and I hopefully hung around the ticket desk. Sometimes I was lucky enough to get free tickets for Mama, Papa and Pearl. We usually sat in the last row in the last balcony (in the stratosphere), but we enjoyed every note. Not only did the music school broaden my musical horizons, but my geographic ones as well. I discovered there was a world beyond my block (Cherry Street) and I totally absorbed the music, opera and ballet. Pretty soon we became the "Music *Mayvins*" on the block.

Mrs. Pearlman, next door, harbored grand illusions of a singing career for herself. She found a voice teacher, and our lives became unbearable. Mama said she would rather go into childbearing labor than listen to Mrs. Pearlman try to sing.

One afternoon while Papa listened to Serge Koussevitzky, he turned up the volume and Mama poured running water into the sink to wash spinach leaves. We still could not drown out Mrs. Pearlman's piercingly shrill off-key voice. A little later she knocked on our door and invited us to her apartment, confiding that she wanted a true evaluation of her voice.

She said she respected our opinion because of our great interest in music. She desperately looked into our eyes and said, "I swear, we should all live and be well, tell me the truth, the whole truth."

Mama and Papa exchanged frantic glances. How could they risk the health of their family and yet, how could they risk telling the truth? Papa solved the problem by relating a story he once heard Deems Taylor tell on the radio.

"It seems," he began, "that a rich matron was determined to become an opera singer, and her husband found the best voice teacher for her. She had no talent at all except to grow progressively worse each week. Her voice had a chilling screech and she was always off key. After a few agonizing lessons, the voice teacher threw up his hands and asked, 'Madam, why is it that when I play the black keys, you sing the white keys and when I play the white keys, you sing the black keys. And when I play both, you sing the cracks?'"

Luckily, Mrs. Pearlman had a sense of humor that was superior to her voice and to our great relief, she soon abandoned her singing career.

Music Hath Charm, Some Violinists Are Another Case

In the Depression years, it was quite common for unemployed musicians (especially violinists) to make the rounds of tenement back yards playing selections in order to earn a few dollars.

They played Yiddish songs in the Jewish neighborhoods and Italian opera pieces in the Italian sections, while the Irish districts resounded with "Danny Boy" and a concert version of "When Irish Eyes Are Smiling."

Most neighbors used to wrap a penny in a small piece of newspaper and throw it out of the window. It usually fell near or at the feet of the violinist.

Mama felt it was undignified to throw coins at a musician. She would give me a few pennies and instruct me to rush downstairs and quietly place the coins in the open violin case resting on the ground.

Mama never lost an opportunity to admonish no one in particular (meaning me). "Practice, practice, if these men practiced more they would be playing in Carnegie Hall today and not in the back yards begging for pennies."

Mama and Papa were delighted when I was awarded a violin scholarship at the Henry Street Settlement School of Music. I was a skinny 11 year-old girl and my violin and case weighed almost as much as I did. Included were free violin lessons with theory and harmony classes given by the then unknown composer Aaron Copland.

Our upstairs (third floor) neighbors, Mr. and Mrs. Berk, had a talented son Georgie. He took private violin lessons from a "genius," Professor Sigmund Wolfmann. They were very ambitious people and felt compelled to convince my parents that I would derive great musical benefits by taking additional lessons from Prof. Wolfmann.

Papa was reluctant. He thought perhaps there would be a conflict in technique.

Mr. and Mrs. Berk were persistent. "Life doesn't sleep, it only sits a minute and dreams a dream. Use every minute wisely and your dreams will come true. Your daughter will make twice as much progress with two violin teachers. The music school need not know and she will double her technique."

Papa did not think it was a good idea, he was not convinced. The Berks were persuasive and Mama relented. "Let her try for a month. What could hurt?" she asked Papa.

Arrangements were made for Prof. Wolfmann to come downstairs after Georgie's lesson to interview me and decide whether he would take me as a pupil. I practiced diligently in preparation. I wanted to be at my best.

After supper on the appointed evening, I helped Mama clear the dishes. The house was especially spic and span, just as if we were expecting a doctor on a house visit.

At 8 o'clock there was a sharp staccato knock on the door. Mr. and Mrs. Berk introduced Prof. Wolfmann and then left immediately so that they would not interfere with the audition.

Prof. Wolfmann made a most impressive appearance with his long hair flowing underneath his wide brimmed felt fedora hat with the brim snapped down in the front and back. He wore a silk ascot knotted loosely around his short thick neck and carried a silver handled cane. His self-awareness was immediately evident and he reveled in the effect he was creating — a genuine impressario.

He put down his cane, took off hat and started to open his elegant violin case. His hand slid slowly over the thick plush lining in the violin case. With a theatrical flair, he pulled out a handkerchief, tucked it under his chin, lifted his violin out tenderly and began to play "Mine Schtayt-el-eh Belz," "Rozh-in-kehs mit Mondlen" and other popular Yiddish songs.

He played with so much schmaltz that I looked for the *greeb-en-ehs* to drop from the bow. Obviously he was trying to melt Mama and Papa without realizing they possessed highly discriminating musical taste.

While Mama and Papa loved Yiddish folk songs, his selections hardly qualified him to be a virtuoso in their eyes or ears.

I stood nearby, violin ready in hand, waiting to be called on to play. He totally ignored me. I found myself intensely disliking this pompous man for not knowing I was there and for his snobbish and patronizing attitude towards my parents. Mama and Papa were polite, but my patience was wearing thin. I waited for a short pause in the music and then I quickly said, "Don't you want to hear me play. Don't you want to know what I'm up to?"

He glared at me threateningly. "*Dar'eh Maidel-eh*" (skinny girl), he addressed me. "I have played for hours before royalty without interruption. Don't you dare disturb an artist. People have paid thousands to hear me play. Open your ears and shut your mouth."

Normally I was a polite child. Suddenly I could not control myself and I blurted out in an angry childish voice, "We listen to many great artists in this house. Jasha Heifetz, Misha Elman and Fritz Kreisler have been here very often. For the small cost of electricity we turn on the radio and their music fills our apartment."

Prof. Wolfmann could not believe his ears, his jaw slackened, his mouth was agape. I was afraid his eyes would pop out of his head. A roar of silence followed. He put away his violin, snapped his fedora angrily on his head, adjusted his ascot and pointed at me uncomfortably close with his silver handled cane. With a pained expression he turned to Mama and Papa (who were speechless) and said in a low, mournful voice. "I extend my deepest sympathy to you. From this *Dar-eh Maidel-eh* (skinny girl) of yours with her *gray-ser pisk* (big mouth), from this you will never live to see *noch-es*. From this snip will never grow a *mensh*."

True, I never grew up to be a violin virtuoso, but Mama and Papa said I gave them *naches* by becoming a *mensh*.

LEARNING AND EDUCATION

A Lesson in Human Kindness

Sex education has been the topic of heated discussion for many years. Experts claim that it enlightens children and eliminates the hazards of learning the facts of life from promiscuous peers in the street. Other experts, equally vocal, say it puts ideas into children's minds at too early an age.

Years ago when I was a child we lived next door to a very progressive mother, Mrs. Weiss. She believed in "telling all" to her three daughters in matters of sex.

The middle daughter, Bella, was very thin and scrawny and even though she stuffed herself with Ovaltine, malteds with ice cream and charlotte russes, she remained skinny as a reed. The kids on the block nicknamed her "Tapeworm." Bella had a steady boyfriend, Solly, who was called skinny Schlaimee. They were inseparable.

On Bella's 17th birthday, Mrs. Weiss took her to the doctor for a physical examination. She pleaded with the doctor, "My daughter took all the tonics you prescribed to help her gain weight and in the past few weeks she lost weight. Please, before she becomes a skeleton, is there anything else you can suggest to put a few pounds on her?"

The doctor replied that as a last resort he recommended that Bella's tonsils be removed. He explained that Bella had a history of tonsilitis and in some cases the diseased tonsils impaired the ability to gain weight. He arranged for Bella to have the offending tonsils removed at a local hospital. Mrs. Weiss was sure this would do the trick.

Bella's tonsillectomy was uneventful. Her boyfriend Solly was constantly at her side. A few weeks later Bella started to gain weight and her mother was overjoyed. The only problem was that she didn't stop blossoming, as she was pregnant. Mrs. Weiss was shocked and a hasty wedding was arranged. Bella gave birth to a fat baby boy, 9 lbs. 8 ozs.

Everyone on tne block was buzzing. Some mean neighbors suggested that Bella name the baby "Tonsillitis." Mrs. Goldstein, the chief gossip and tongue wagger, smirked all through the event and made snide remarks in her nasal voice as she rolled her eyes toward the sky, "That's what happens when you have such a progressive mother."

Mrs. Goldstein's complete lack of sensitivity and compassion for Bella and her mother offended Mama. She reminded Mrs. Goldstein, "You are the mother of four little children, keep in mind the wise saying, 'If you have children in the cradle, it is best not to point a finger at others.'" Mama continued, looking right into Mrs. Goldstein's eyes, "You must always lean backwards to give someone the benefit of a doubt if it will lessen another person's pain. And it is wrong to feel joy from someone else's *tzuris*. Listen carefully to this tale, Mrs. Goldstein, it is a folk tale, but there is a lesson in kindness. We can all learn from it."

Mama told this story without taking her eyes off Mrs. Goldstein for a second. "A young innocent scholar was stunned when his wife gave birth. He ran to the rabbi and blurted out, 'An extraordinary thing has happened! Please explain it to me. My wife has given birth although we have been married only three months. How can this be? Everybody knows it takes nine months for a baby to be born.

"The rabbi, a world-renowned sage and kind soul, put on his silver-rimmed spectacles and stroked his beard. 'My son', he said, 'I see you haven't the slightest idea about such matters, nor can you make the simplest calculation. Let me ask you, have you lived with your wife for three months?' 'Yes.' 'Has she lived with you three months!' 'Yes.' 'Together, have you lived three months?' 'Yes.' The rabbi's eyes twinkled. 'Then in all human kindness, three months plus three plus three — what is the total?' 'Nine months!' 'Your question is answered. Go home to your wife, and *Mozel-Tov!*'"

Never Too Late to Learn

I read her name in the obituary column. Bessie Hemmendinger, age 96.

My mother-in-law and father-in-law lived in Newark when I was a newlywed. My husband and I lived nearby in Irvington in our first apartment. It was always a real pleasure to visit my new groom's parents. We did so frequently for we loved to schmooze, to laugh, and just enjoy being together.

My mother-in-law, Mom Rose Bressman, was an exceptional woman. She was extremely bright and possessed a wonderful combination of real strength tempered with infinite kindness. Her dignity, wisdom, and sheer common sense always impressed me and I secretly vowed to someday grow in all her special ways.

One day we were sitting in her warm inviting kitchen while making kasha varnishkehs when she suddenly turned to me and wistfully said. "If I could have a wish come true—naturally after asking for good health for my family and friends, and of course, peace on earth—do you know what I would really want?"

"No, Mom," I answered quietly, sensitive to the seriousness in her voice.

She wiped her hands on her apron, sat down opposite me at the kitchen table and took my hands in her's. "I would want to become a good speller," she said. Mom confided that she was very uncomfortable with her spelling and knew there was room for improvement.

She came to America at age sixteen, and with very little help she practically taught herself to read and write English, including English newspapers. I assured her that I thought she was wonderful—spelling and all. Her spelling never bothered me. In fact it endeared her all the more to me. I knew that Mom spelled the way she heard words. She once left a neatly written reminder to her husband, reading, "Louie, be sure to pay your texas early."

Landscaped became 'landskate.' Nostril was 'nozzel' and she turned a multi-millionaire into a 'malted' millionaire. I could feel her frustration and was touched by her strong desire to improve her spelling. I promised to find out where she could get some expert help.

After several inquiries, I found an Americanization course at Weequahic High School in Newark. The next day I called the school and they said they had open enrollment all through the term and would welcome Mom in the class. I excitedly called to tell her the good news. She suddenly had a case of cold feet and haltingly said, "I'm not sure I can keep up with the others. Maybe I won't be right for the class."

She needed confidence. "Mom," I urged, "I'll go with you for the first few times and you'll see how you like it. I'm sure I can learn something too."

She replied, "We'll go together, I like that." For the next few days we both went to class. The teacher was a wonderfully kind and perceptive soft-spoken woman. Her name was Bessie Hemmendinger. She knew the students personally and was attuned to their every need. I learned a great deal, too.

Mrs. Hemmendinger had a deep respect for simple, direct, uncluttered English and extolled the lyric quality of everyday common speech, She taught her students to zealously guard against the malady of swollen language. She gave as an example, "Never call a library 'a study materials resource center.' This malady has turned janitors into custodians; street cleaners into sanitary engineers, and ear, nose and, throat doctors into otorhinolaryngologists."

She cautioned her students. "In swollen language we don't talk to anyone. We should try to 'establish a meaningful dialogue'. There is so much beauty to be found in simple language without embroidery. Learn to appreciate and use simple classic words and sentences." She often repeated this sound advice.

Mom grew more confident and told me she was ready to go to class alone. She loved learning and pretty soon she was the brightest student in the class. Mrs. Hemmendinger enjoyed Mom's inquisitive mind and challenging questions. Mom worked diligently on her homework assignments. She completed them plus a little extra. She could not stop. Her spelling improved beyond her greatest expectations.

My father-in-law encouraged her and was very proud of her dedication and progress. We jokingly promised Mom a big graduation party at the end of the year. She went back to class the following year to "improve my improvements." Mom now loved civics, American history, current events, spelling and especially her teacher.

As I read the obituary, 'Bessie Hemmendinger, age 96,' I enjoyed imagining that Mom would joyously greet her in heaven and resume some serious studying.

A 'Good Neighbor' Policy

When I was a little girl I used to accompany my mother to her Adult Education Class at the Henry Street Settlement House on the Lower East Side. She could not afford a babysitter. How well I still remember the classroom, the colors, the smells and the furniture. Around an enormous oak table in the center of the room sat a group of massive women.

The womens' hands and fingers were all red and swollen from their heavy housework. The pencils looked strangely small and alien in their puffed hands.

One day the teacher distributed narrow strips of yellow paper for a spelling test. "Number your papers one to ten going down. Ten points for each word spelled correctly, and ten points off for each misspelled word," she instructed the class.

Even as a child, I could feel the tension mounting in the room. The teacher slowly and carefully pronounced each word, giving her class more than ample time to write them.

At about the third word, I noticed one woman write her word on her yellow sheet and immediately slap her other hand down to cover it. The heavy-set auburn-haired woman next to her seemed to be leaning over trying to catch a glimpse of her classmate's paper.

Each time the hand-slapping paper coverer concealed her words, her neighbor's annoyance grew more intense.

Finally, in sheer desperation she blurted out, "Mrs. Pearlman, what kind of friend and neighbor are you? A few times a day you are in my apartment to borrow an onion, a potato, a piece of garlic for your *cholent* or something else you forgot to buy. Don't I always lend you with an open heart? Now here I forget a little word to spell, and you won't even lend me a peek — some friend — some neighbor!"

Mama Studies Hard to Take the Big US Citizenship Test

Our whole country is responding enthusiastically to the Statue of Liberty Ellis Island Foundation. The establishment of the museum (open to millions of visitors) serves as a testament to the heroism and triumphs of the immigrants who came to America.

Certificates of registration for family members who arrived in this country may be purchased from the foundation. This enables your *mishpocheh* to be recorded on the Centennial Edition of the American Immigrant Wall of Honor at Ellis Island.

From the moment that Mama arrived in this country as a young girl, her goal was to become an American citizen. She immediately registered at night school to learn English and took every course offered. Meanwhile, she worked long hours in a dress factory, met her future husband, married and raised a family.

I was 11 years old when I accompanied Mama to apply for her citizenship papers. "You must study the history of the United States," warned the austere clerk. "You have to be prepared to pass the Big Test." Mama felt that if she flunked the test, she would automatically become an illegal alien—and who knows—God forbid be shipped back to Russia. Actually she did hear such rumors at her kosher butcher shop.

Mama set out to study for the Big Test with the motivation and determination of a Rhodes scholar. She enlisted the aid of the senior librarian at the Seward Park Library who supplied Mama with an endless source of books on American history. My young life changed drastically from that moment on. Every day when I came home from school, Mama sat me down, thrust a book in my hands and asked me to quiz her on the chapters she studied. She could name all the United States presidents in the right order along with their term of office.

In her own inimitable way, Mama endowed the historical figures with a personal flavor. Mama must have been sure the fourth U.S. president was also a doctor as she pronounced his name James Medicine. And Bessie Ross, the wonderful woman who sewed the American flag was very special in Mama's heart, not to mention the first president, Judge Voshington and his wife, Mosha Voshington.

One day I came home from school and my mother greeted me with "Test me, test me." She closed her eyes as she recited the name of all the signers of the Constitution. The next day I arrived after school and was barely in the door when she greeted me with, "Nu, now I remember all the states—when they came into the union—and their population." She gave me the reference book and I followed her accurate rendition. She also knew about the Senate and the House of Representatives.

I had given up playing in the park playground after school for the duration of Mama's serious studies. One day she caught me daydreaming and glancing out of the window. Gently, she brought me back to the mission at hand. "Please don't look out of the window. Follow what I'm saying in the book on your lap. Try to catch me in a mistake, and correct me. *Gottenyu*, that could be the very question the examiner will ask me on the Big Test!" I followed the text carefully; she was letter perfect. Although I didn't appreciate my role as offical tester, I had to admire her determination and hard work.

Finally, the day arrived for Mama to take the Big Test. To reassure her I told her, "I know you will pass. By me Mama, you are an American history *mayvin*."

"Maybe by you," was her nervous retort, "but not by the Big Examiner. I would be so disappointed in myself and ashamed for Papa and my children if I do not pass. Besides I want to be proud to be a 100 percent American citizen."

Mama and I had mistakenly assumed that the examination would be given in a classroom with about 10 to 20 people and that the test would take several hours. To our dismay when we reached the address on the card it turned out to be a large courtroom on Madison Street with a presiding judge and more than 200 anxious test takers.

The judge was a distinguished looking, handsome man with a gray moustache and warm friendly eyes. He appeared eager to process the applicants quickly as he called out names from a list on his bench. The judge asked each person a question, nodded, and rapidly called the next name. The fast process in which each person answered one quick question and then moved on confused Mama. Soon the judge called Rose Pinchik Bernstein.

Mama's cheeks flushed and her body tensed. The judge looked at Mama who was holding on to my hand for additional support. "Is this your little girl?" he asked.

"Yes," whispered Mama, barely finding her voice.

"Now, Mrs. Bernstein, can you tell me the name of the president who freed the slaves?"

Suddenly Mama stood erect, her voice clear and the answer began to flow from her lips. "Abraham Lincun freed the slaves. He was president number 16 of the United States from 1861 to 1865. He was born in a lock cabin in Kentucky, but he sure worked himself up. He became a lawyer and was called Honest Abe because he always told the truth."

Sensing the urgency in Mama's recitation, the judge did not interrupt. Without stopping for a breath, Mama bemoaned Lincoln's unhappy marriage to Mary Todd and the tragic death of three of his sons at an early age.

"Judge," Mama said sympathetically, "even though he was the president, he just did not have any *naches* from his family. A crazy actor John Vilkes Boot shot him to death on April 4, 1865. That is all I studied on Lincun. What is the next question?"

The judge leaned over and said, "I am not going to ask you any other question." He looked at me standing by Mama's side and asked while smiling, "Do you know your Mama knows more about President Lincoln than many Americans? And I am proud to welcome her as a citizen of this country"

I squeezed Mama's hand and shyly replied, "I'm proud too!"

On Mama's Own Meaning of 'I.Q.'

My daughter and I were visiting Mama and we were discussing the latest developments in the Nature versus the Nurture controversy on the origins of intelligence.

In the late sixties a number of research psychologists began publishing work indicating that intelligence is predominantly an inherited characteristic (nature) and that environmental factors (nurture) played a relatively small role in determining a child's intellectual function.

Prof. Jerome Kegan of Harvard University, once an ardent "environmentalist," said at the time, "Nobody denies the importance of environment, but I now believe that inherited sequences of growth are more powerful than we had thought."

Then there are the controversial findings of Dr. Arthur Jensen. He stated that heredity is the major determinant of intelligence and that I.Q. test scores indicate innate differences by race. This set off a furor in 1969 and in liberal circles, his name was synonymous with racism.

Jensen's theory was strongly refuted by other scientists who claimed that society limited the opportunities for blacks to learn white middle class vocabulary and skills and that this environmental deprivation caused the lowered I.Q. scores. They assert that tests are not unfair. Life is unfair and tests measure the results.

Prof. Kagan and other psychologists were asking more complicated questions about both heredity and environment. The challenge of the next 10 or 20 years would be to understand the interaction of the two. Careful evaluation and compilation of the data were the measuring tools used by the researchers. Essentially, we are not much closer now in settling the Nature versus the Nurture controversy than we were many years ago.

Beth and I were engrossed in our discussion when suddenly we both felt we were excluding Mama from the conversation. Mama seemed to be listening very attentively. We thought she was merely trying to be polite.

Just as we were about to change the subject to a lighter vein, and much to our surprise, Mama said, "I betcha you didn't know that I understand maybe a little bit about intelligence testing too!" It was our turn to listen as Mama related the following. She addressed my daughter.

"One morning, when your Mama was in Junior High School, there was a knock on the door. I called out, 'Who's there?'

"A man replied, 'I'm Mr. Anderson from the Board of Education.'

"Oy, did I get scared. I let him in and he asked me whether I would be kind enough to answer some questions for him. 'Sure,' I said. But I kept thinking, 'Oy vey I hope there is no trouble with the teachers or with playing hookey.'

"In a serious tone Mr. Anderson told me, 'Your daughter Lillian has the second highest I.Q. in New York, and her first cousin, Lily Ritz has the highest I.Q. in New York. We are trying to formulate some correlation with family history and environmental background.'"

Mama continued, "All of a sudden I started to *shuk-kel* (shake). I guess it was from fright. I tried to compose myself as I said through chattering teeth, 'I know you are here from the Board of Education, so it must be on important business—but what I don't know is—what is an I.Q.? *Gottenyu*, does I.Q. mean "In Quarantine?" Is it a contagious disease? And more important, can it be cured?"

After telling us that Anderson explained to her that I.Q. stood for Intelligence Quotient, and that it was the result of a test given to measure a person's intelligence, Mama sighed and said, "Don't ask—was I relieved! And I was happy to answer his questions about our whole *mish-poch-eh*, grandparents, great grandparents, and great-great grandparents. He was especially interested in the same grandparents we shared with number one I.Q. cousin Lily Ritz.

"Mr. Anderson then asked me to show him around my home, 'the total physical environment.'" Mama laughed as she recalled, "It took me one minute to show him everything in the *pitzele* (tiny) apartment.

"Then his eyes fell upon the claw-footed bathtub next to the sink in the kitchen. It had a removable white enamel top that doubled as counter space and the bathtub also served as a washtub."

According to Mama's telling of the story, Anderson then said, "Please don't think I'm nosey, but even the smallest detail is important in this in-depth survey. Tell me, how often does Lillian take a bath?"

Mama told him, "How often, you ask? Like every normal person—in the winter—once a week—on Friday night. As for 'in-depth', as deep as the tub will allow."

Mama looked directly at my daughter as she continued. "Then Mr. Anderson questioned me about your mother's nutrition. "What does she eat?" he wanted to know.

"I almost laughed and asked him, 'Have you seen her? She's a skinny *malink*. She's a terrible eater. She eats not more than a fly. And this holds true for her cousin Lily Ritz too. The two of them together on a scale hardly weigh enough for one thin person."

Mama recalled that Anderson took copious notes all through the interview. She said that suddenly his eyes flashed and he wrote excitedly on his official pad. "Aha," he said, "maybe we stumbled on something of scientific value. Perhaps we can establish a positive correlation between being very skinny and being very intelligent. Perhaps too much food interferes with the flow of oxygen to the brain. Who knows, this could open a Pandora's box in scientific annals."

Mama continued: "Exactly what he meant by those fancy words I didn't understand, but we had a nice friendly conversation over a glass of tea and home-baked Russian cake.

"Mr. Anderson made sure to write down in his notes that we drank tea from a glass (actually a *yur-tzeit* glass), not from a cup. He noticed every-thing. Also, he told me that statistics show that the percentage of Jews among Nobel Prize winners is much greater than for other groups. I didn't know this, but I sure was proud to hear it from him."

Anderson closed his notebook at last, screwed the top on his Waterman's fountain pen and as he was ready to leave, Mama said to him,

"Frankly in my eyes she's very special. She's my child, but I must be honest with you. If you knew all the foolish things she does that didn't show up on the test, hoo-ha! And as the saying goes, 'We don't need intelligence to have luck, but we do need luck to have intelligence.' Please don't think I'm ungrateful, for right now in my heart I have a new meaning for I.Q. I'm *qvelling*, but I plan to keep reminding her whenever she does something foolish. For I could not stand a child with a big head. It would be a problem because our apartment is too small and we have no room!"

Anderson smiled as he said goodbye. Mama ended by telling us that Anderson said that he had enjoyed the interview so much he would like to come back just to talk to her and have some more of her tea and Russian cake.

LANGUAGE AND HUMOR

Those Colorful Yiddish Curses

After a good deal of soul searching, I came to the conclusion that in one respect I had a deprived childhood. Both my mother and my father would not permit cursing in our home. Mama insisted that only *prust-eh men-shen* (coarse people) cursed and she was always on guard to enforce the no *shel-tin* (cursing) rule.

When we were naughty children and sorely tried Mama's patience, she would cry out in exasperation. *"Oy, zult yir nor zine ge-zunt!"* (Oh, may you only be in good health). This outburst could hardly be classified as an expletive to be deleted. Secretly I longed for Mama and Papa to be more like our neighbors.

We lived in a tenement teeming with immigrants who came to America with an extensive repertoire of curses. It probably was one form of lashing out at the absurdities and cruelties of life. It was an immediate release for pent-up frustrations. Physical fighting was non-existent. Hostility was verbalized with the use of wits instead of fists.

My friend Tillie Goldstein's mother made an indelible impression on me. Papa said she had a sharp tongue that could clip a hedge. She was a master curser. Mrs. Goldstein was so skilled I'm convinced she had a Ph.D. in colorful cursing.

She possessed the rare talent of constructing every sentence around a well-turned curse. I made every excuse to spend as much time as possible in Tillie's house. My ears were constantly attuned to Mrs. Goldstein's sharp voice spewing out wrath with gusto.

Because cursing was forbidden in our house, it added to my complete fascination. When I was ready to leave Tillie's house I would say Goodbye.

Mrs. Goldstein would answer, *"Gay, gay, gay tzum tei-vul."* (Go, go, go to the devil).

Immediately, I would rush to our apartment to write down the juicy curses in the back of my homework assignment notebook. That is how I started my collection of colorful curses.

Many years later I came across a chapter in Maurice Samuel's In Praise of Yiddish and I was astonished to find almost all of my notes in his book. I have a strange suspicion that he also knew Mrs. Goldstein.

Here are some examples. Of course there is the basic, *Gay in drerd* (Go into the earth or go to hell). *Ver geh-har-get* (Be killed). *Krenk-en zol er* (May he sicken). And the stronger, *Zol er krenk-en un ge-day-ken* (May he sicken and remember). *Kine dokter zull im nit helfin* (May no doctor be able to help him).

A dokter zol im darf-en (May a doctor need him). This has many implications. May a doctor need him for what, diagnosis? Or possibly more offensive, for an autopsy! Then there is the all encompassing, *Oif doc-toy-rim zol er es oll-es oys-gay-ben* (May he spend it all on doctors). *A vay-tik em in kup* (May he have a pain in his head). *Shtek-en zol im in de zeit-in* (May he have stabbing pains in the sides). *A cholehr-yeh oif im* (May a cholera come upon him). *Krich-in zol er ahf alleh fear* (May he crawl on all fours).

And the more inspired morsels: *Zol im drik-in in hartzen* (May he have clamping heaviness of the heart). *Redin zol er fun hitz* (May he talk from fever, in delirium). *Geschvol-len zol er ver-rin vee ah barg* (May he swell up like a mountain). *Fargelt un fargrint zol er ver-rin* (May he turn yellow and green, jaundiced). *A duner zol im trefin un a blitz im in kup* (May a thunderbolt hit him and lightening strike in his head). *Er krenkt un krenkt, un' siz nit tuh vem-in tzu bar-grubbin* (He ails and ails, yet there is no one to bury). *Meh zol schoyn zit-tzen shiveh noch im* (It is time they sat in mourning for him).

Several years ago I came across an interesting article stating that there was a course in Jewish Folklore that included cursing, given at the University of Pennsylvania. It was exciting to read that cursing was now elevated to a college course. The distinguished professor of history and folklore, Dr. Barbara Kirshenblatt Gimblett, presented the course.

Mama never knew about my carefully guarded collection of curses. After reading the article, I decided to tell her all about it. She was amazed. It was the right time to show her the article. She read it slowly; then read it again and replied, "*Az-och-in-vay*" (It's painful). Mama shrugged her shoulders, sighed, and said through clenched teeth, "A distinguished professor, Dr. Gimblett, she wastes her time on teaching curses, *zult zee nor zine ge-zunt* (may she only be in good health)!"

Who's Afraid of a *Kine-Ahora*?

When Mama came to America, she was surprised to find many of her friends and relatives clinging to their old ingrained European folk superstitions. Mama could not intellectually accept them at face value, but then again,·why look an evil eye in the eye?

Many immigrants retained their beliefs in the power of the supernatural to fulfill their need for something familiar after their arrival in this country, an unknown place with a new language and strange customs.

Superstition flourishes when man seeks to grasp and control the forces of nature and events that he does not understand. It borders on magic on the one hand and on religion on the other. The Jews through the centuries have had their share of superstitions, particularly at times when they had the least security.

Learned scholars, including Maimonides, denounced superstition. However, it had a strong hold on the large population of the *shtetl* and was handed down from generation to generation.

An ancient sage once said, "One should not believe in superstitions, but still it is best to be heedful of them." This was exactly Mama's attitude.

One of the most important things to avoid was the *kine-ahora* (the evil eye). The eye was considered the most powerful means of transmitting disaster and *tzurris* (trouble) to another person.

The demon and evil spirits were believed to emerge through the eyes. An envious, jealous mortal could cast an evil spell on another's luck or health with one withering glance!

"*Kein*" is derived from German, meaning "no." "*Ayin ha-rah*" is Hebrew for "the evil eye". Over the years *kein* and *ayin* were blended into one Yiddish word, *kine*. Simply by adding *kine* in front of another Yiddish blend, *ahora* (from *ayin ha-rah*), it was possible to ward off any dire consequences and provide instant protection to a child or loved one.

As soon as one was threatened by an evil eye (usually cast by a bitter enemy, or worse yet, an envious friend), it was customary for the mother or a concerned friend to repeat the magic phrase *kine-ahora* three times. And then she would kiss the endangered child or person three times on the forehead, spitting after each kiss.

Over the years, the variation on this theme was refined to merely spitting softly three times in the air and at the same time whispering *"Poo! Poo! Poo!"* Strong believers attest to the fact that this gesture is guaranteed to thwart any demons lurking about. Above all, it is best to shun all praise regarding appearance, health and success. To extol or admire is considered perilous.

Every Shabbos, Mama dressed us in colorful starched dresses and we went for a *schpatzeer* (walk) in the park. We had a friendly plump neighbor, Mrs. Shapiro, who specialized in very fluid spitting.

My sister Pearl was particularly pretty. If anyone remarked that we looked cute, Mrs. Shapiro would suddenly appear from out of nowhere and shower us with a profusion of *kine-ahoras* and spit to shoo away any evil demons that may have heard the compliment. She spit so effectively that the starch in our dresses wilted.

Mama had completed her courses at the Settlement House in Health and Nutrition where she learned that bacteria and infection could be carried in the spray of saliva. Poor Mama was torn between protecting us from germs or letting Mrs. Shapiro protect us from a calamity. She settled on the former more scientific belief and we tried to avoid Shapiro the *shpyerkeh* (spitter) like a plague.

On the fifth floor lived Mrs. Finkel. Her life was one constant misfortune after another — a condition that creates a fertile climate for unlimited belief in a myriad of superstitions. As a child I found it fascinating to listen to Mrs. Finkel. She was a walking encyclopedia of mysticism and interpretations. She always had a mystical explanation for all her bad luck.

Looking back, I can see that it gave her some semblance of control over the fates and provided her with answers to many unanswerable questions.

She was certain that her first born son, Izzy, became a sickly child and passed away because a neighbor took him out for a walk in his carriage when he was an infant without realizing that little Izzy was not wearing his *royte bendle* (red band). The red band was supposed to distract the evil spirits.

She also knew why her brother Moishe died suddenly. She was with him the day before he passed away when he was speaking of his departed wife. Suddenly Moishe sneezed, but he forgot to pull his left ear lobe. She explained that a sneeze is a momentary departure from complete control and consciousness. If one should neglect to pull the ear lobe on the side of the heart when speaking of the dead, it was perfectly logical (to Mrs. Finkel) that the speaker would soon join the departed one in an extended state of unconsciousness.

Mama sewed all our clothes on her foot treadle Singer sewing machine. She would pin and baste a dress directly on us in order to get a proper fit. It was considered unsafe to sew clothes on a person as this would surely sew up the brain.

However, if a person chewed on a piece of thread, that supposedly kept the brain intact. Mama was not one to waste thread, and between fittings told me, "Save the thread until I need you for another fitting." I immediately went to the kitchen and carefully removed the piece of chewed gum I had previously placed in a cup. I took the thread out of my mouth and placed it in the cup for safekeeping and resumed chewing the hardened wad of gum.

Many of our neighbors and friends had their own favorite omens. Some examples are:

"If you sing before you get out of bed, you'll cry before you go to sleep."

"If a pregnant woman likes to eat the *schpitz* (end) of a bread, she will most likely have a boy."

"Even numbers are bad luck (except for 18, *Chai*) and odd numbers are good luck."

"If you step over a child it will stop growing. To make a child resume growing, recross it."

"Always begin an undertaking or journey or move on Tuesday. *Dinstig iz mozeldik* (Tuesday is lucky)."

"If, on returning from the *chuppah*, the bride takes the groom's hand first, she will dominate in family matters. If he takes her hand first, he will direct affairs."

The breaking of a glass at weddings was actually a move to scare off the demons (who, naturally envy and try to destroy the happiness of humans) by making a loud noise. In the course of time, people rationalized this tradition and the superstitious custom was explained or purified. Thus the breaking of the glass subsequently became a symbol of mourning for the destruction of the Temple in Jerusalem.

One ritual most everyone took seriously was, "When starting a journey, always go with the right foot first and the journey will end right." Strange, but somehow I find myself stepping on a plane with my right foot and hoping the pilot did the same!

Mama considered herself an enlightened woman and often spoke humorously about people who actually believed in these *mishegossen* (crazy ideas), but she always spoke quietly as there was no sense in stirring up anything, just in case.

Mama once asked me, "Did you ever hear the superstition? 'If the palm of your hand keeps itching, it means you are going to get something (hopefully, money). But, if your head keeps itching, it means you have something already (presumably, lice).'

Mama continued, "I always prided myself on the fact that I had sense enough to see through that hocus-pocus, *Kine-Ahora*."

I softly echoed, "*Poo! Poo! Poo!*"

Sigmund Freud, Meet the Ladies

My mother-in-law was a wonderful woman, may her soul rest in peace. She was strong, yet gentle and extremely bright with an endless reservoir of common sense. It was a pleasure to be in her company. I learned a good deal about life by observing her, both practical and beautiful. We shared a loving and deeply enriching relationship.

Mom Bressman was 16 when she left Poland to come to America. Her posture was regal and she had an inner grace that touched everyone she knew. A good student, she learned to speak and read and write English in a short time.

Every day she read an english newspaper. Rose Bressman, however, was a 'Master of Malaprops.' They flowed out of her mouth as naturally as poetry from Robert Burns.

When my daughter was an infant, we visited "Bubbeh Rosie" often. My mother-in-law and I had a great time playing with, hugging, singing to and cooing the baby. Mom held the baby's cheek close to her cheek and said to me, "I can see that you read Dr. Spock's book. He says you should always give a baby a lot of love and 'infection.'" She solemnly continued, "To help a child grow up to be a happy person, the parents have to have the right 'latitude' towards life."

I mentioned that the baby was very fretful for several nights.

Mom replied, "When a baby cries two nights in 'concession,' it wears you out from lack of sleep. Maybe she is crying because the sore from her vaccination is 'irrigating her'.

The conversation turned to food.

Mom advised, "As soon as the baby gets a little older, instead of candy and cookies, she should eat lots of raw carrots and 'strokes' of celery."

One day Mom phoned and said, "Better dress the baby in warm clothes when you take her out in the carriage. I just heard the weather report—20 degrees in the city and 15 degrees in the 'subways.' It's a good day to make hot pancakes from Aunt Jemima's 'battery.'"

In the spring we took a ride in the country and stopped to admire the rolling hills of New Jersey. Mom breathed the fresh air deeply and said, "Such natural beauty. You can see for miles. What a lovely 'landskate.'"

When my niece Marilyn called to tell Mom she had landed a job, Mom couldn't wait to tell me the good news. "Marilyn is working for a company, I think the name is Don Brodskys. I was so excited for her. I'm not sure, maybe she said 'down on Broad Street.'"

It turned out that Marilyn was employed by Dun and Bradstreet! Somehow these expressions endeared Mom all the more to me and added to her specialness.

My own Mama had a cheerful, lively friend, Sadie Moskowitz. She also specialized in verbal blunders. If there was a new wrong way to say something, she invented it. We called her 'Mrs. Malaprop.' Sigmund Freud attached deeper, darker meanings to slips of the tongue and claimed that malaprops and misnomers are not entirely innocent or accidental. Now Mom Bressman and Sadie could have easily kept Dr. Freud busy for many years interpreting the reaches of their verbal doozies.

Sadie once went to a concert in the park with Mama. The orchestra was playing and Sadie was swaying in her seat. She leaned toward Mama and said "Oy, that Wiennese composer, Johann Strauss, he wrote my favorite waltz, 'The Blue Daniel.' I get so carried away with his music that I feel dizzy and breathless and almost need 'artificial perspiration.'

"I read somewhere that Johann was a regular ladies man in his day, a real wolf in 'cheap clothing.' You know how people like to gossip, but I always say, 'people in glass houses shouldn't get stoned.' But if the shoe fits, buy it."

Just then Sadie started to cough and to blow her nose. Mama asked if she was chilled. She replied, "No, I'm not cold, and I don't have a cold, it's just that my 'sciences' are all stopped up."

During the recent rainy spell Sadie spent a good deal of time with Mama. I was visiting Mama when Sadie rang the bell. She greeted me with a warm hug and kiss, and twirled about the kitchen showing her new crisp, cotton dress. She was very generous in giving to charities, but she could not bear to throw out torn stockings. Her stockings always had runs that look like Eiffel Towers stretching from her ankles to her knees.

It didn't take long for Sadie to launch into her favorite hobby, talking. She asked us, "Did you see that former prizefighter, 'Rocky Galitzianer' on TV? He's a regular 'malted-millionaire.' Now this *zhlob* without an education made so much money that he bought his wife a beautiful white 'vermin' fur coat. And to think that my nephew, a college graduate, works in the post office and is only a 'civil serpent.'"

"Of course, my son-in-law is a 'sodified public accountant' and every year he sends me, for my birthday, a United States Government 'Bomb.'"

I couldn't believe my ears. It was clearly evident that I was in the presence of an expert of parody of the English language. She sailed forth with pure aplomb and assurance that made listening to her a delicious experience. Slowly peeling a banana, she went on, "I just mailed to my daughter Toby in Long Island, a sun dress I sewed for her. I always mail my packages 'partial post.' Toby's air conditioner broke down, but she has a big 'addict fan' to keep the house cool."

Sadie is getting on in years and suffers from many ailments. She adores her doctor. He treats her with great tenderness and looks forward to her visits to brighten his busyday.

Coincidentally her doctor is a good friend of our family. He has asked Sadie if he could share some of the highlights of her visits with others.

She was very complimented and gave him blanket permission. He described a typical office visit. "Sadie ususally enters the consultation room with a big bright smile, closely followed by a deep *ziftz* (sigh). She needs no prodding and immediately starts, 'Dr. Zecker, let's get down to 'brass roots.' I know you are honest with me. One thing I learned: you have to take the bad with the worst. Look up in my chart, the 'tantalizers' (tranquilizers) you prescribed for my nerves haven't helped me. But the anti-biotic helped, because the 'inflation' in my ear is gone. I realize that my 'existence' must be low and sometimes the body develops 'anti-taxis.' I must have taken too much of a laxative because now I have loose 'vowels.' To be perfectly honest, what I need at my age is a good 'plaster surgeon' to make me over again. But the best medicine, Doctor, is talking to you. Dear Dr. Zecker, you are such a wonderful doctor. If they gave out a special award, you would for sure win the 'Pullet Surprise' in Medicine!"

Yes, Sigmund Freud could have had a full career.

Yiddish Proverbs Mirror 'Delicious' Wisdom

Some children grow up in luxury, others are surrounded by sports and still others cut their teeth on politics. I grew up nurtured by Yiddish proverbs. Delicious wisdom is found in Yiddish proverbs. As Leo Rosten said, "They make you laugh, smile, and think. They reflect our fears and crystallize our hopes. Yiddish proverbs mirror the longings, the strivings, the trials and tribulations, the joys and griefs of the Jewish people." Shakespeare said, "We patch grief with proverbs."

Mama and Papa cherished proverbs and believed in teaching them to their children. Papa felt that proverbs revealed the soul of our people. My sister Pearl and I grew up with proverbs being tossed around us like tennis balls.

There were few moral dilemmas that Mama could not explain or illustrate by using an appropriate proverb. Papa was cautious by nature and he was fond of saying, "Look before you leap."

Mama's reply was "He who hesitates is lost."

Mama, an incurable romantic quoted, "Absence makes the heart grow fonder."

Papa, the realist, countered with, "Out of sight, out of mind." True, proverbs often take opposite sides, which only proves that life is full of contradictions.

For years I kept a loose-leaf proverb notebook. Here are some of Mama's and Papa's and my favorites: (The full sharp flavor of the proverb in its original spoken form in Yiddish is diluted in the translation, but it is hardy enough to retain much of its flavor even in English.

- On someone else's beard it's good to practice barbering.

- Better an honest slap than a false kiss.

- For a long happy life, breathe through your nose and keep your mouth shut.

- If you sit home, you won't wear out your shoes.
- If a horse had anything to say he would speak up.
- Little children don't let you sleep; big children won't let you live.
- An imaginary ailment is worse than a disease.
- Laughter is heard farther than weeping.
- A boil is no trouble under someone else's armpit.
- A half-truth is a whole lie.
- What is on the lung is soon on the tongue.
- With a child in the house, all corners are full.
- A wise man hears one word and understands two.
- Love is like butter, it is better with bread.
- You can't chew with somebody else's teeth.
- Houseguests and fish spoil on the third day.
- Enemies cannot do a man the harm that he does himself.
- For luck you don't need any wisdom.
- Drive your horse with oats, not with a whip.
- When the heart is full, the eyes overflow.
- A liar must have a good memory.
- You can't dance at two weddings at the same time, nor can you sit on two horses with one behind.
- A fool grows without rain.
- Never show a stick to a beaten dog.
- A clock that doesn't go at all is better than one that goes wrong.
- When you are scalded by the hot, you blow on the cold.
- At a distance you fool others; close at hand, just yourself.
- No choice is a choice.

- Man is stronger than iron and weaker than a fly.
- If you grease the wheels, you can ride.
- You can wash your hands but not your conscience.
- The highest wisdom is kindness.
- Jews are just like everyone else only more so.

Mama heard this from her mother. "A wish half fulfilled leaves one half empty."

Papa heard this from his father. "Half a wish granted is better than none."

Papa often told one of his favorite folk stories about the rabbi who prayed long and hard. His wife asked what he prayed for that day. The rabbi answered that his prayer was that the rich should be more generous to the poor. His wife asked if God heard the prayer. The rabbi answered he was sure He heard at least half of it because the poor have agreed to accept!

Yiddish proverbs are truly a treasure-trove expressing life in a special way. They are alive and well and endure even today.

Wait for the Right Time

Robert celebrated his Bar Mitzvah in 1928, a year before the Depression. It was a lovely Bar Mitzvah, followed by a festive affair at the Avon Caterers in Newark. Relatives and friends brought the usual gifts. But the most impressive gift, by far, was given to Robert by his rich uncle. With an appropriate flourish, the uncle presented him with a 14-karat gold Waterman's pen and pencil set elegantly encased in a beautiful box lined with red velvet.

Everyone admired this generous gift which cost $25, a small fortune in 1928. However, little did the new Bar Mitzvah boy realize at the time that this splendid gift would play a continuous part in his life.

After the excitement of the event was past, young Robert asked his mom to let him take his new 14-karat gold pen and pencil set to school. "After all Mom," he said, "now that I am a man, I'd like to use the beautiful set and show it to my classmates."

His mother turned pale and was visibly shaken. She tried to control her voice as she replied, "Son, you are still much too young to be entrusted with such a valuable possession. You are active in school sports; you love to play ball with the fellows. Who knows, you'll jump up to catch a fly ball and the pen and pencil will pop out of your pocket. You must try to understand. Now is not the right time. The set is safe in the vault." Young Bob bit his lower lip and quietly said, "I'll try to understand."

He was graduated from grade school with honors and was about to enter high school. Again he asked his mother if he could have the 14-karat gold pen, and pencil set. "My precious son," she crooned, "in high school there are some wild adolescents. I read somewhere that they even steal valuables from lockers. Why do you have to worry about your gold pen and pencil set? Better concentrate on your studies. Now is not the right time. The set is safe in the vault."

Robert was graduated with high honors and was accepted at a college in Michigan. Once more he spoke to his mom and told her he would like to take his pen and pencil with him. "Think it through," she reasoned, "you're going to a strange place, there may be many *meshuggenehs* in Michigan. Who can vouch for the honesty of the 'total stranger' who will be your roommate? It is not wise to put temptation right under his nose. Believe me, now is not the right time. The set is safe in the vault."

Robert was graduated again at the top of his class and entered medical school in Montreal, Canada. Once more he mentioned the pen and pencil set. His mother looked at him, unable to conceal the great pride she felt.

She replied in a loving voice, "Not because you are my son, but you are a gifted person, a genius, and geniuses are so involved in high level thoughts that they sometimes overlook simple and practical facts. In medical school you will be wearing a white jacket. You will put the gold pen in your pocket, the rubber bladder (sack) in the pen may leak, and before you know it you will have ink all over your white jacket. Your teachers, your professor will think you are not neat and most unprofessional looking with all that ink staining your white jacket. In the best interest of your future career, now is not the right time. The set is safe in the vault. "

Robert developed into a kind, sensitive, compassionate human being, and by now he had gained enough insight, with a strong sense of humor to somehow understand his mother's passionate concern over the safety of the "set."

Finally, when Dr. Robert first opened his medical office he jokingly asked her, "Nu, Mom, do you think I could place the pen and pencil set on my desk?" He waited for her reply with bemused anticipation.

She answered, "I was afraid you would ask me, and I gave it serious thought, and came to the conclusion that you are just starting in your new office and you cannot afford a nurse. Naturally, you are anxious for a new patient and I could just picture your excitement when a new patient comes in. Let us assume the patient is a lady. You will lend her your pen to fill out her personal history and forget to take it back. Why should you have to worry about the set? Better you should worry about building up the practice. Now is not the right time. The set is safe in the vault."

At this point, Dr. Robert could barely contain a smile. His mother possessed so many wonderful qualities that she was entitled to this one idiosyncrasy.

Four years ago, his mother passed away. When the vault was opened, Dr. Robert found the never used set resting peacefully in its red velvet lined case safely tucked in the bottom of the box. A short time later, Dr. Robert and his wife read an advertisement in The New York Times classified section, "Wanted, Antique Waterman's 14-karat gold pen and pencil set, circa 1928, mint condition, will pay $5,500."

Dr. Robert and his wife made arrangements to take the set to New York to consummate the sale. When they arrived, they looked at each other and decided against parting with this special heirloom.

On the ride home they discussed the future of the set. Dr. Robert's face lit up. "I have a wonderful idea, our grandson will become a Bar Mitzvah in a few years. Wouldn't it be a meaningful symbol of continuity if we gave him the set on that wonderful occasion? Provided of course, that we keep it in the vault for him until it is the right time!"

A Rose by Any Other Name

William Shakespeare said, "What's in a name? That which we call a rose by any other name would smell as sweet." He was right. Oh, how right he was!

A few months ago, I attended an all-day seminar on Jewish Folklore. It was an interesting and worthwhile day. Sitting next to me at one of the workshops was a warm, friendly, talkative woman. In the 15-minute intermission we became good friends.

My new found friend, Ethel, talked *kine-ahora*, a blue streak. "Isn't it wonderful," she said in a rich velvety voice, "that Jews have maintained the beautiful tradition of naming newborn children after a beloved relative so that the name can live on from generation to generation? Eastern European Jews (Ashkenazim) select the name to honor a respected departed person who lived a long, fruitful life. It is believed that the new baby will take on the exemplary characteristics and emotional qualities of the person he or she is named after. Among the Sephardic Jews, the baby is named after a living relative who is bright, successful and highly regarded."

When Ethel paused for a breath of air I asked her "Do you know that some people go to *shul* to rename a member of their family who is critically ill? This is done as a desperate measure when all else had failed in a hopeless situation.

"The rabbi bestows on the sick one, a different Hebrew name than the one he or she has had all along. Superstition holds that the angel of death, the *malach ha movess*, will be totally confused by the strange new name when he comes to claim the sick person and his mission will be thwarted. Usually the new given name is one of a strong person, like Gideon."

Ethel smiled and said, "Yes I know about this folk custom. It's not easy to outwit a determined *malach ha movess*, but it can't hurt to try."

She paused for a second and then went on, "Yes, continuity is the very essence of a people. Take my *ay-nek-loch* (grandchildren). My granddaughter was named after my late beloved mother *Chai-yeh Tzippeh*, may she rest in peace. Only in English my granddaughter is called Chandra Tammey.

"And my new grandson was named after my great uncle, *Moishe Yussel.* He is called Montgomery Jordan. Believe me, I get goose pimples each time I say his name and feel the ring of continuity resounding in my soul," said Ethel with tears welling in her soft, blue eyes.

I gave her a fresh tissue and told her, "I strongly feel that in perpetuating a name in our family we feel the flow of our own immortality."

We then proceeded to recount the original given names and their English counterparts of the many children and grandchildren we knew. *Yankel-Laib* became Jacques Lance, *Layeh-Mindel* is Lindsey Meryl, *Tevye-Shimmon* answers to Tyrone Sean and *Channeh-Pessel* is known as Amanda Paige.

Also, *Shaineh Mollkeh* is Stacey Melissa, *Chaim Beryl* responds to Claude Bernard, *Surreh-Rifka* is Sherryl Roxanne and *Avrum-Schmulik* is Ashley Scott.

Also, *Velvel-Itzik* is called Vance Ian, *Pesheh-Faigeh* replies to Pamela Francine, *Schlaimee-Reuven* is now Sylvester Rocky and *Tybee Yenta* is Tiffany Yolanda.

We both laughed at the far flung English translations. "You know something Ethel," I said, confiding in my new friend. "You are so right, it is a beautiful tradition — children flowering, keeping alive the name of a beloved person from generation to generation, from century to century, it touches my heart."

As for the loud ring of continuity each time the name is sounded, I can't help but question if in some strange way our departed relatives could hear the new translations, would they be able to recognize themselves? It would take a very sophisticated and astute *Yankel-Laib, Avrum-Schmulik, Shaineh-Mollkeh,* or *Schlaimee-Reuven,* to know they are being remembered as Jacques Lance, Ashley Scott, Stacey Melissa and Sylvester Rocky!

Litvaks and Gailtzianers—*Oy Vay* or *Eye Vye*

When our ancestors came to America, the first and most important thing they had to learn was to speak *Engulsh* (English). In the United States we have southern, midwestern, New York and Brooklyn accents. Similarly, the immigrants reflected their regional accents.

Mama came from Lithuania and Papa came from Bruk, a little town in Poland. There was quite a difference in their dialects, especially in the vowel sound. Mama said *shayn* (beautiful) while Papa pronounced it *shoyn*. Mama said *hayzn* (trousers) but Papa said *hoyzn*. Bread and butter were *brayt un putter* to Mama, *broyt un pitter* to Papa.

Mama felt that Litvaks spoke with a more lyrical, softer sound. To her ear, the Polish, GalitziANER accents were harsh and unpleasant. She made a pact with Papa to raise her children to sound like pure Litvaks.

When new immigrant neighbors moved in, Mama needed only a short conversation with them before identifying their place of origin. "Good," Mama said, "they are Litvaks, just like us." Or, if from another region, she pretended to be crestfallen as she whispered, "They are *nebech* Galitzianers."

Some people categorize others as "Haves" or "Have Nots." Our world consisted of two classifications: Litvaks and Galitzianers. Litvaks pronounced the Yiddish letter for S, *shin* as *sin*. In Litvakese, *a shayner Shabbes* (a beautiful Sabbath) comes out as a *ssayner Ssabbes*. When you stood close to a Litvak, you risked being *sspritzt* (sprayed) as he spoke.

Note the different pronunciations of the same words, *kayfn a shtik fleish* (to buy a piece of meat). Litvaks said, (stand back now and watch out for the spray) *kayfn a sstik flayss*. Papa said, *"Koyfn a shtik floysh."* The Galitzianer always accented the sound "ei" and it came out as *keifyn a shtik fleish.* You could identify a Galitzianer a mile away simply by listening for *eye vye* instead of *oy vay.*

As a child I developed a keen ear for the various accents and the color-ful, lilting but fractured English. How they struggled with strange sound-ing vowels, verbs and words. The letter W was pronounced as a V and the V as a W. For example, "I vould trust her vid my life for she is a wery vun-derul voman."

The regional differences in the immigrants' accents spilled over into their English pronunciation, often inventing new patterns for the creation of new words. They developed a lexicon of Yiddish-Yinglish words, some of which became part of the English language.

Many Hebrew words (and subsequently Yiddish words) start with a *tzadi*—the TS or TZ sound. The Yiddish-speaking new arrivals clung to this familiar sound and wove it into their new language. Years ago I heard a wonderful entertainer and comedian, Emil Cohen, give his version of the TS and TZ sound as it was incorporated into English. His fine ear impressed me and I am firmly convinced that he must have lived in our apartment house.

Bessie Zimmer, our neighbor next door, often came to borrow some *tsuker* (sugar) for her *tsimmes* (cooked prunes, carrots and sweet potatoes).

Tsimmes can also mean making a big fuss or a big deal out of anything or nothing.

After a few years in this country, Bessie, now Americanized no longer borrowed *tsuker,* instead she asked for *tsugar* (sugar).

Tsatske, Yiddish for toy, can also refer to a girl of questionable repute (a plaything). For instance, "Her *tsister* (sister) is some tough *tsatske,* with one look she can make her husband's *tsitses* (fringes) twirl."

Bessie Zimmer would often exclaim, "If more people were *tzadiks* (men of extreme virtue) and went to the *tsinagogue* (*syna*gogue), this would be a better *tsivilization* (civilization)."

Bessie lamented, "If my husband Harry didn't smoke so many *tsigars* (cigars) and *tsigarettes* (cigarettes), he would not be so *tsedrayt* (mixed-up, confused), *tsetummelt* (discombobulated) or *tsedoodelt* (wacky)."

"As for me," Bessie moralized, "I don't want my money should go up in smoke. Instead I take a *tsubvay* (subway) and go to the uptown *tseenyer tsitizner tsenter* (senior citizen center) to hear a good *tsinger* (singer)."

A *tsenter* can also refer to the tenth man needed for a *minyan*.

William Safire, the celebrated word *mayvin* for *The New York Times,* is an authority on the use and misuse of new and old words.

Just imagine the challenge Mr. Safire would face with Yinglish usage.

He may have a lot of *tsores* (trouble) translating the above glossary of words, that's for *tsertain* (certain)!

Jewish Humor—a Treasure Beyond Measure

The New York Times recently printed an interesting article about the Nobel Prize-winning Yiddish writer Isaac Bashevis Singer. It seems his tombstone engraving had several errors: The word Nobel was written as Noble and Bashevis was misspelled. Also, he was buried next to his wife's first husband.

His son protested vigorously and a new stone with the correct spelling replaced the original one. However, Singer still remains next to Alma Singer's first husband.

If Singer could have witnessed these events, he probably would have been greatly amused and surely would have spun this scenario into a marvelous story.

When my beloved Mama died, I ordered a tombstone with the inscription: "Her Beauty, Grace and Loving-kindness Illuminated Our Lives." Luckily, I paid close attention to the proof mailed to me by the engraver. I opened the envelope, read the inscription and could not believe my eyes. The proof read: "Her Beauty, Grace and Loving-kindness Eliminated Our Lives." The correction was made before it was carved in stone.

Both Mama and Papa had a delicious sense of humor and we often talked about the special quality of Yiddish humor. Because the Jews have gone through so much and our history is filled with tragedy, we use humor as an arsenal of defense, as a means of survival. It is a kind of balance wheel in life and people who can laugh at their own shortcomings and foibles are people who are human. We know what Jews think and feel, and we sense some of their deepest emotions by what they find amusing.

In *Wit and Subconscious,* Freud tells us that a veneer of civilization surrounds us whether it has to do with religion, sex, government or our way of life. We break through the veneer when we tell a funny story and when we laugh at it. We relieve the tensions of life through humor.

Yiddish humor can even spoof and laugh at subjects relating to the cemetery and death. One of Mama's favorite stories was about poor Abe, who was on his deathbed. Every breath was an effort for him. His wife, Sadie, sat close to his bed, afraid to leave even for a minute. Suddenly, Abe motioned weakly to Sadie to come closer and in a faint, raspy voice said, "Sadie, I want you to go upstairs and put on your blue chiffon evening gown and your blue sapphire earrings and your antique broach." Abe took a labored breath and continued, "Then I want you to put on some make-up and comb your hair."

Sadie was bewildered. "Abe," she said, "You must be delirious. I won't leave you for a second."

"Sadie dear," he implored, "do not deny me my last wish."

Sadie ran up the stairs, hurriedly put on the blue chiffon dress, blue sapphire earrings, antique broach and quickly dabbed on some make-up and combed her hair while flying down the stairs. She was relieved to hear that he was still breathing. She sat down close to Abe; his eyes were closed and his color poor.

Suddenly, he half opened his eyes and reached for Sadie's hand. Sadie trembled with fear, but she could not keep herself from saying, "Abe, you must not go until you tell me why you sent me upstairs to get all *farputzed* (dressed up) at such a critical time."

With great effort, Abe summoned every ounce of strength to explain: "Sadie, I know the end is near and the *molech hamoves* (angel of death) is coming to take me any minute now. I thought maybe if you sat near me and looked so good, maybe he would take you instead of me!"

Mama and Papa both enjoyed telling these stories. Another one was about Harry Hirschkowitz, who lived until he was 99. At his funeral, two of his neighbors were discussing Harry. "What was so special about living until 99?" they asked. "He didn't do anything worthwhile in his whole life except to get old, and it took him such a long time to do that!"

Teddy Tomashevsky of the famous Teddy's Ties made a fortune in the tie business. He credited his success with his lifelong policy of postdating all his checks. Upon his death, his headstone was engraved with this immortal description: HERE LIES TEDDY TOMASHEVSKY, DIED DEC. 15, 1996—AS OF JAN. 1, 1997.

And the tale of Phyllis: She died, and before she was accepted in heaven, the gatekeeper said she would have to answer a few questions to establish her good character.

He asked her whether it was true that she married her husband because he was a millionaire. "Absolutely not," an indignant Phyllis replied. "Actually, I made him a millionaire."

The gatekeeper asked, "What was he before?"

She answered, "A multi-millionaire!"

Laughing with tears in your eyes or with joy in your heart is all a part of Jewish humor. It is a treasure way beyond measure.

Jewish Humor Mirrors Life

Papa possessed a keen, dry sense of humor and viewed the world through kind, tolerant and bemused eyes. He delighted in telling a wealth of humorous stories. He felt that Jewish humor was special and unique for it mirrored and reflected the whole cycle of life from birth to death. Papa believed that humor that is not afraid to look death in the eye and laugh in its face must be taken seriously.

Here are some of Papa's and my favorite stories.

Richest Man

The richest man in town died and a great number of mourners came to his funeral. At the cemetery, the rabbi noticed that among the mourners was Yussel, the town cobbler, who cried as though his heart would break.

"I noticed you weeping. Were you related to the deceased?" asked the rabbi.

Yussel said with a loud wail, "No, I wasn't related at all."

The rabbi asked, "Then why do you weep."

"I just told you," sobbed Yussel, "that is why."

Putting on Weight

Tillie Cohen's husband Jack died. Although she had personal misgivings, Tillie had Jake's body cremated according to his last wishes. She never told a soul what was in the urn. When asked, she would say that it was merely an unusual ashtray. Many friends came to visit her and they would often flick their cigar and cigarette ashes into it.

One day as Tillie was cleaning the house she picked up the urn in order to dust under it. She muttered to her self, "I know it is not my imagination. I'm sure that Jake is putting on weight."

Grave Error

Mr. Goldberg, a wealthy garment manufacturer lay dying. His wife Bella sat nearby anxiously listening to his every labored breath. Suddenly Goldberg motioned Bella to move closer and he whispered, "I neglected to draw up a will. Listen carefully and pay attention to my last wishes."

Bella wept, "Yes, Sam, anything you want-it will be done."

Goldberg said, "First, I'm leaving my business to Sheldon."

"Sheldon!" shrieked Bella, "You're making, (you should pardon the expression) a 'grave' error. Sheldon is a compulsive gambler and he shuttles between the casinos in Las Vegas and Atlantic City. In six months time he'll ruin the business. It would be much wiser if you left the business to Harry; he is mature and level headed."

"All right, let it be Harry," sighed the dying man. He continued, "And to my grandson, Jayson, I leave the house in the Hamptons."

Bella's eyes widened, "That is another (again you should excuse the expression) 'fatal' mistake. Jayson needs structure and discipline. He'll get in with the Hampton playboys and playgirls and he'll play the rest of his life away. Better leave the house in the Hamptons to elderly Tante Sadie. The ocean air will be good for her in her few remaining years."

"O.K. give the Hampton house to Sadie," Goldberg said in a faint voice. "But I want the warehouse in Soho to go to Phillip."

Bella tried to keep her exasperated voice down, "Phillip has no imagination. The warehouse will depreciate into nothing. Definitely the warehouse should go to Sidney. He is a real swinger and he has flair and style. He will convert the warehouse into a combination Soho art gallery and disco and in a short while Sidney will become a great success."

With a weak nod, Goldberg agreed and added, "One thing for sure, I leave all my clothes, my entire wardrobe to Izzy, who is my exact size."

Bella gritted her teeth and spoke through them, hardly moving her lips, "Why does Izzy need your clothes? Where does he go? Day and night he is glued to his TV set. Take my advice, better you should leave your clothes to Bernie. True, he is 30 pounds lighter than you, but with a few alterations, a nip here and a tuck there, they will fit him beautifully." Goldberg wanly consented.

By this time his patience had worn completely. Raising himself off the pillow, and summoning his last ounce of strength, he implored, "Listen Bella — who's dying around here — you or me?"

Why Wait

Bernard Baruch amassed millions in the stock market. One day he fell gravely ill and his trusted partner Michael sat faithfully at his bedside.

Mr. Baruch said, "Michael, my friend and partner, I'm afraid my time has come. I'm 79 years old and I'm dying."

"Oh no," said Michael, consolingly, "with your constitution you'll live to 120."

"What sort of silly remark is that?" retorted Baruch, the successful financier. "Why should God wait until I go all the way up to 120 when he can get me now at only 79?"

Yes, Papa was right. Jewish humor is unique and really something special.

Never Say Died

My mama and all her relatives had one thing in common. They knew hundreds of ways to convey the message that someone was near death, or had died, without mentioning the word died.

In retrospect, I think it may have had something to do with the constant fear of pogroms and the imminence of death in their little *shtetl* (village) in Russia. They always cushioned the fatal words and did not say them outright in conversation.

Never did I ever hear my mother simply say, "Mr. Goldstein died." Instead, she would wait until after dinner, and then decide to wait until morning, (after all, why should she impart such bad news before bedtime). She would clear her throat and say, "It is such a shame, Mr. Goldstein is very ill."

This meant he was not long for this world or he is near his last breath. When you heard adult teeth clicking, it meant someone was momentarily alive.

If you listened to a deep sigh followed by, "She is not far from heaven or paradise," you knew it was near the end.

Uncle Itzhak often sat in our kitchen, sipping a glass of tea through a lump of sugar held securely between his front teeth. When he told us about a cousin who had one foot in the other world, we knew it would not take too long for the other foot to follow.

All of the above held true when Mama said someone was very sick. When she softly said someone was very, very sick, it meant they had already died.

Recently I heard a story that brought a reminiscent smile. Two brothers had a close relationship. They worked hard and became extremely successful. One brother, Sam, lived a full, happy life. He frequently took vacations and traveled all over the world with his family. The other brother, Jack, was a bachelor who was completely devoted to his dog Lucky. Jack never took a vacation because he did not trust anyone to properly care for Lucky.

One day his brother Sam prevailed upon him. "Jack, you worked hard all your life, yet you never allow yourself any pleasures. Please go to Europe. See the world. I'll take care of your dog as if he was my very own child."

After much apprehension about Lucky's care, Jack reluctantly went on his first vacation. His attachment to the dog was so great that he felt compelled to make a Trans-Atlantic call to Sam every night to ask about Lucky. "Did he eat — is he depressed — does he miss me?" he anxiously inquired. Sam assured him that Lucky was fine and was romping about with other dogs and having a good time.

The daily phone calls continued through the third week, and this night Sam was very upset and nervously said, "Lucky is dead." There was complete silence on the other end of the telephone, then deep, irregular breathing. Sam was alarmed, "Jack, Jack, are you O.K.?" he shouted into the phone.

After what seemed an eternity, Jack faintly answered, "Sam, how could you break such news to me so abruptly. A man could go into shock or at least have a coronary. You know what Lucky meant to me."

Sam was contrite, "So tell me, how else could I tell you the dog was dead? By me, dead is dead."

Jack had regained some of his composure and replied, "First you should have said Lucky is playing on the roof! The next night when I called, it would have been more discreet if you said Lucky had an accident. The third night you could have said poor Lucky's condition is worse, and then when I called the following night I would have been conditioned when you told me 'Lucky passed away.' Bad news should always be broken gently."

I'm really sorry," said Sam, I'll know better next time."

"All right," said Jack, "I'm not one to carry grudges. I forgive you. I won't belabor the point. In fact I'll change the subject completely. Tell me, how is our beloved Mama feeling?"

After a long, pregnant pause, Sam carefully answered, "Mama is playing on the roof!"

Mama and 'Jawge Burnod Shor'

When Mama set foot in this country from Russia, she was determined to register for the Americanization class at once. Her sister Lena accompanied her to the local school where the English language and preparation for the United States citizenship examination were the two major courses of study.

Mama was wildly enthusiastic. She could read and write Russian fluently, and she could not wait to sit down at a desk to start her lessons in "Engulsh" and "citiznership."

Lena tried to restrain her: "But you can't rush right into a classroom, first you must register." They went to the school office and waited until they were summoned to the inner cubicle. The registrar started to ask questions in English and began to fill out a printed form. She asked Mama's name.

"Rose Pinchick," replied Lena, acting as the interpreter.

"How do you spell it?" the registrar asked matter-of-factly. Mama asked Lena what the conversation was about.

"She wants to know how to spell your name," Lena patiently explained.

Mama was alarmed. "We better go to another school," she suggested. "If they couldn't teach her how to spell a simple name, what can they teach me here?"

Russian is a phonetic language, and it never occurred to Mama that the same sounding words could have different spellings. But Mama turned out to be a star pupil. She never stopped going to school. She absorbed courses in history, current events, the labor movement and health and nutrition like a hungry sponge.

She still had a problem with spelling. How often I would hear her ask, "So why do you need a 'K' in knife?"

The word "daughter" was the bane of her existence. She was frequently assigned to write a composition as homework. The teacher urged her class to write about their own lives. It was not unusual for Mama to sit around the kitchen table with my sister Pearl and me — all doing our homework.

Mama's composition would tell about her family, her husband and two daughters. "Daughters should be spelled like it is said — 'dutters.' Who needs the 'au,' the 'g' and the 'h'? You can't hear it, can you? It would be easier for my spelling if I had 'sons' — or do they spell it in American, suns? *Meshugge* (crazy)!"

In 1950 I was still a newlywed, and I always looked forward to my visits with Mama and Papa in New York. One day I came to find Mama excited. An awesome blush covered her cheeks. She waved the newspaper in front of me, pointed to an article and immediately started to read out loud:

George Bernard Shaw strongly supports the universal use of phonetic language; words should be spelled as they are spoken."

"I am letting the world know," the article continued, "that what remains of my fortune of 300,000 pounds, after death duties are paid, is left in a trust for research on a proposed phonetic alphabet." Mama's beautiful eyes were aglow as she read on.

"All civilized people should adapt the use of phonetic spelling as this would encourage an understanding and closeness of people the world over."

Shaw was further quoted, "Let us pass an international law abolishing the stupid spelling we now employ, and replace it with phonetic spelling."

Mama could not contain her elation. She felt she had found a kindred soul. She hugged the newspaper to her chest and wistfully said, "One heart reaches out and touches another heart."

She wanted to give him her support and encouragement. She would write to him immediately. Papa gave me a warm wink and asked, "Do you think 'Judge' Bernard Shaw will be excited to hear from Mama?"

Mama pretended she didn't hear. She sat down and wrote him a long, passionate letter, in her own special phonetic spelling, telling him of her many years of frustration with the English language. Mama implored him to go on with this vital movement and liberate the world from needless, soundless spelling.

George Bernard Shaw died shortly thereafter on Nov. 2, 1950. Although he lived to a ripe old age, I strongly suspect that the strain of trying to decipher her letter may have shortened the poor man's life!

HEALTH AND DOCTORS

Hoping for a 'Big' Doctor

Behavioral scientists have long found that we are a society greatly influenced by peer pressure. This applies to children, adolescents, mid-lifers and seniors.

Some time ago Mama kept hearing from her friends at the senior center and on the park bench that the New York Eye and Ear Infirmary was the best place for the care of eye problems. She reasoned that her friends have had so much experience that they are specialists in knowing good specialists.

Mama was bothered by a burning sensation in her eyes and her friends persuaded her to go to this clinic. She went several times and they prescribed various salves and ointments. They did not seem to help.

Mama didn't tell me a word about her visits to the clinic. She thought she would spare me the trip to the doctor with her by attending to this problem herself. If anything, her eyes felt more irritated, and after a while she confessed all to me and told me she was going to keep her appointment the following day. Perhaps she would be lucky enough to be seen by a "big" doctor. All doctors in New York are "big" doctors, none are ever "small."

Early the next morning I decided to go to Mama's house so that we could visit the clinic together. I wanted to find out exactly what was happening and was concerned that she should get the proper treatment. I reached Mama's house at 10 in the morning.

Her appointment was scheduled for one o'clock. She was glad to see me although she admonished me, "Why did you have to *shlep* here, I can go by myself."

At 11 o'clock Mama started to pack a lunch for us. "What are you doing?" I inquired.

She looked at me as if I had asked a foolish question and answered, "Everyone takes lunch. We want to get there early, and usually there is a long wait, so it is best to take lunch along." She packed two cold chicken sandwiches on whole wheat bread, carrot and celery sticks, a banana for her and an apple for me. Also tucked into the bag were two bran muffins and a small baggie with raisins and nuts plus paper napkins and several Wash'n Dry packets.

We took the bus and arrived at the clinic a little before noon. Although the clinic didn't officially open until one o'clock, the patients (mostly elderly) were rapidly filling the seats. We sat in a huge waiting room containing row upon row of chairs. At 12:30, I was amazed to see most everyone unwrap a lunch and start eating. Mama spread a napkin on my lap, then put one on her lap and we nonchalantly ate our chicken sandwiches.

There were warm friendly exchanges of, "Here's some of my carrot. "I'll taste a piece of your pickle." "Sample a *shtikeleh* salami. Even if it repeats on you, it's worth it." I was completely taken in by the *haimish* (homey) social spirit and soon I was exchanging my bran muffin for a piece of homemade strudel.

July first was the date of Mama's appointment and we learned that it was also the first day the brand new residents (fresh out of medical school) were starting to work in the clinic. Needless to say, this did nothing to instill confidence in us.

At precisely one o'clock, a nervous young resident came out. He actually blushed and cleared his throat two times before he called the name on the chart. Mama whispered to me, "He's scared, it's his first day, *nebech* (poor thing). I'm so glad he didn't pick my chart."

Then another resident appeared and called another name. He looked even younger and slighter. Mama heaved a sigh of relief when she heard him pronounce a strange name. In between a senior doctor would appear and call a name from a chart. This went on for several hours.

Each patient was hoping for an experienced doctor to pull his chart. It was like a lottery. There was a nervous atmosphere in the clinic and everyone kept munching on the last remnants of lunch, polyseeds, Hershey bars and antacid tablets.

A heavyset man in front of us said in a loud voice, "How is this for a play on words in an eye clinic, by me the young *boychik* doctors are not so *eye y'eye y'eye.*" He laughed uproariously at his own wit. No one else smiled. His wife glared at him and gave him a *chmallyeh* (a clout with her hand) and ordered him to keep quiet.

At 3:30, I asked Mama, "Do you think we should have brought supper too?" It was 4:00 P.M. and Mama's name was still not called. She was *oysgematert* (worn out) from hoping to hear her name called by a senior 'big' doctor yet dreading to hear her name called by a young doctor.

At 4:10 P.M. Mama looked at me in despair and said, "You know I'm not a complainer but the young ones look like regular babies to me and I'm afraid to trust my eyes to a 'baby' doctor."

I looked back at her and tried to calm her fears. "Mama dear," I said, "If we sit here any longer the young doctors won't be babies any more. They will be old experienced men by the time they call your name!" We both laughed and hoped for the best.

When Mama's name was called at long last, as luck would have it, she was approached by a young resident and Mama's heart fell. Her fervent prayer for a senior doctor calling her chart was unanswered. With a complete lack of confidence, we followed the timid young doctor into the examining room.

He read Mama's chart, put his hand over his chin and uttered an impressive sounding "Hmmm." Then he started to whistle an off-key tune through his teeth. We realized he was nervous and was probably unaware of his whistling. But we were not exactly relaxed either, and it was unsettling.

He proceeded to crack his knuckles, wash his hands, and very gingerly lift Mama's eyelids before flashing a little light in her eyes, whistling all the while. I watched him set his young face in what he must have assumed was a dignified, professional expression. Again he read Mama's chart and with all the authority he could muster, he informed Mama that he recently read in the medical literature that washing the brows and lashes with Johnson's Baby Shampoo would eliminate the problem that caused the burning in her eyes. He solicitously asked, "Do you want me to write a prescription for the Johnson's Baby Shampoo"

I assured him that I would have no trouble obtaining it in the local pharmacy without a prescription.

Mama and I both thanked him and we were happy to get out of the clinic. It seemed as if we had been sitting there for a week. We were pretty skeptical about his prescription but Mama explained, "Just before we came here today, his mother probably washed his hair with Johnsons Baby Shampoo so it was still fresh in his head."

Some time later I took Mama to a fine eye doctor, Dr. Greenfield, and we told him about the trip to the clinic. He recommended special drops. Mama was greatly relieved to put her eyes in the hands of an experienced doctor.

On our way home Mama told me she was reminded of a humorous doctor story she heard many years ago. It seems there was a young doctor in Moscow in his first year of internship. He had an inflated ego and already believed he knew more than any other doctor did in the large state hospital in Russia.

One morning he strode into the orthopedic ward to examine two Jewish men who were suffering from the same type of injury, a dislocated shoulder. The intern examined the first man's shoulder, turning and twisting it with a heavy hand. The poor patient screamed with the pain. Then the young doctor turned to the other man and went through the same procedure, but not a sound escaped the injured patient.

When the intern left, the first patient said to his neighbor, "Comrade, Boris, where did you ever find the courage to endure such pain without uttering a single cry?"

"Courage, who has courage?" answered Boris. "I just used some old fashioned *say-khel* (sense). After what that young, inexperienced doctor did to you, do you think I was fool enough to let him touch the shoulder that was injured?"

As Mama said, "Experience is the best teacher, and wisdom comes with the years — sometimes!"

The Making of a *Mayvin*

The high cost of medical care has become a major domestic issue in this country.

We are living in an age when the Federal government is subsidizing behavioral research on the sex lives of cats. Yet no one seems to be doing serious research on how to reduce spiraling medical costs. People are alarmed and frightened that one major illness can wipe out a lifetime of savings. Mama's senior citizen group talked about this problem at its weekly current events discussion group.

Mr. Goodman had the floor: "The reason people are burdened with such high medical costs is that we neglect to make use of all the knowledgeable people in our own families who sometimes have as much experience as any doctor. Let me give you an example.

"For months my nephew Sheldon had persistent sneezing and a hacking cough. I told his mother, 'The lad would be cured if he eliminated pepper from his diet.' I know the same thing happened to me when I was a young boy, and a *feldsher* (folk doctor) in Poland told me the cause of my sneezing and coughing was pepper. I figured maybe my nephew took after me and inherited the same problem.

"But no one listened to me and they schlepped poor Sheldon to internists, ear, nose and throat specialists, and allergists. After exhausting all the professional advice with no apparent lessening of the symptoms, they finally tried my suggestion, and Sheldon has not sneezed or coughed since he threw away the pepper-shaker."

Sam Lieberman was next to volunteer medical advice. Sam had a pacemaker implant and he considers himself an authority on the same level as Dr. De Bakey. Sam paused until he had everyone's undivided attention before speaking.

"Just the other day I was visiting my brother Izzy and he complained about poor circulation and an irregular heart beat. I told him, 'Izzy, you can benefit from my experience and save yourself a lot of money. You don't need a lot of advice from doctors, schmocktors. What you need is a pacemaker and you'll feel like a new man. Izzy, don't ask for consultations, better ask the man who owns one. Eliminate the middleman and go directly to the man who will put in the pacemaker!"

Next, tiny Mrs. Klein contributed to the discussion. "I have back problems, upper and lower back, neck and shoulders, and all connecting joints. When I go to the doctor, I ask a lot of questions. The trick is to listen very carefully to every word the doctor says. In this way, I have been able to advise every one in my family (or close friends) with similar ailments. They have saved a fortune of money in doctor bills. Believe me, I may not have an official medical diploma, but when it comes to the upper and lower back, neck and shoulders, and all connecting joints, I'm a real specialist. I should have so many good years as the many people I've helped. Recently I had someone come to me with a minor backache plus a little heartburn on the side. I took care of the back and referred the heartburn symptoms to our own heart specialist, Mr. Sam Lieberman." Mr. Lieberman beamed at the professional recognition.

Mr. Pearlman, a handsome 85-year-old man with thick, wavy white hair spoke up. "Almost 50 years ago a doctor told my wife she needed a hysterectomy. I am a firm believer in letting nature take its course. I felt it was against nature to 'tinkle with the ivories.' *Oy*, I always get those words twisted. This has nothing to do with playing the piano. I didn't mean to say, 'tinkling with the ivories,' I meant, tampering with the ovaries.' I advised my wife to wait and respect nature. She went to another doctor and he agreed with me. 'No operation,' and here she is almost 50 years later with her own 'ivories' intact." He proudly pointed to his wife sitting happily and healthily by his side.

Mrs. Minnie Tennenbaum, a sturdy woman in her early 70s, held up her hand to be recognized and strode to the front of the discussion group with her ample bosom leading the way.

She smiled warmly and said, "I took a course in positive thinking and assertiveness and I am no longer intimidated by doctors. I ignore minor aches and pains and they go away. Last week I woke up feeling blue. Instead of brooding or going to a psychiatrist I went to a corset store and brought myself a fancy brassiere. I felt uplifted immediately."

Minnie grinned and waited for her audience to fully appreciate her play on words. She continued, "Seriously though, positive thinking helps keep my medical expenses down."

Mr. Pollack is the official poet for the senior group and enjoys putting everything into rhyme. Throughout the discussion he jotted on his pad. He stood up and declared "I just wrote a hasty poem that sums up our feelings."

He proceeded to read:

It's an umglick (tragedy)
To be sick
We ask the Lord
To keep from us bills we can't afford.
We love the doctors
But fun der vite-en (from afar)
May we enjoy good health
Fun alleh zite-en. (from all sides)

The group responded with a loud "*Omein.*"

Doing What Comes Naturally

My daughter Beth came home from school for a weekend. We took an early bus into New York and looked forward to visiting Mama. It was a beautiful, sunny day and we spent the afternoon on Mama's favorite park-bench.

My niece Lois was expecting a baby and Beth said to Mama, "*Bubbeh*, this will make you an *Ur-Bubbeh* (great grandmother)."

Mama was delighted. Somehow the conversation turned to the various new methods of childbirth. My niece and her husband were taking lessons in natural childbirth and Mama wanted to know more about it.

Beth explained it was a course of training in which the husband and wife are both involved. The expectant mother is taught to cooperate consciously with the delivery of the child, and breathing techniques are used to help her cope with the painful contractions.

In this way the mother is able to deliver her child with as little anesthesia as possible. The couple spends weeks going to classes to learn proper methods and the husband plays an important part in the birth process. He acts as his wife's coach throughout the delivery. Beth continued to explain the kinds of breathing accompanying the various stages of labor.

Mama looked astounded as Beth's jargon became more technical and Mama exclaimed in disbelief, "In America, *mocht min fun yayder klay-neh-kite a gray-sen tzimmis*" (In America, they make 'Much Ado About Nothing').

Quite by coincidence there was an interesting article in the paper I was reading that morning on the bus to New York. I had the paper with me and I turned to the page to read aloud to mama. It was a review of a book titled "Expectant Fathers" by Betty Parsons, one of Britain's most prestigious teachers of preparation for child birth.

The reviewer described it as a practical guide to pregnancy for the anxious male. Its key aim was to educate the man so that he could share with his wife "the incredible miracle they are achieving." Mrs. Parsons wrote, "When a man does participate, he feels much more a part of the child, and the couple can see the birth as something they are doing together."

Mama listened very carefully, "I don't want to appear unfeeling for the nervous fathers, but in all my years I never heard of a man dying in *kinpit* (childbirth). I can also understand that it is a great moral and psychological comfort to have a husband in the delivery room. Even if he got an A+ in the course — let's be practical and realistic — physically speaking — what else can he do except *helfin krech-tzen* (help her moan and groan)."

Mama continued, "I bet the couples taking the natural childbirth courses think it is a new invention. Childbirth used to be a natural thing. Now it has to be practiced, studied and learned. If you ask me, this makes it artificial. I guess the people in Europe were too busy having children to worry about how to have them."

I mentioned that Lois was planning to nurse her baby and was attending meetings of La Leche League. Mama's ears perked up. "I'm almost afraid to ask, what's that?"

We explained that La Leche International is a volunteer organization of mothers interested in promoting and publicizing the value of breast-feeding. Nursing mothers often find the support of their peers particularly valuable, and local groups meet to discuss their mutual problems and distribute literature on breast-feeding.

Mama shook her head from side to side. "All these years mothers managed to breast feed their babies without an international organization; even without the support of their peers. Who knew from peers, shmeers? You were lucky if your husband could support your family."

Mama was unsuccessful in trying to hide a bemused smile. She asked, "Tell me, *ver lerent a katz tzu zaygen ketz-a-loch*? (Who teaches a cat to nurse her kittens?). Today I wouldn't be suprised if there is a La Leche Society for *ketz-a-loch*!"

Beth was enjoying Mama's wry humor and wanted to witness her reaction to Dr. Frederick Le Boyer, an obstetrician who came here from France to publicize his new book, "Birth Without Violence." She proceeded to tell Mama about Dr. Le Boyer's concepts. He believes that those first cries of the newborn that we're all so glad to hear are really screams of terror. Birth is a trauma that persists for life and everything that is done in the delivery room with its glaring lights, sounds and strange environment increases the trauma. To take the terror out of birth, he developed a gentle birth method. To be suddenly thrust into a new environment is very frightening to the newborn, Dr. Le Boyer explains. He emphasized that the baby must be born into a calm, quiet atmosphere where talking, if necessary, is in hushed reverent tones, and there must not be any bright lights. Everything must be done to eliminate sharp contrasts and maintain the condition and security the baby had in the mother's body. He recommended that right after a baby is born, it should be placed on the mother's stomach to maintain physical contact with the mother. In this way the trauma of separation is lessened. The baby should then gently be massaged with rhythmic stroking and immersed in water to ease the transition from the mother's water sac. If these procedures are followed, Dr. Le Boyer claimed the baby then relaxed completely, and tensions that the baby might have carried all through life are released. The book stresses over and over again that the newborn baby is already a person with strong emotions, a person who has feelings and is aware of what is happening.

Mama said she found it very hard to believe all this scientific *narrishkeit* (foolishness).

Beth then asked Mama if she remembered the details of my birth.

"Like it happened yesterday," Mama replied. "But better Dr. Le Boyer shouldn't hear about it." Mama started to unfold the story of my entrance into this world. It was a hot Friday night in August, at 2 A.M. to be exact. Mama felt a sharp labor pain. She gently shook Papa, trying to awaken him from a deep sleep.

He half-awakened and asked what time it was. When Mama told him, he looked at her incredulously and said, "In the middle of the night you pick to have labor pains and wake a hard-working man who slaved in the shop all day? Try to go back to sleep, it may be a false alarm, maybe a little indigestion."

These were hardly words of comfort to a woman in the ninth month. But Mama felt sorry for Papa. He did work hard and he looked so tired. She tried to follow Papa's advice, but the labor pains continued. They were sharper and more frequent. She half apologized and woke Papa again.

Papa put on his pants over his underwear (men used to sleep in underwear, never pajamas). He told Mama he was going up to the third floor to summon a *lantzlady*, Gussie, to stay with Mama as prearranged. Gussie was to act as midwife.

Leaving Gussie at Mama's side, Papa ran two blocks down the street to a public telephone. (A private telephone was considered a luxury.) Papa called Dr. Newman and asked him to come right away.

Gussie was very hard of hearing and she spoke in a thunderous voice. She stood by Mama's bed lamenting, "Of all times to have a baby, you picked the worst time. Don't you realize it is *Erev-Shabbos* and aside from taking care of my six children, I chopped gefilteh fish, made knaydlach, baked challah, washed floors, spread newspapers over them and bathed the children too? I am *ois gematert* (exhausted). This baby should have had the sense to wait until the morning. I'm afraid I'll fall asleep in middle of the delivery."

Mama felt guilty about waking Papa and this warm reception didn't make her feel better.

Papa rushed back from the phone booth and a little while later Dr. Newman, also half asleep, knocked on the door. Water was boiling in readiness and suddenly Mama's labor pains subsided. She was petrified lest it was a false alarm. Dr. Newman instructed Mama to get back into bed so that he could examine her. A few minutes later I was born, an easy delivery with no complication.

Papa's first comment was: "I hope it's a boy."

Dr. Newman answered, "Better luck next time."

Then he took a close look at me and said, "Your sample was much prettier," (meaning my older sister Pearl).

Then Papa said to the doctor, "It was such a quick delivery, only a few minutes. Is the fee still $50?"

Dr. Newman wisely replied, "If your wife had *mu-chet* (struggled) with a long and difficult delivery, would it be worth it?"

I guess Papa didn't think another girl was worth $50. Please bear in mind that all these comments were made after I was born, and according to Dr. Le Boyer I was already aware and listening. To borrow his phrase, it could have been very "traumatic".

Maybe I was half asleep and escaped hearing these "welcoming" comments. I know my father loved me deeply and I couldn't have loved him more.

However, it was gratifying to recently read a child psychiatrist's views regarding Dr. Le Boyer's assumptions about the newborn's sensitivity to light, sound and touch. He wrote, "The newborn's nervous system is very primitive at birth. It's probably so underdeveloped that Le Boyer's methods couldn't make much difference."

Other obstetricians feel that there is no proof that the baby's first cries are full of terror. "The whole thing doesn't ring true," they claim, "a gross generalization." I heaved a sigh of relief.

While taking all the classes, my niece Lois and her husband Peter became apt students. They had twins; a handsome boy, Benjamin, named for my father, and a beautiful girl, Jasmine, named for a special uncle.

When Mama heard the joyous news, she said, "*Mazel-Tov, Mazel-Tov!*"

Oh, Those Home Remedies, They Would Cure or Kill You

I read recently that a government grant was being given for worldwide research on the effectiveness of home remedies, known as folk medicine. Eminent people in the medical profession discovered that these home nostrums warranted more credence than they had been previously accorded.

I thought back to my mother's own brewed secret cough syrup made with buxor, honey and special herbs that stopped coughs. The lining of my lungs is probably still coated with it. For a mild throat tickle, rock candy was recommended instead of cough drops.

Another favorite was the use of a mustard plaster to get rid of a persistent cough and to loosen heaviness in the chest. Mama made a paste of strong dry mustard, oil, flour and boiling water, spread it with the back of a tablespoon onto a piece of old flannel, folded it over, placed it on the chest and covered it with a towel to retain the heat.

This procedure required precision timing. The healing effects were immediately apparent. The powerful mustard fumes wafted up to clear the sinuses and serve as an eye wash by causing tears to flow.

My dear mother-in-law had seven children and helped her husband in the store. She would make a strong home concoction that acted as a laxative. Every Friday she lined up her brood of seven children and gave each a heaping tablespoon. She was too busy to keep track of their regularity. In this way she was secure in the knowledge that they were "cleaned out" weekly.

Another remedy was to place a piece of garlic into a homemade little pouch that was hung around the neck like a pungent pendant. This was supposed to ward off germs (particularly in the scary infantile paralysis era.) True, it did ward off germs in this respect — people didn't come too close to anyone wearing garlic.

There was an interesting regional difference. Galitzianers believed in garlic while Litvaks swore by the curative powers of a piece of camphor similarly worn.

Preventive measures were skillfully employed. After washing the hair, adding a drop or two of kerosene in the last rinse would guarantee a clean scalp and prevent nits.

For a sore throat and cough, a *guggle–muggle* was prescribed. This consisted of melted butter and honey and the beaten yolk of an egg added to boiling milk. If you could swallow and retain it, you forgot about your throat. There was a sure cure for laryngitis. Mama put a teakettle on the stove until the steam came through the spout. Then she put a towel over your head and gave orders to "breathe in" (never out). If you didn't suffocate, you survived.

Boiling cow's neck meat (which was thought to contain a lot of blood) and then straining the broth made beef tea. This rich broth was the approved tonic for pale children. It was automatically assumed that any skinny kid with a sallow complexion was anemic.

The most dramatic treatment for a lingering illness — when all else failed — was *bahn-kes* (vacuum cups). Usually the barber came with a cigar box filled with special glass cups and a long wire with a cotton tip. He would dip the tip in alcohol, ignite it and insert it into the cup to create a vacuum. He then quickly placed the cup on the patient's back or chest. After a specific time for the *bahn-kes* to "take," he would remove them, leaving many reddish-purple circles (the size of a half-dollar) on the skin. The purpose of this was to bring all the impurities to the surface of the skin and thus rid the body of any ailment. Everybody seemed to recover, and the barber vowed he never lost a case. The fee was usually fifty cents.

If any research foundation would like to use the carefully recorded data in this scientific paper, they may feel free to do so!

Also a Doctor!

Have you ever heard of a physician in New York who is simply "a doctor?" Never! It seems that all New York medical men fall into two categories, "big doctors" or the "biggest doctors."

Mama's *next-door-ek-eh*, Mrs. Rifkin, is bright, lively, and 92 years young. She is very proud of her three sons who are to quote her, "the three biggest, finest doctors in New York."

Hardly a day passes when she doesn't tell Mama a dramatic tale of how her sons routinely save the lives of desperately ill patients when no one else can help them.

"Geniuses," "Golden Hands," and "Miracle Men" are some of her more conservative descriptions of her children.

Her oldest son is "the greatest neurosurgeon ever born" her middle son is a "stomach specialist," and her youngest son is an orthopedist.

So you can readily see that she is medically covered from head to foot!

Mama was greatly surprised when Mrs. Rifkin told her she had severe pains in her right leg and was planning to see a local doctor. She asked Mama to go along with her.

"I can't understand your going to another doctor. Why don't you ask your sons about the pain in your right leg?" Mama asked.

Mrs. Rifkin's voice reflected her irritation. "Because," she said, "would my sonny boys tell me the truth if it is something serious? They would want to spare me."

She continued, "but a strange doctor will tell me the true nature of illness. Mama understood perfectly.

They went to see Dr. Grossman. Mama sat in the waiting room while Mrs. Rifkin went in for her examination. When she emerged from the consultation room, Mama helped her put her coat on and asked what the doctor said.

With a sharp, exasperated look Mrs. Rifkin announced, loud enough for all in the waiting room to hear, "Let's get out of here, what does a local doctor know?"

Mama hastily ushered her outside. She couldn't wait to hear the doctor's findings.

Mrs. Rifkin didn't waste a minute. "Do you want to hear something ridiculous? Dr. Grossman took my case history. His ball point pen ran out of ink when I was half through."

"He asked my age. I never lie. I told him 92. Then he told me that the pain in my right leg was probably due to my advancing years. Also a doctor!

"So what did you say?" Mama asked innocently.

"What did I say to him? I told him the only logical thing a sensible person could reply. I said, 'Doctor dear, my left leg isn't any younger—so tell me why it never hurts me?'"

Remembrance of Days Past

How vividly I remember that Sunday. It was a hot July morning, and I was packing a sandwich and fruit to take for lunch. I was 17 years old and eagerly looking forward to meeting my friends. How refreshing it would be to get out of the sweltering city, on to the Sea Beach Express and to finally reach the cool inviting ocean at Coney Island.

I wore my bathing suit under my dress. We wasted no time or money on bathing lockers. My lunch and towel were neatly packed in my bathing cap. The attached strap to my bathing cap served as the handle to my "luggage."

I was early for the appointed meeting, and while waiting, I felt a sharp pain in my abdomen. It grew progressively worse. My mother came into the kitchen just then. She took one look at me and said, "You look green and yellow — let me feel your forehead. You're running a fever and I'm going to call Dr. Solomon because *eppes* (somehow) to me you don't look good."

With these reassuring words I abandoned my Coney Island plans and could hardly wait for Dr. Solomon's knock on the door.

Kindly Dr. Solomon was the society doctor. Not Park Avenue society— he simply belonged to my father's lodge. He had a poor memory and could not remember names. He solved this problem by calling everyone "kiddie," including my mother. After a few painful pokes, he announced, "Kiddie, you have to have your appendix out. I'll call the hospital and make arrangements. Take your time, but be there soon." And to my mother he called over his shoulder, "Kiddie, be sure to take her in a taxi."

With the word "taxi" I first became alarmed. You simply did not take a taxi unless you were dying. Our neighborhood was noted for its non taxi-riding public, and no sane taxi driver could be found for miles around. Fortunately, a neighbor who was a part-time cabby decided to come home for lunch that fateful day and he drove us to the hospital.

They took me to the emergency room. The day was Sunday, and doctors were scarce. In the meantime, my mother and father were desperately trying to locate the big surgeon, Dr. Isaacs, only to learn he was away on vacation. A young, timid resident doctor took my history and haltingly told me that he was going to remove my appendix. He appeared nervous, and his complexion seemed no better than mine did, green and yellow.

I feebly attempted some funny remarks. He smiled wanly. I recalled reading an article about a noted New York surgeon who had an extensive collection of gallstones he had personally removed. He had them mounted, framed and hung in his study. I casually asked the young doctor, "Will you add my appendix to your collection?"

He looked at me and soberly replied, "Yours is the first one I am doing." This comforting thought stayed with me as they wheeled me into the operating room.

Even though I was a strong young girl and recovered nicely, it was then the general rule to keep patients in the hospital for ten days following surgery. On the second day, they brought in my roommate. She was a beautiful European woman in her early thirties. Rachel was a rebbitzen who was married to a handsome Orthodox rabbi. She spoke not a word of English. We conversed in Yiddish and became very friendly.

Every day the rabbi would come and offer a blessing for his wife's speedy recovery and, as he passed my bed, he would offer one for me too. After the young green surgeon, I gratefully accepted any blessings thrown my way.

On the tenth day I was preparing to leave the hospital. The rebbitzen took my hand and searched my face. "My dear friend," she said in Yiddish, "I feel toward you like my very own. Please forgive me for being so forward but you must do something about it — and soon."

"What is it, *rebbitzen?*" I asked.

"Dear friend," she continued, "you are a young girl, just in the bloom of 17 years — you are in America — you should get yourself a nice fine young American boy to marry. "*Folg mir*," (listen to me) she said, "do yourself a favor and learn to speak a little English!"

I often think of my rebbitzen friend. I would like her to meet my fine American husband. She'd be delighted to know that I look forward to sharing Yiddish with him for the rest of my life.

Food

Ess, Ess, Don't *Fress*: Some Food for Thought

Our whole country has become aware of the need for sound nutrition. Every week we read about the danger of foods that raise cholesterol levels, the ill effects of too many carbohydrates, the perils of excessive eating and vitamin deficiencies, and the health hazards of being overweight.

Organic, natural food is big business now.

Many years ago Mama attended a class in nutrition at the Henry Street Settlement. The teacher, Miss Brechen, had great difficulty in conveying to her class (consisting of European women), the importance of cutting down on the *schmaltz, cholent* and other very heavy foods. But the nutrition teacher had a strong influence on Mama and we were the victims. We appealed to Mama: "How come Miss Brechen is still *on olteh moid* (an old maid)?"

Papa had the answer: "Because she gives her suitors a sample of her nutritious cooking and scares them away."

The teacher made up little rhymes, "My my, don't fry," "Say scat to the chicken fat," 'Don't oil it, broil it," "*Ess ess*, don't *fress*" (eat, eat, don't gorge) and worst of all, "If it tastes too delicious, it can't be nutritious."

Mama took this last rhyme very seriously, and on that day she threw out the jar of chicken fat and broiled everything. Our mouths would water as we walked up the steps in the hall of our apartment. Delicious aromas of foods being fried and *ge-dempt* wafted through the doors and assailed us from all sides. When we reached our, apartment, Mama would be broiling liver, which somehow had the odor of hot rubber. "It's rich in iron,"she would explain.

Papa had so many "greens" served (schav and spinach) that he often complained he was eating grass. "I don't see any great contributions made by cows and they eat grass all the time," Papa exclaimed as he chewed on his broccoli.

Mama could not be swayed. We drank "certified milk" and rarely ate anything out of a can.

The Ices man made his daily rounds and it was a treat to watch him shave the ice into a paper cup and sprinkle the colored flavoring on top. Mama disapproved of the artificial coloring and could not understand why he didn't crush fresh strawberries, blueberries and cherries, and use this natural fruit to flavor the ices.

When the Frankfurter man came around with his colorful stand and umbrella, Mama looked at him scornfully. My sister and I watched him in awe as he opened many mysterious compartments, pierced the hot dog, put it on a soggy roll, swabed it with mustard and relish, and masterfully topped it all with limp sauerkraut.

To us it was a gourmet's delight that was strictly forbidden. To Mama it was "regular poison" that should be served with individual stomach pumps.

"Come upstairs with me," she urged, "and I'll make you some spinach *latkes* that will make you forget those frankfurters." We didn't quite forget.

Mama told me, "Do you know that today some new brides do not even know how to peel an onion or mince a piece of garlic—everything is dehydrated. And better we should not know what kind of *chozzerai* (junk) they put into the dehydrated soups and mixtures."

I replied, in jest, "With the steady growth of overpopulation, it may someday be necessary to dehydrate people in order to save space on this earth."

"Don't laugh," Mama answered. "With so many *meshuggeneh menshen* (crazy people) around," her voiced trailed off.

When we were little girls and Mama was attending nutrition class, Papa took us aside and explained that Mama was doing all this because she loved us and wanted to safeguard our health. He asked us to understand and to respect her efforts and we did.

However, in self-defense we made up our own rhyme to counteract Miss Brechen's poetry. "In any language that is *schprechen* (spoken). From her *essen* (food), *ken mir brech-en* (you can vomit)."

Papa set these words to fit a melody by Shubert. We sang it to Mama again and again.

Mama sang back softly, "If Shubert ate properly, you see — he would have lived to finish his symphony."

Art of *Challeh* Baking, No Simple Matter

Mama wasn't feeling well and she stayed with us for several weeks. Normally, Mama is very active and creative. Her doctor's order to "get as much rest as possible" was not easy for her to follow. As soon as she felt better she looked for something to do.

One day she mentioned that she did not like the taste of the salt-free bread recommended on her diet. Mama said it was missing a major ingredient, *tam* (flavor). I was trying to think of a project that would not be too strenuous for Mama and I asked her, "How about baking a salt-free *challeh* with yeast?" Her eyes lit up.

In no time at all I returned from the market with all the necessary ingredients. Mama was a little unsure. "I haven't baked a *challeh* in years, I hope I still remember how to make it."

"You will bake it by instinct," I replied, "it will come back to you as soon as you start." Mama put on a colorful *far-toch* (apron). This simple gesture seemed to invest her with an immediate sense of confidence and total recall.

She poured out the flour in the shape of a circle, forming a well for the eggs and then added the other ingredients. Before long she was kneading the dough in graceful, rhythmic movements. She had beautiful hands and I always told her, "You weave love into every knead." I now watched as she gently shaped the dough on my kitchen table. When the consistency was right and ready for rising she looked around my kitchen with a puzzled expression on her face.

"*Oy vay*," she exclaimed, "what am I going to do with my dough now? I always placed it right next to my coal stove where the temperature was perfect for the dough to rise." She glanced around again and then looked into my eyes sympathetically as she spoke. "Nebech my child, you don't have a coal stove, how can I have the correct temperature for my *challeh*?"

I agreed with her. "Mama," I answered, "I hope my husband is aware of the sacrifice I made when I married. Imagine taking a girl out of a home with a beautiful coal stove and having her make do without one. It hasn't been easy, but I'm still trying to adjust," I jokingly added.

Meanwhile, the dough was standing. Mama, by necessity, was always a genius at improvising. She asked me to fetch a water bag filled with hot water and encased it in a fresh pillowcase with a small feather pillow. Then she arranged the dough next to the hot water bag and lightly covered it all with another feather pillow.

Mama hoped her makeshift incubator would work. After waiting for one-hour intervals, she kneaded the dough two more times while I refilled the water bag with hot water to maintain the warmth. *Kine-ahora* the dough doubled and tripled in size.

Mama was pleased and said, "*Unzer mozel zull a zay vock-sen*" (Our luck should grow so successfully.) I watched her braid the *challeh* with sure deft hands, and with a flourish she brushed on beaten egg yolks as a finishing touch to "give a shine to the crust."

Mama carefully placed the *challeh* in the oven and asked us not to walk through the kitchen while the baking was in progress, not even "tipsy toe" lest the *challeh* fall. The house smelled delicious and the *challeh* turned out superbly.

Mama taught me knitting, crocheting, embroidering, and many other skills, but I never did master the art of making dough. It always stuck to my hands and fingers. When I added more flour in an effort to dislodge the dough, the end result was a piece of dough as hard as a rock.

Mama good-naturedly teased me and remarked, "When it comes to making *taig* (dough), you have *tzvay linkeh hent*" (two left hands).

As I watched Mama make the *challeh* in my kitchen, I asked her, "One last time, would you try to teach me again?"

Mama had infinite patience and she started from scratch. I was determined to learn, but alas the results were the same. Mama observed the ball of rock I held in my hand and shrugged, "I guess you just weren't meant to make a dough."

My husband was sitting nearby reading a book. He overheard our conversation and much to my surprise he turned to Mama and asked, "I wonder if I can learn to make a *challeh* dough?"

"Aha," I thought, "just let him try, he'll soon find out it's not as easy as it appears. Then he will understand my frustration."

Mama was delighted with the request. She truly loved my husband. They had a warm, easy relationship and in a few minutes she infused him with confidence, smiling and telling him she was sure he would be successful in making a *challeh*.

I observed in amusement, certain of the disastrous outcome, as my husband washed his hands, rolled up his shirt sleeves and started to follow Mama's instructions, the very same instructions she had given me earlier.

It didn't take long before my amusement started to turn sour and completely disintegrate! I watched in despair as everything went smoothly.

Mama was *qvelling* as she said to my husband, "You are a natural born *challeh* maker, you have *gold-en-eh hent*." (golden hands) I looked on enviously, particularly noting that not one piece of dough stuck to his fingers.

Then in patronizing tones, they both-urged me to "keep trying, don't give up." They assured me, "By the time *Meshiakh* (the Messiah) comes, you'll learn how to make a *challeh* dough."

I smiled along with them and answered, "Not a day sooner!"

Food, Food, Glorious Food!

Mama was not a great cook. She was very involved in her nutrition courses at The Henry Street Settlement where her teacher stressed; "If it's too delicious it's not nutritious." Looking back, Mama's method of cooking was avant-garde. She prepared meals the natural way, meats in natural juices, plain boiled chicken, broiled fish, green and yellow vegetables, and leafy salads.

Papa hated green vegetables and salads. "Grass," he called it, "fit for cows." But Mama was so enthusiastic about all the health benefits derived from eating them, that he didn't have the heart to dampen her spirits, so he ate *gruz* (grass).

Reading, sewing and attending educational lectures were Mama's true enjoyments. She wasted little time *potch-kee-ing* (fussing) with involved recipes. She made them only on rare occasions.

Today the tables have turned. Cooking is in! It is fashionable for educated and sophisticated young people to take great pride and interest in cooking. They are purists and start each recipe from scratch without easy shortcuts. Witness to this fact are hundreds of flourishing cooking schools where, in addition to the actual lessons, eager students wind up buying huge restaurant-size cooking pots, gadgets, special utensils, and exotic ingredients. The graduates cook up a storm, entertaining large groups of friends. The conversation is sprinkled with names of rare recipes, superb spices and epicurean feats.

Years ago, butter was butter, cream was cream, and *greeb-en-ess* were pieces of chicken skin rendered in chicken fat. Today's new products are labeled, "real imitation." This must be a notch above "fake imitation." For our cholesterol conscious society, margarine or polyunsaturated oil is often used instead of rendered chicken fat, real *shmaltz*. Mama's neighbor, Yetta, says that substituting polyunsaturated oil for *shmaltz* is like substituting a muskrat coat for a mink.

With so many electric gadgets: stove, mixer, blender, chopper, sifter, liquefier, it helps to be an engineer as well as a cook. Modern cooking enthusiasts buy automatic pasta machines that roll out uniformly even strips of pasta with no individual personality.

One hand-made specialty made by both my dear Mama and my husband's late beloved Mama was *luck-shen* (noodles). I never ceased to be fascinated by watching the deft performance of rolling and stretching the dough as thin as it could be stretched, the sides hanging over the kitchen table, then swiftly wrapping it around the rolling pin, gently placing it down again and stretching it still some more. The dough would be left to dry for about one half hour after which it was rolled like a jellyroll. Then with the fingertips of the left hand placed perilously near the knife-edge, the slicing began. The knife hit the cutting board in a steady staccato beat, never losing a beat or a fingertip. The last step was tossing the noodles lightly to separate the freshly cut strands for final drying. A human hand personally touched each strand.

The *meichel* (delicacy) that I vividly remember was unborn chicken egg yolks. They were encased in a membrane and were delicious beyond description. Every Friday night Mama cooked them with the chicken soup and gave half to my sister Pearl, and half to me. If, heaven forbid, there were seven eggs; Mama gave three to Pearl, three to me and carefully split the extra yolk down the middle to divide it between us.

My first learning experience in counting (even fractions) came from these egg yolks. Mama tried to teach us discipline. "Don't be pigs," she would tell us. "Don't eat all the egg yolks at once. They could last for a few days." Our discipline dissolved. Maybe they could last for a few days if she kept them locked in a bank vault; but not if they were seductively floating in a pot of chicken soup atop our kitchen stove.

Once in a blue moon Mama made *gefilte helzel* (stuffed neck of the poultry). The filling was made from grated potatoes; onions and beaten egg and Mama sewed up the ends with coarse white thread making beautiful even stitches.

Money was scarce and women were judicious shoppers. Fresh fish was carefully inspected, the gills opened and checked for color and smelled for freshness. Fruits and vegetables were thoroughly examined for perfection, plumpness and crispness.

Unlike our neighbors, Mama didn't try to stuff us with food. She considered it morally wrong to overindulge in any form — overspending, overprimping, etc. Overeating fitted this excess and she frequently admonished, "One must learn early (in every aspect of life) when *genug iz genug* (when enough is enough)." She tried to teach us the wisdom of a happy medium.

Mama's theory was "you eat to live—you do not live to eat. It is more important to feed the soul than it is to feed the stomach. One cannot get fat from reading a heavy book whereas a heavy meal dulls the mind and broadens the hips."

Wise words (for new and old cooks) that should be digested slowly and carefully.

'Scat' to Recipes Rich in Chicken Fat

Many years ago in the era before cholesterol, Jewish *balabustas* cooked with a heavy hand. Iceboxes were filled with butter, sweet cream and chicken fat. A Shabbos meal consisted of chopped liver made with fried liver, hard-boiled eggs, onions and chicken fat. Often, *gribbenes* (pieces of chicken skin rendered in chicken fat) were strewn on top of the chopped liver for added *geschmokeit* (deliciousness). Then came the chicken soup with knaidles or kreplach, followed by *gedempt* (roasted) chicken and *flanken* with lima beans.

When company was expected, *hockflaish* (chopped meat) wrapped with sweet-and-sour cabbage and stuffed *helzel* and *kishka* were added. Add to that the traditional *tzimmes* that was offered as a side dish. The next course was a parve noodle *kugel* (pudding) made with egg noodles, six eggs, sugar, cinnamon, apples and raisins.

Now it was time to cleanse the palate with a fruit compote, and to clear the stomach with stewed prunes. At this point the table was cleared once more to make room for a light fluffy sponge cake (made with a dozen eggs). Naturally the cake was washed down with a glass (usually a saved *yahrzeit* glass) of tea with lemon.

The tea was sipped through a cube of sugar held firmly between the upper and lower front teeth. Papa used to ask, "Why is it that we boil the water to make hot tea, blow on it in a saucer to make it cool, add sugar to make it sweet and then add lemon to make it sour?"

After the meal described above, it was not easy to get up from the table.

Eating the marrow that was carefully scooped out of the marrow bones was another delectable treat. This morsel can be classified as PC (pure cholesterol).

Strange as it may seem today, I never ate out in a restaurant with my parents. Mama invited relatives and friends to eat at our house and we were invited back. When I started to date and was taken out to dinner, I noticed that the soup was ordered first, before the main course. After witnessing this several times, I asked Mama, "How come the soup is served first and the main course is eaten after the soup when dining in a restaurant? You always serve the chicken or meat first and the soup afterwards and all your relatives and Papa's relatives serve this way."

Mama explained the custom. There were frequent pogroms in her little shtetl in Russia. Many times the hoodlums would storm in at mealtime, especially during Shabbos dinners, and devour the food prepared for the family. Mama's mother told her, "Better we should already have the chicken and meat in our stomach and leave the soup for the pogromniks."

Sometimes I think that perhaps we exaggerate when we recall the high level of cholesterol-forming diets we consumed many years ago. I decided to put these doubts to a test. My sister-in-law Birdie is a hale and hearty 87 years young. She exercises, swims and eats everything. Lots of red meat, rich sauces and a daily nightcap of ice cream are the staples of her diet. She often makes a mouth-watering noodle kugel. I asked her for the recipe.

BIRDIE'S NOODLE KUGEL
1/2 lb. fine egg noodles
1/2 lb. cottage cheese
1/2 C. whole milk
1/2 lb. block cream cheese
1/4 lb. butter (melted)
1/2 C. heavy sour cream
5 jumbo eggs, well beaten
1/2 tsp. salt
2 tsp. vanilla
1/2 C. sugar
1/2 C. white raisins
Grease large glass baking dish generously with butter. Pour in mixture of above ingredients. Top with cinnamon. Bake in preheated 350-degree oven for one hour.

To be scientifically accurate, I conducted a double-blind study (without telling the participants the purpose of my research). I simply asked Miriam Plafsky Stamen for her noodle kugel recipe. Here it is exactly as she told me:

MIRIAM'S NOODLE KUGEL
1/2 lb. medium noodles cooked, not too soft
1/2 lb. farmer cheese
1/4 lb. cream cheese
1 lb. cottage cheese
6 jumbo eggs, well beaten
1 C. sour cream
3/4 C. sugar
6 Tbsp. melted butter
2 C. whole milk
I tsp. vanilla
1/2 tsp. salt
corn flake crumbs

Mix all the cheeses together. Add sugar, sour cream, butter, vanilla and salt to noodles. Add well-beaten eggs to milk. Fold everything together. Bake in preheated 350-degree oven for 75 minutes in big glass baking dish. When pudding is three-quarters done sprinkle top with corn flake crumbs mixed with a little cinnamon. Best time to eat it is about 15 minutes after taking it out of the oven.

I was shaken to find that these two recipes confirmed my original memories of high-fat consumption of yesteryear. I also marvel that I survived to tell this tale.

However, when analyzing the scientific data presented in this rudimentary research, there is a bright side to these cholesterol laden noodle kugels. If a person stops eating them, his or her cholesterol count is sure to drop at least 50 points!

Cholent Is *Cholent,* Until You Make a *Tsimmes*

Orthodox Jews do not light the oven during the Sabbath, although it is permissible to keep a dish warm over a previously lit fire.

When I was a child, a favorite Sabbath treat in tradition-observing homes was *cholent,* a perfect dish because its flavor was enhanced by long, slow cooking. *Cholent* is a hardy, heavy meal-in-one stew consisting of meat, chicken fat, lima beans, barley and potatoes. It was put into the warm oven of the neighborhood bakery before sundown on Friday, baked at low heat all night, and taken out on Saturday morning.

Mama never made *cholent* after she learned in her nutrition class that it was too heavy for the digestive tract and had no vitamin content due to the long hours of cooking. Mama convincingly said, "It bakes for 18 hours in the oven and stays in your stomach for 36 hours."

However, we were not convinced and we begged her to make an exception to her anti-*cholent* policy. But she would not relent, we lost and her nutrition teacher won. Forbidden fruit is always sweeter, and our mouths watered and our nostrils quivered as neighbors passed our door carrying huge pots of this delicious smelling *meichel* (food delight).

Mrs. Zimmer, our next-door neighbor, was a free thinker and her husband Yankel was an observant Jew. He was frequently unemployed, and instead of looking for work, he spent most of his time in the synagogue asking God to find a job for him. His needs were few, but he insisted on a *cholent* every week.

Poor Mrs Zimmer had only a handful of pennies and she prepared what she could afford. Her *cholent* turned out to be a weak mish-mosh made with lots of water, plenty of lima beans, barley, onion, garlic, a snip of *miltz* (spleen), *hartz,* (heart), *puppicks* (navels), *helzel* (neck of chicken) assorted *chozzerai* (junk) and anything else she *schnorred* (begged) from the butcher. Usually the butcher threw in the above with the purchase of a big order. Since Mrs. Zimmer's meat orders were infrequent and meager, she always got what the butcher was ready to throw out. At best it was an ersatz *cholent* to the eye as well as to the palate. The kindest comment one could make after tasting her concoction was *Feh*!

Mr. Zimmer worked less and earned less and his wife grew more and more desperate. She watched the proud *bol-botisheh* (respectable) women bring their *cholent* to the bakery and enviously noticed the diamonds shining in their pierced ears and the fancy cameo brooches pinned to the lace collars on top of their ample bosoms. The pots they placed in the oven were always made of fine heavy enamel without a scratch on them.

Mrs. Zimmer's old pot was mostly chipped. Her senses reeled with the smell of the genuine meat-laden cholents brought in by the others. After some soul searching, Mrs. Zimmer resorted to going to the bakery early on Saturday in order to take out a good one, any *cholent* but her own.

When her husband came home from shul Saturday at noon and sat down to a feast filled with tender *brust*, he was suspicious. "Minnie, my dear wife, he softly asked, "for three weeks I haven't brought home a penny. Where did you get the money to make this thick, meaty cholent?" When he saw the beautiful pot, his suspicions were confirmed.

His wife blushed beet red, wiped her hands on her apron, and feebly explained, "It was dark in the bakery and I must have taken the wrong pot out of the oven. What's the difference? I left mine there, and a *cholent* is a *cholent*."

A few weeks later Mrs. Zimmer made the same mistake. As she was serving her husband from another strange and beautiful new pot Mr. Zimmer held up his hand.

"Stop, Minnie, this is not your *cholent*!" he cried, as the heavenly aroma engulfed him. Mrs. Zimmer feigned great surprise.

"A person is only human, and to make a mistake is human," she replied. Then she asked defensively, "Why are you making such a *tsimmes* (issue) over a *cholent*?"

Her husband glared at her and tried to control his anger. "I'm talking about a *cholent*, not a *tsimmes*. Take it back," he pleaded, mustering all his will power.

"First of all," she wearily replied, "I'm thoroughly exhausted and I don't have enough strength to *schlep* back to the bakery with the heavy pot, and secondly, it is too late; all the *cholents* are gone by now. It would be sinful to waste this delicious food."

She started to serve her husband.

"Then don't give me the first biteful," he said with a resigned sigh.

"Why?" She asked.

Yankel continued, "It's like a story the *shammes* (Synogogue caretaker) told me in *shul* about a poor woman who bought some giblets to make chicken fricassee. Another woman bought a fat, tender roasting chicken. The butcher made a mistake and interchanged their orders. As soon as the women reached their respective homes and emptied their shopping bags they realized the error. It was too late to make an exchange because the butcher closed early on Friday. When the man who was expecting to come home to a plump *ge-dempt-eh* (roast) chicken found a skimpy fricassee on his plate, his wife explained the mix-up in the butcher store. In his great disappointment, he blurted, 'Whoever is sitting tonight feasting on my chicken should only choke on the first bite!'"

Yankel tucked his napkin in.

"So Minnie," he said, "if you'll excuse me, I'll start with the second bite."

INTERGENERATIONAL EXPERIENCES

Bubbeh and the Hippies, Yippies and Zippies

This piece was written in the sixties when the Hippies, Yippies and Zippies were demonstrating in Florida.

My mother-in-law lives in Florida and she writes that the Hippies, Yippies and Zippies made their headquarters in Flamingo Park during the Democratic National Convention. This park is but a few blocks away from where Mom and a great number of senior citizens live.

Mom was an intelligent woman with an alert, inquisitive mind. She was curious to get to know, understand and perhaps befriend a member of this controversial group.

"After all," she wrote, "they are someone's *ayneklach* (grandchildren) too!"

So it was with pure and trusting hearts, equal to any of the idealistic flower children, that many of the senior citizens made strange friends that convention week. They held long conversations and had no trouble communicating.

The following is a mythical dialogue I overheard one night in a dream:

Bubbeh: "Mr. Hippie, excuse me, but you look so *oiyse-ge-dart* (emaciated). It just so happens I have some sandwiches in my shopping bag."

Hippie: "Sure, lady. I haven't had decent grub in a long time."

Bubbeh: "I don't know how to make grub, but I hope this will do."

Hippie: (taking a bite) "Man, this is so delicious it can blow your mind. What is it?

Bubbeh: "Just something I had in the house, freshly rendered chicken fat with *gribbenehs* and salt on Jewish rye."

Hippie: "Wow, what an ethnic trip. I sure dig it. What is your name, lady?"

Bubbeh: "You can call me Bubbeh."

Hippie: "Mind if I call you Bub?"

Bubbeh: "Not at all, and I'll call you son."

Hippie: "Those *gribbenehs* turn me on, but they really make me thirsty."

Bubbeh: "Don't move an inch." She dug into her big canvas shopping bag. "Here is some home brewed tea I took in a thermos. I also brought a glass. You know tea never tastes right in a cup."

She poured the tea, unwrapped saran wrap from a slice of lemon and dropped the fresh lemon into the glass.

"Wait, wait," (she reached into a far corner of the bag) "here is a packet of fresh honey, it's much better than sugar."

Hippie: (visibly impressed) "Boy, Bub, you certainly are a hip chick. Are you on a nature kick too?"

Bubbeh: "Nature, schmature, this is how we ate in Europe — everything natural — and we were as strong as oxen."

Hippie: "You have the right vibes. You're a swell guy."

It was the first time Bubbeh was called a guy, and strangely enough, she liked it. He spoke softly, "You know, Bub, I'd buy you a complete volume of Zen poetry if I had some bread (money)."

Bubbeh: "I don't have any more bread, a piece of challah, maybe?"

Hippie: "You're beautiful, real cool. Who knows, maybe if you were my Bubbeh, I wouldn't be here in this pad. I'd probably be one of the nominees for the Vice Presidency."

Bubbeh: "So where is your Bubbeh?"

Hippie: "Come to think of its she lives somewhere near here in Miami. Her name is Faigeh Pesheh Lefkowitz."

Bubbeh: "I don't believe my ears! Faigeh is my next-door neighbor, my very best friend."

Hippie: "Really? I should look her up. Where do you think she is now?"

Bubbeh: (embarrassed) "Right now she is here in Flamingo Park talking to my grandson, Heshie the Hippie!"

End of Dream.

A Liberated Woman, Mama Tells It 'Like It Was'

Mama was sitting and reading the paper. She called to me, "Listen to this article, 'Women libbers not satisfied with child centers to look after their children. They are now demanding infant care centers that will take babies from one week old.'"

The high-power lady executives seemed to find that taking care of a newborn infant is less stimulating than their jobs. The newspaper quoted the owner of the Park Avenue Professionally Trained Nannie Agency. She claimed that women executives were anxious to return to their exciting career jobs soon after childbirth.

I asked Mama, "What do you think of this new trend?"

"She replied, "By you this is new. By me this is old. Everyone is telling it like it is. Let me tell it like it was. In our little *dorf* in Russia we had Christian neighbors, the Kovalchiks. They were good, kind and hard working people who spent all their time tilling their soil and raising crops in the fields. It was a large family, the grandmother, grandfather, mother, father, nine single sons and one married son and his wife with two children.

"I remember one special day when I was 14 years old. I heard a gentle knock on the door. It was Monya Kovalchik, our neighbor's beautiful daughter-in-law. She asked for my mother. I told her my mother was out. 'Then you'll do,' she said, looking at me very seriously.

"Monya was nine months pregnant with her third child. She put her hands on my shoulders and told me, 'I think I will need your help today. Please stay close to your house so that you can hear me if I call.'

"I did not quite understand what she meant, but I did sense the urgency in her voice. A few hours later I heard her calling my name, 'Rochell, Rochell, come quick.' I ran out to the field just in time to see her spread a clean sheet on the ground. Then she lowered herself on her knees and remained in that position.'

"I asked, Monya, why are you kneeling? She replied, 'The baby will be here soon and I don't want it to fall a distance. I can help it to be born easier while I am on my knees.' Her voice was calm and composed. I was scared stiff. In a little while the baby was born and the afterbirth came out. I was terrified and started to tremble, *Gottenyu*, I thought, 'her *kishkehs* (intestines) are falling out!'

"She saw how frightened I was and assured me that everything was fine. Soon she took a small clean knife out of her apron pocket and cut her own umbilical cord. Out of her other apron pocket she took a piece of white thread and in a deft, skilled manner proceeded to tie the cord.

"I was a *tzittering* (shaking), totally inexperienced assistant, but I soon took hold of myself and helped her by doing whatever she told me. Next she poured a cup of water out of a keg and gently washed the baby's eyes and face with a small clean cloth she tore from a white sheet.

"I felt my heartbeat in my ears as I watched her unfold another clean sheet and wrap it around the entire baby, including the head. When she reached the baby's nostrils she quickly snipped two little holes in the sheet to allow the air in. I asked Monya, 'Where did you learn all this?'

"She told me her first child was born in the winter and she had the luxury of a midwife. 'I am a very careful watcher and I have an excellent memory,' she said. Her second child was born in the summer, in the field, and she applied everything she learned from the midwife.

"Now, with the birth of her third child, she was a real professional, even with a *koll-yek-eh* (inept) assistant. She neatly kept all her supplies in a small wicker basket. After attending to the important matters, Monya said she was going to take a rest.

"My eyes darted nervously from the mother to the mummy-wrapped infant. I sighed with relief when Monya dozed off and the baby was quiet. She awoke after two hours and said it was time to go back to the farmhouse, a distance of about three short blocks. I helped gather everything together and carried all the stuff, the basket, water keg, etc.

"Monya carried the baby and leaned heavily on me as I saw them safely home. Somehow I felt very grown up and not frightened at all. Instead I was filled with the wonder of nature."

Mama told me that Monya stayed home for three days, helping with light house chores while waiting for the milk in her breasts to flow abundantly. On the fourth day she packed a collapsible tripod stand which had a little folding hammock suspended from a hook at the top. Mama helped her carry the tripod, hammock and netting plus food, the water keg and the baby back to the field.

Monya hammered the tripod stakes securely into the ground, hung up the hammock on the hook, tenderly placed the baby into it and gave it a loving push to start it rocking. She placed netting over the entire tent and then put in a full day's work, taking time out only to eat, drink water, and to breast feed her baby.

Mama left the memories of her *dorf* and came back to the newspaper. "Today these independent woman libbers need so much help. It is not their fault. It is simply the way of life in modern society. They need doctors for prenatal care and delivery, postnatal care day centers for childcare and domestic help for home care."

Mama wondered out loud, "Are these women really liberated when they are so dependent upon others for day-to-day living?"

"It seems to me," Mama continued, "Monya was ahead of her time. Not only was she back to her career job working in the field after three days, but at the same time she also managed her own portable infant care center. She was almost totally independent — a truly liberated woman!"

A *Dybbuk* in the Appliances

Tuesday

Lillian: "Hello, Mama, I'm sorry I can't visit you today. My clothes dryer is broken and I have an appointment with the service man. He promised to come to fix it before noon today and I don't dare leave the house."

Mama: "It's a shame to be stuck in the house on such a lovely day. Goodness knows that's one problem I didn't have. I never had a clothes dryer. Right outside my kitchen window—strung across the back court-yard—I kept my dryer—my clothesline. I can't ever remember waiting for a service man. Whenever the line wore thin, Papa made a *knippel* (knot) and repaired it. Every few years we were big sports and bought a brand new clothesline."

Wednesday

Lillian: "Hello, Mama. The service man never came to fix my dryer. And now my washing machine is not working. It's leaking and I've been busy mopping up the puddles of water."

Mama: "I feel sorry for you, but I can't say I know how you feel from my own experience. I had the same washing machine, a hand *vosh-brettel* (washboard) for more than 40 years. It worked fine and never leaked. They don't build appliances like that any more!

"As for the service man breaking his promise to come yesterday, you know the expression, 'To promise and to love cost no money.'"

Thursday

Lillian: "Mama dear, first the good news. The clothes dryer man finally came and fixed it. But I have no clothes to dry because I'm still waiting for the washing machine man to come. The puddles are growing. They almost look like a calm lake. And, you won't believe it—my refrigerator stopped working. My next door neighbors now have my food stored in their refrigerators. So I'm also waiting for the refrigerator repair man."

Mama: "Sounds like a *dybbuk* (demon) crept into your appliances. You know I'm only kidding. I don't really believe in *dybbuks*. When I was a young woman I never laid eyes on a refrigerator repairman. We bought a sturdy icebox and it lasted for years. If you kept it supplied with a cake of ice and remembered to empty the *shissel* (pan), there were no further problems."

Friday

Lillian: "Mama, I know you were joking, but I'm almost convinced there is a *dybbuk* lurking in my appliances. My gas oven is not right and the Public Service Company promised faithfully to send a specialist to find the gas leak. And to top it all, my air conditioning is *fun-ferring* (acting funny.) Meanwhile I'm glued to the house. I'm virtually a prisoner and am even afraid to go to the corner to mail a letter lest I miss the servicemen. It's a frustrating feeling. There's nothing I can do but wait."

Mama: "*Oy mein kind* (child), sometimes I wonder, is it worth it? Modern technology makes a person totally dependent upon others. As for your air conditioning not working right, on a hot night, I bet you wish you had a nice cool fire escape to sleep on.

"Meanwhile, don't worry over being tied down to the house. You can always find something good in a situation if you look hard enough. Remember, if you stay at home you won't wear out your shoes. Seriously though, when I had my own coal stove, I was my own boss. I put in the coal, adjusted the damper, and the house was filled with warmth. Not only did it heat the apartment, but at the same time it cooked a delicious *ge-dempteh flaysh* (roast meat), and *luck-shin* (noodle) and potato *kugels*. And believe me, the baked apples and baked potatoes had a special taste that you just simply can't get in a *modrin* oven."

I hated to interrupt Mama in the midst of her tender reveries, but I said, "Mama, please excuse me, but I must hang up. Someone is knocking on the door."

I ran to open the door. There stood the washing machine, refrigerator and oven repair men. They said, in unison, "Lady, we tried to ring your bell but it is out of order. You better call the electrician!"

Big City Experts Take in the Scenes of Suburbia

Once she left the *dorf* (farm) in Russia, Mama essentially became a city girl. We consider it a treat when she visits us here in New Jersey.

"Millburn is such a small *shtetl* (little village)," Mama says, "you could sit by the window for half a day and a car hardly passes by. People — never!

"By me in New York, I see a whole world when I look out my window across from the park. I can tell right away when Mr. and Mrs. Klein had a spat — they sit on different benches.

"Mrs. Zimmer has such a perfect attendance on her favorite bench that I know she is not feeling well if she is not there. When I visit her and find her not feeling well, she is always surprised at how I knew she was sick.

"I must have ESP, she insists. ESP, Schmee S P, I look out my window, and I know right away. When I saw Mr. Kaback put his arm around the back of widow Shapiro's bench as he sat near her, I knew for sure it would be a *shiddach* (match). To look out a window and see nothing but quiet — that's for farmers.

"How I wish my dear friend Mrs. Chonin was here," Mama said wistfully as she looked out of my dull suburban window. So I telephoned Mrs. Chonin in New York. She missed Mama too. I invited her to take the next bus out to Millburn for a joyful reunion.

Mrs. Chonin is a delicious, delightful person. She is intelligent, full of enthusiasm and has a wry sense of humor. I was glad to take the "girls" on a tour of local sights.

We visited the Y and they were busy making comparative notes. In their opinion the New York Senior League group had less card playing, less bingo, and more intellectual pursuits. We spent some time in neighboring synagogues. They were duly impressed.

One day we passed Saks and I asked them if they would like to see the lovely store.

"Of course," replied Mrs. Chonin. "In my many years of employment I used to work with the leading designers of the finest fashion houses."

Mrs. Chonin still sews most of her own clothes, and her skill and craftsmanship are of the highest caliber. I parked the car and we started to walk towards Saks.

They were in deep conversation. It seems they were both surprised that some high-ranking executive did not take a forthright stand to change the name of the store.

"After all," said Mama, "I'm a progressive woman, and certainly not a prude, but a name like 'Seks', belongs more in the bedroom." Mrs. Chonin solemnly agreed.

Right near the entrance stood a display mannequin bedecked in a glamorous evening gown of white silk brocade. The belt was a mass of colorful mock jewels. It was dazzling.

But Mrs. Chonin was not to be taken in. She aimed straight at the jugular vein. She grabbed the collar, turned it inside out and loudly exclaimed, "Not even hand-stitched. In my day such workmanship we wouldn't let an apprentice do."

Then, as if on cue, both Mama and Mrs. Chonin put on their reading glasses to see the price tag. This elegant costume was priced at $899.

I didn't say a word as I watched the scene unfold. Mama looked at Mrs. Chonin who looked back at Mama. They held a private conference. Finally they came over to me and said in unison, "Surely there is missing a dot after the number eight!"

Mrs. Chonin was still firm in insisting, "Even at $8.99 it is not a bargain — not with machine stitching!"

MAMA'S VIEWS

Mama, A Four Letter Word

Since the days of Philip Wylie's "Momism," to Philip Roth's "Portnoy's Complaint," moms have had a pretty rough time in contemporary literature. It is both fashionable and profitable to picture Mom with a series of scathing four-letter words.

I also have a descriptive four-letter word for my Mom — love. Mama is a beautiful woman who has not had an easy life, yet she has always maintained a delicious sense of humor.

Two years after Papa passed away, Mama's neighbor Mrs. Stein, was sipping a glass of tea in Mama's apartment. She cleared her throat and said, "Mrs. Bernstein, I would like you to meet my cousin. He lost his wife two years ago and he is very lonely. This poor widower is hungry to have a deep conversation with a fine, bright woman. And don't think he is *a gornit* (a nothing), he is a progressive man, a former writer for The Jewish Daily Forward and a genuine intellectual."

Mama couldn't help but be impressed. "Also," continued Mrs. Stein, "he is visiting my husband now and since I am right next door I'll be back in a minute."

Before Mama could clear the tea glasses off the kitchen table, Mrs. Stein was back with her cousin, Mr. Jacobs. She introduced him and five minutes later made a hasty stage exit, exclaiming: "Excuse me, I must leave now — something is burning by me on the stove."

Jacobs was a chipper, dapper man. Mama was delighted to have a real live writer sitting on her sofa. She started to discuss Tolstoy. Jacobs abruptly changed the subject.

"Mrs. Bernstein," he asked, "what do you think of dancing?"

Dancing, Mama thought — he wanted to discuss maybe the famous Russian ballet dancer, Nijinsky? Mama followed his career with great interest.

"Ah Nijinsky," she said, "what a graceful dancer. Never did another dancer leap as high. And such a tragic life he led," Mama added with feeling.

Jacobs was quick to explain, "Perhaps I did not make myself clear. I was talking about social dancing. You know, the fox-trot, the waltz, the box step. It's so easy to learn; one, two, feet together."

Mama was puzzled. She simply could not understand how a man who was "hungry to have a deep conversation" could start an "acquaintance-ship" with such a frivolous matter, such *narrishkeit* (foolishness).

Jacobs did not receive the message and was intent upon pursuing the subject. "Mrs. Bernstein," he asked, "do you know how to dance?"

Mama replied that she knew all the Russian folk dances but she never learned the American steps. "You're a progressive woman," Jacobs said in a determined voice. "Don't be a watcher, be a doer! Let me teach you the box step and you'll be dancing at all *simchas.*"

He turned on the radio, found some dance music and eagerly started the lesson. After a few preliminary instructions he placed one hand on her shoulder and with the other hand he pressed her lower back towards him in an attempt to do a "dip." Suddenly he kissed her on the side of her neck. Mama was shocked. She stepped back and could not hide her disappointment. Trying hard to control her voice, she told him, "I'm surprised at you Mr. Jacobs, from such a cultured person I expected you should act like a gentleman—not like a *pruster yung* (coarse youth). And, as for the kissing, what do you think I am, a *Mezuzah?*" Mr. Jacobs apologized and they remained intellectual friends for a long time.

A few months after this episode, Mr. Jacobs suffered a heart attack. When he returned from the hospital to his apartment, he stubbornly refused an aide. Mama felt sorry for him and brought him his meals and helped him in his slow recovery.

His apartment was filled with books and albums. He proudly told Mama he was the father of the famous actor Lee J. Cobb. Mr Jacobs saved every clipping about his son and kept them neatly in his albums. He enjoyed leafing through the rave reviews of his son's talents and he shared them with Mama.

A month after Mr. Jacobs' illness, Mama received a long distance call. It was Lee J. Cobb calling from Hollywood. He thanked Mama for her kindness to his father and added, "My father tells me you are not a rich woman and you bring him such nourishing food and good company. I can never repay you for all the care you are giving him and I would like to show my appreciation. Can I mail you some money?"

The sheer beauty of his voice overwhelmed mama. She replied, "Thank you, but I cannot accept any money. It is no problem—whatever I cook for myself—I just cook a little more. Seeing your father get stronger gives me great pleasure—it is payment enough."

Every few weeks Lee J. Cobb called Mama to ask about his father and to talk to her. She looked forward to his calls with great excitement. He told her how much he enjoyed talking to her and drinking in her wise common sense. He admired her lively interest in music, poetry and the legendary dancer, Nijinsky.

Mama told me she was relieved Lee J. Cobb never asked her to dance!

Mama's Views on Monkey Business

Dr. Jane Goodall is an animal behaviorist who has done remarkable research with chimpanzees in the African bush. The chimp is man's nearest living relative, and he resembles us more closely than does any other primate species. His brain is very much like our brain and there are striking similarities between chimp and human conduct.

The purpose of Dr. Goodall's research is to learn something about humans by observing our anthropoid relatives in their natural habitat. A good deal of what has been considered uniquely human may be rooted in our evolutionary history since humans and chimps share a common heritage of behavioral tendencies.

When a chimp is alarmed or upset, he will reach out to touch another chimp or to take its hand. Male chimps are very aggressive and dominant and the females assume a submissive role in the community. So far, the female chimps have not organized a woman's liberation movement!

Dr. Goodall has written a fascinating book on chimpanzee life, "In the Shadow of Man," and there is a remarkable film shot and edited by her photographer husband, Hugo Van Lawick.

Mama was visiting us when one of Dr. Goodall's films was shown on television. We watched it together. It was a segment dealing with chimps and aggression. The movie opened with a view of the chimps leading peaceful, orderly lives in contented structured groups. Each chimp was productively gathering his or her food, picking bananas and peeling and eating them. They appeared relaxed and friendly and some were tenderly grooming each other. The scene was serene.

In this particular experiment, Dr. Goodall wanted to find out what would happen if she placed bunches of bananas in the area where the chimps usually sought their food. Now ample food was available to all the chimps without any work or effort on their part. Each day she returned with more bananas and she carefully watched and recorded the reactions. It wasn't long before all havoc broke loose.

The stronger, more aggressive chimps gorged themselves and hoarded the bananas they were too full to eat. The small, weaker chimps were reduced to begging for a tiny piece of banana.

We were alarmed to see how the strong chimps enjoyed the role of power and grew greedier each day. The former tranquil existence soon disappeared and the chimp society was divided into two factions, the haves and the have-nots.

Mama watched the film intently. I gathered from the perplexed expression on her face that she did not understand the point being made. I explained the experiment and told Mama that Dr. Goodall had gathered data for many years to see what scientists might learn from animal behavior that could subsequently be applied to human beings.

Mama shook her head from side to side in utter disbelief and said, "So what is she trying to prove? She wasted years making such a *tzimmes* (fuss) with the monkeys.

"What is this *moishe kapoyr* (topsy-turvy) world coming to that we have to learn from monkeys. Let the monkeys learn from us! Believe me, the monkeys don't need Dr. Goodman (she subconsciously changed Goodall's name). They need her to mix into their lives like one needs a *schlech-teh schvigger* (bad mother-in-law). *Nebech* (unfortunately), she got those poor monkeys all *tsetummelt* (confused). And if Dr. Goodman knew what we Jews have always known about human nature, she could have saved herself a lot of time."

"What do you mean," I asked, not having the vaguest notion of what was so obviously clear to Mama.

She explained that when chimps or people do not have any purpose or meaningful direction in their lives, when everything is handed to them without any labor like those chimps had the bananas given to them with no effort on their part, bad things happen to them.

Mama then smiled and said, "If only Dr. Goodman had a Yiddisheh mama to tell her this old Yiddish expression, she would not be *potchkeeing* (messing) around with the monkeys."

I impatiently asked, "What old Yiddish expression are you talking about, Mama?"

She slowly replied, "*Meh vert meshugge far gootzkite*". (You can go crazy from having it too good).

How Mama Voted—And Why

Mama was very involved in the 1976 presidential election. Her right to *vute* (vote) was something she had long treasured. For many years, Mama's and Papa's citizenship papers, properly framed, hung proudly on our living room wall.

I recall our immigrant relatives fresh off the boat visiting us, and looking at the citizenship papers with great awe. To have this splendid and meaningful paper adorn their wall some day was their goal.

Mama always took her responsibilities as a naturalized American citizen very seriously. In this campaign, as in all others, she carefully read a great deal of campaign literature and listened to every word of the TV debates.

Mama said she had to be honest with herself and admit she could not forgive Ford for pardoning Nixon. But still it was her duty to be well informed and "hear out" both sides with an open heart, if not with an unprejudiced mind.

Mama was visiting us when Carter's controversial interview with Playboy magazine was in all the news headlines. She was puzzled and asked me, "*Vus maynt* lust (what does lust mean)?" I tried to tell her in a delicate way.

To my surprise she replied, "It's not so *prust* (coarse) to have a little lust. A person is only human! To look at someone with feeling is not so terrible and especially to look and not touch — what harm can there be?"

The following day I was having breakfast with Mama and we both watched President Ford being interviewed on TV. The interviewer asked Ford whether he read the Playboy article.

President Ford replied, "Yes, I did."

The interviewer probed more deeply. "Mr. President, did you read an excerpt from the magazine, or did you actually read it in the Playboy magazine?"

The camera panned in and Ford replied in close-up. "I read it directly from Playboy magazine." He paused a minute and in a serious and righteous tone added, "But I didn't look at the centerfold, not even a peek."

I immediately knew what Mama's next question would be. A second later, Mama asked, "Tell me, what is a centerfold?"

I started to explain. She saw me groping for words and said, "Be honest—I'm not a baby. I was not born yesterday." I told her the naked truth.

She thought for a long time and said, "Now I'm really worried. A man who is human would normally take a look or at least take a peek, and President Ford can sit there and stiffly say he didn't open the centerfold page. To me that man must be made of a *schtick holtz* (a piece of wood) and frankly, I couldn't *vute* for a piece of *vood!*"

Initials, Fashions of the Times

When the immigrants came from Eastern Europe they often arrived with only the clothes they wore and a small straw suitcase containing all their worldly possessions.

Mama came to America with three pairs of handknit stockings, two undershirts, three pairs of bloomers, two handkerchiefs, two ruffled petticoats, a pink shawl, and an embroidered skirt and blouse. Home baked cookies and a small pack of polly seeds were carried separately in a knapsack. These were emergency supplies to avoid hunger pangs. Mama hardly had to be concerned about overweight luggage.

The new arrival had many situations to cope with, like finding suitable lodging, (usually with relatives) and a job. Buying new American clothes was often postponed. Mama washed and ironed the few things she had and wore them over and over again. Nobody in her crowd was a fashion plate. They lived by the motto *rain iz shain*, (clean is beautiful). Extra money earned was carefully saved for the future and not frittered away on fancy clothes.

An exception to this rule was Tessie Zimmerman. She came over on the same *shif* (boat) with Mama and she spent every last cent she earned (or borrowed) on new *dress-kehs*. She was addicted to fashion, but not to cleanliness. Each day she would bedeck herself in her latest creation and lavishly splash toilet water all over her body.

Mama tried to convince Tessie that the smell of soap was even nicer. Secretly, she was referred to by the neighbors as "Klessy Tessie, *Ay-vin Putz Un-ten Schmutz*" (classy Tessie, fancy on the surface and unclean underneath). Poor Tessie's *mazel*, she married a man who was crazy clean. She changed her habits but kept bemoaning her fate: "My skin is shedding, I'm bathing and scrubbing myself to an early grave!"

Today, it is not unusual to see a man carrying a purse. Over 50 years ago, most men carried their money in a *teis-ter*, a small leather purse with two top openings, one for bills and the other for change.

For safety sake, some ladies kept their currency in a pocket they sewed on the underside of their petticoat. The open end was securely fastened with a large safety pin. Women also carried money rolled in a knotted handkerchief (a *knippel*) tied just under the knee. They then pulled the stocking up over it for added security. Probably the expression "she's saving everything in her *knippel*" (building up a nest egg) originated from this practice.

Fashions have changed a great deal. Once I took Mama to an elegant luncheon. Some of the ladies were carrying handbags with the interlocking "G" (Gucci) initials on them. Mama pointed to one woman and whispered to me, "That lady must have a name like Gussie Ginsburg or Gertie Goldstein."

"No, Mama," I replied, and proceeded to explain that it was the initials of a status designer, Gucci.

Just then Mama's eyes fell on several Louis Vuitton bags with the initials "LV" imprinted all over. She commented, "There must be a big bargain sale on these pocketbooks, there are so many of them."

I told her the initials belonged to a famous designer, Louis Vuitton and that they were not on sale. When I gave her some idea as to the high cost of these handbags, she almost fell off her chair. She was quiet for a long while, then she shook her head and said, "I can't understand why people would pay such a fortune just to wear someone else's initials." She looked straight into my eyes and continued, "I think you missed the whole point entirely. There is a much deeper meaning to the popularity of these pocketbooks."

I was completely befuddled, but I could sense the wheels going around in Mama's head. Mama spoke with great assurance: "I figured it out, it's pure logic. Nowadays psychiatrists are constantly warning us that we are in great danger of losing our identity. These ladies are smart and are doing something about it. They are identifying themselves proudly to the whole world. The ladies with the pocketbooks with the "G" are telling us they are Galitzianers and the ladies with the "LV" initials are for sure Lit-Vaks!"

New School vs. Old School

The rainy Monday was a perfect day for cleaning out my desk drawers. Mama was sitting nearby knitting and urging me to throw out the accumulation of papers and assorted literature I didn't absolutely need. (A saver by nature, I find it particularly hard to part with papers, clippings, poems, etc.)

Each time I paused to read a clipping yellowed with age, Mama encouraged me to "throw it out and make room for the new stuff you keep putting on top."

She was right, and I really was trying to reduce the pile when I ran across a brochure listing courses given at The New School Human Relations Center. Leafing through it I read aloud the titles of the courses to Mama. "Building Self Esteem, Improve Your Functioning and Well-Being."

Mama commented, "Sounds like an advertisement for a laxative, maybe Ex-Lax or Milk of' Magnesia. Self Nourishment, The Art of Nurturing Yourself, must be some good recipes in this course," Mama remarked. "A *kugel* or a *tzimmis?*"

"De-programming and Re-programming Our Responses, The Act of Creation versus the Act of Destruction."

Mama asked, "Is that like telling a child to do his homework instead of *klopping kup in vont* (hitting his head against the wall.)?"

"Become Your Independent Self, Learning to Move from Dependence to Independence."

Mama said, "Everybody is moving nowadays."

"Liberated Parents Workshop, How to Enhance the Quality of Our Everyday Lives with Children, Learning through Role Playing and Group Discussion to express anger helpfully rather than hurtfully."

"*Oy*, that needs some thinking through," Mama said with uncertainty. "Like when a little child is really naughty, are you supposed to say,

'Hershaleh, please accept this *potch* in the helpful manner in which it is applied?' Do you remember our upstairs neighbors, Berkowitz the butcher? They had four sons. His wife, Hendel, was very strict with them. She had one motto she always used, 'More children are ruined by parent's saying yes than by saying no'. She felt that denial helped to build character. She would repeat over and over to her children, 'Better you should cry now than I should cry later!'"

"Mind-Body Integration, Self Evaluation Consciousness Training to awaken and stimulate our sense of connection to the larger world around us."

Mama looked completely bewildered, "So who is disconnected?" she asked. "Touch Therapy, that doesn't need an explanation," Mama smiled. "That was practiced all the time—*a potch, a knip, a frosk.* (a slap, a pinch, a wallop)."

My throat was getting dry as I continued to read the other titles. "Gestalt Theory and Technique, Behavior Therapy, Transactional Therapy, Bioenergetic Therapy, Jungian Analytical Therapy, Existential Therapy, Psychodrama, Encounter, Transpersonal Therapy, Rorschach Testing Technique, and Primal Therapy."

Mama's head was whirling. She begged, "Give me a for instance. I don't even understand the first one. Explain to me what is the last one, Primal Therapy?"

From the pamphlet, I read to her, "Primal Therapy was developed by Arthur Janov. He claims that neurotic behavior is the result of very early experiences of deprivation. This unfulfilment of basic needs causes the child to repress his true self and substitute his neurotic self. The therapeutic process requires the patient to directly experience these early situations, at first in marathon individual sessions and later in regularly scheduled group sessions. The cathartic effect of re-experiencing these primal scenes leads to the remission of neurotic behaviors. Primal screams liberate and free the patient from his repressions."

Mama asked in all seriousness, "From this Janov makes a living? Come to think of it," she continued in slow measure, a spark of recollection coming through. "It's almost beginning to make sense to me. Years ago we lived right next door to Bessie and Jake Zimmerman. They were always screaming, yelling and hollering on top of their lungs. The walls would shake. And in those days, not for one minute did I have any idea or understanding that they were really not arguing but were practicing *gevalt, geshray* and *qvitch* Primal Therapy." Mama shrugged her shoulders, "*gey vaise.*" (go know). And what is the next to last one on the list, the Rosenberg test?"

"You mean the Rorschach test," I replied, reading on. "The Rorschach test is a set of 10 ink blots of different shapes. The test involves instant responses by patients as they view each of the ten blots in succession. "From the patterns of the responses, a trained professional can translate the results as a useful diagnostic tool. It can assist the therapist to understand better the underlying anxieties of the patient as well as reveal many personal characteristics."

Mama held her hand up to her forehead, "It's spinning by me the head, so much meaning over an inkblot! I never knew there were so many ways to look for the root of what makes a person tick-tock."

Her eyes shone with excitement as she recalled. "Now I'm really sure that there is nothing new in this world. Many, many years ago when I was a young girl in the old country, there was a test that was handed down from one generation to the next. The results were 100 percent perfect."

"C'mon, Mama," I said. "Are you telling me a *Bubbeh-meiseh* (tall tale)?"

"No, *emmes*" (the truth), she replied. Mama then told me that this method of finding out about a person's character was common in her small village in Russia. In those days when a young man courted a young lady, he brought her to his home so that his family could look her over. At the dinner table, his mother and father would ask her questions regarding her family and background. If his mother felt the young lady was a suitable prospective daughter in-law, she would then give the girl an ancient psychological test.

Beforehand, the mother prepared a large ball of yarn that she tightly snarled and knotted. After dinner she handed this ball of yarn to the young girl and asked her to please unravel it.

At this point, the older woman busied herself at the other end of the room, and through the corner of her eye, would carefully observe the young girl. If the young lady slowly and calmly tried to unravel and untangle the yarn and the knots, it was soon apparent that she was a patient person. But if she tightly tugged, pulled and broke the yarn she was not considered a good prospect. (According to Rorschach, this was instant response.).

Mama posed her last question in jest, "So why are you keeping that brochure from The New School? It doesn't even list a course on 'Character Analysis' to help young girls pass a future *schvigger* (mother-in-law) test. That course you can find only in The Old School!"

Mama the Decorator—A Step Ahead of Her Time

When the immigrants came to America in the early 1900s, they brought with them precious few worldly possessions. Brass Sabbath candlesticks, lace, embroideries, tablecloths, and sometimes a beloved *peh-reh-neh* were carefully transported to this country by the newcomers. Young married couples scrimped and saved in order to pay the rent and furnish an apartment. In the process of becoming Americanized, many immigrants developed an eclectic style of decorating. The result was usually a melange of various periods incorporating European *shtetl* taste with Yankee trends.

These thoughts came to mind as I was browsing through an issue of *Architectural Digest* and found an article titled "Minimalism in Manhattan."

I read that the new wave in interior design leans toward a minimalist approach to space. Less is more and clutter is out. Bare walls, clean surfaces, and large plants make a statement, and are considered pure sculptural form. Matching, coordinated furnishings are contrived and *passe'*. The magazine article stressed that each piece should characterize the decor with the look and feel of an honest 'found object.'

I smiled as I pored over handsome illustrations showing a scattering of unmatched assemblages against stark settings. Even the curtains and draperies were 'found pieces' picked up by the decorator on her extensive world travels. The pictures vividly brought back memories of my own Mama's avant-garde decorating scheme.

Our family once lived in a tiny New York apartment that aptly fit the article title, "Minimalism in Manhattan." Our interior decoration was state-of-the-art, determined at that time by the state-of-Depression. This state was largely instrumental in Mama's not cluttering up her place with artifacts. Mama and Papa were happy to clutter up the kitchen table with bread, milk and pot cheese.

In our family, literature and music were considered to be essentials along with food. Despite my father's meager salary, he managed to accumulate an amazing number of serious books and classical records. Papa would not allow a popular phonograph record in our little apartment. "No room for junk," he explained. "It would be an insult to Caruso, Elman and Heifitz." Surely, his attitude foretold the magazine's instructions to strive for pure quality in every sphere of the home.

As for multi-functionalism, now so fashionable, Mama and Papa's bedroom doubled as Mama's sewing room. Her Singer sewing machine stood regally in the far corner. Mama made a flowered tapestry slipcover with a ruffled bottom that gracefully concealed the foot treadle. The colors and design blended with the bedspread she had hand-crocheted. I loved the hues and patterns that danced in the room, especially when the sun streamed through the windows. That room was my favorite place in the tiny apartment. There I had a feeling of complete contentment as I sat nearby rocking my doll to the rhythm and hum of the sewing machine treadle.

And when Mama sang Russian folk songs as she sewed, the room seemed to take on a special enchantment. All was serene in my young world. Here too, Mama unknowingly preempted the advice in the magazine to create a cheerful and peaceful ambience.

Mama and Papa's bedroom had two windows facing the front street with a glorious view of the East River. My sister Pearl and I shared the other tiny bedroom that barely accommodated the three-quarter bed and a miniature dresser. Our bedroom had one window, also facing the front with the same view. I would sit at the foot of the bed and daydream for hours while looking out of this window watching the boats pass by on the East River.

The small combination dining room and parlor were not lived in much. Our kitchen was the heart of the apartment with the coal stove as its "warming core."

For the windows, Mama sewed all the curtains using a string pulled through the top seam heading. We owned no metal curtain rods. The nails on either side of the windows served as anchorage. Mama would deftly wind the string around the nails, secure the ends, and adjust the gathers of the material. The three front windows facing the street had curtains that did not match. I asked Mama why they were not made of the same fabric and she replied, "I found these remnants on Orchard Street. True, they don't match, but such good *vareh* (fabric) and such a bargain — I couldn't resist." Little did Mama realize how stylish unmatched found objects (even from Orchard Street) would become in later years.

Mama always loved nature. In a rare moment of reckless economic abandonment, she impulsively bought a rubber plant. I fell in love with this only item of pure luxury in our apartment, lavishing all my attention upon it. Mama sensed how important the plant was to me and she put me in full charge of its care. I was proud to have this honor and vowed to help my precious plant grow to the ceiling.

From the public library Mama took out a book specializing in the care and nourishment of houseplants. In it we found the chapter on rubber plants and I followed the directions faithfully, taking care not to overwater. Every day I gently brushed the leaves with a soft rag that I first dipped in a saucer of milk. Once a month I tenderly wiped a thin coat of castor oil on the leaves giving them a healthy sheen. I can still feel the sense of beauty this plant brought into my young life. To me it symbolized a green oasis that wiped out the harsh reality of the cement world outside.

Each year Papa brought home a calendar from his *landsmanshaft* organization, The Zaromber Young Men's Progressive Society. Mama hung this calendar prominently on the kitchen wall where we could all admire the change of seasons in the picture appropriate for each month. No valuable work of art had a more appreciative audience.

In this same kitchen, directly above the combination washtub and bathtub on legs (with its removable white enamel top) hung a cupboard with glass doors. Wooden strips divided the glass into eight-inch squares. One day on a trip to the local Woolworth store, I discovered and bought a package of "cockamamie" decals depicting colorful clusters of strawberries, cherries, green grapes, and apples. It was the week before Passover and Mama was busy with holiday preparations. When she was out marketing, I pasted one "cockamamie" in the middle of each glass panel. They gave the cupboard a cheerful Pennsylvania Dutch look. Mama was pleasantly surprised when she returned, and Papa and my sister Pearl loved the improvement. It brightened our *yontif* (holiday).

In a recent issue of a prestigious design magazine, I saw a layout of a home in Santa Fe, N.M. Its owners were noted collectors of folk art. Lo and behold, in full color there was a photograph of an old glass-paned hanging cupboard with clusters of strawberry, cherry, green grape and apple "cockamamies" pasted in the center of each pane. This was a collector's item! It looked exactly like the one we once had in our kitchen. Who knows? Maybe this was Mama's old cupboard.

All through her life, Mama's attitude toward acquisitions and possessions was minimalist. Over and over again she would remind us, "Things are only things and can be replaced. People are important." After reading the articles in the magazines, I excitedly told Mama that unbeknownst to her, she was ahead of her time, a real pioneer in decorating ideas. Isn't it nice to be first, to be important?" I asked her.

With a smile, she replied. "But it's more important to be nice." Mama understood minimalism in its purest form.

What's New at Watergate

Mama was not a television addict. However, she was glued to the TV set watching the Watergate spectacle unfold during Nixon's trial in 1973. For an immigrant coming to these shores, America is the "Land of the free and the home of the brave." A person fleeing from persecution feels very strongly about his adopted land.

Mama became deeply distressed while viewing the accusations and recriminations. As each witness testified, again and again she deplored the display of individual greed, the passion for power and the total lack of honor.

At one point in the Watergate hearings, John Dean III offered to take a polygraph lie detector test to prove that he was telling the truth to the Senate Investigating Committee. Mama asked me what this test entailed. I once read an article giving all the details on the operation of the test and I tried to explain what I read.

I told Mama that the suspect sits in a chair beside the instrument. A blood-pressure cuff similar to the one physicians use is wrapped around a suspect's left arm. This records his blood pressure and pulse. Next, a strip is attached to the palm of the right hand to record skin responses or increases and decreases in moisture. Last, two tubes are attached around the chest and stomach to measure the rate and depth of breathing. The devices record the body changes with pens that write on moving graph paper, hence the name polygraph, Greek for "writing much." Any sudden changes in heart rate, pressure, moisture and respiration (and these can be evoked by the emotions) are registered on the graph chart and interpreted by highly trained and skilled experts.

Mama tried to follow each step carefully and at this point she said, "It seems to me if you are a heavy breather or a big *schvitzer* (a person who sweats a lot), you're in trouble. Do you know where they stole the basic idea for the lie detector test?" Mama caught me completely off guard.

"No, Mama, do you?" I asked.

"Of course," she answered. "While you were explaining the test, I figured out exactly where it came from."

I listened as Mama began. "Many many years ago, in a small *shtetl* in Russia there was a poor young rabbi and his class of *chedar bochers* (students). The class was overcrowded, the young rabbi underpaid and overworked, and to add to the daily problems, there was a *gonnif* (thief) among the students. Every day something else was missing, a pencil, a notebook, a few *groshen* (halfpennies). The rabbi tried his best to impress upon the class that it was sinful to steal. He promised that God would forgive the thief if the stolen articles were returned. This met with no success and the daily petty thefts continued.

"The rabbi was at his wit's end. He pleaded, he threatened and he cajoled. His pleas fell on deaf ears and the *gonnif* persisted in his sneaky and elusive ways. This made the rabbi more determined to find some way to catch the thief.

"All the students wore *yarmulkehs*. A *yarmulke* is also called a *hittlel* (hat). After a grueling day, the rabbi's voice was soft and droning. The class was lulled into a hushed quiet by the repetitive lessons.

"Suddenly, without warning, the rabbi shouted excitedly, '*Ahfen gonnif brent de hittel!*' (The thief's hat is burning and it is on fire!) Instinctively, without a moment's hesitation, the hands of one student flew up to his *yarmulkeh* and he furiously began to beat out the imaginary fire. The rabbi's lie detector test worked successfully and the culprit was finally caught.

"See," Mama explained, "That was the beginning of the lie detector test."

Mama Goes to an Art Auction

There are so many worthwhile causes today that it is difficult to say no to any of them. For several months I have been deluged with tickets to art auctions. The admission price and a percentage of the profits go to deserving organizations.

Mama came to spend a week with me and I bought two tickets. It was her very first art auction and she was filled with enthusiasm. We arrived early, earnestly looked at the exhibits and then sat down to await the auctioneer. Mama surprised me; she even liked the "modrin" paintings.

We were surrounded by a group of very talkative women. Mama and I sat quietly and listened and observed the ways of the experienced art auction ladies. Their conversation was sprinkled with avant-garde arty phrases such as: "soft sculpture is the 'in' thing," "pop art is on its way out" and "Andy Warhol is too campy." Mama's head bobbed left and right as she tried to make some sense out of what she overheard.

"What do they mean?" she asked me. "Art is 'in' and then 'out' and then Andy Warhol goes to camp? You should excuse me, I don't understand," she confided.

Most of the ladies were lovely and seemed very refined. One woman was outstanding. Physically, she stood out in all parts. And vocally, she was blessed with a set of lungs that Caruso would have envied.

All eyes and ears were the captive victims of her enormous presence. Without a doubt, she thought of herself as a *mayvin's mayvin*.

We'll call her Mrs. Schtultz. She talked about her extensive art collection and wasted no time telling everyone within earshot (about two blocks) that she was a collector of all types of objects d'art. She had a decorator and a dealer and they both traveled the world to shop for rare things for her.

When Mama heard this, she whispered to me, "*Nebech*, (alas) poor woman, she must be ill. She has to send other people to do her shopping. I hope she is able to do things for herself soon."

I answered, "I'll explain later, Mama."

Mrs. Schtultz launched into a lengthy explanation of how it took her dealer six years to compile a complete set of a dozen very rare glasses. This was the only remaining set in existence. It was priceless and was considered a museum treasure. She went on and on raving about the glasses ad nauseam.

The one thing Mama never developed was a tolerance for braggarts. Mama leaned over and whispered to me, "Nu, are you going to let her brag on and on? Think of some way to stop her."

I took the hint. I looked Mrs. Schtultz in the eye and told her, "I also have a very rare set of two dozen glasses. I believe they are the only complete and perfectly matched set in the country."

"Really, how interesting," Mrs. Schtultz said, noticing us for the first time. She started to fire questions at me in rapid succession. "Are they authenticated — what circa? Could they be French Baccarat or rare Russian cut stemware? Where did you obtain them? I must alert my dealer. Tell me, how did you collect them?"

With as straight a face as I could keep, I answered, "They cannot be amassed at once. They must be collected privately, year after year. They have a long history. They are called *Yortzeit* glasses."

Mama smiled and winked at me. I winked back!

Photo Sent To David, Marvin and Larry

Mama's Negative Advice

During World War II, American patriotism was at its height. The whole country was behind the war effort. We were convinced that this was definitely the war to end all wars. I was a young single girl living at home. Our family saved every penny we could spare to buy U.S. Savings Bonds. A $25 bond sold for $18.75. It was also de rigueur for those of us on the home front to write frequent letters to the servicemen. I did my part to keep up their morale by writing to several young men that I knew who were serving their country in the Armed Forces.

Night after night I sat glued to the kitchen table writing individual letters until the wee hours. One night Mama awakened and came into the kitchen. She asked, "It is past midnight and you are still writing to the whole U.S. Army? Your hand will become attached to the pen. Why do you have to write a different letter to each young man? It will take you half the time if you just write the same letter to all."

"But Mama," I protested, "it just doesn't seem right. Now they have each asked that I enclose my photograph in my next letter. I have to look for three different pictures to send."

Mama's voice echoed her exasperation. "A different letter, a different picture—next it will be a different stamp to each one. *Gottenu* (dear God) you are spending your whole life sitting at the kitchen table and writing."

At first I felt that if I followed her suggestion, it would somehow not be a personal response. However, the more I thought of it, the more logical Mama's advice seemed. Instead of going through the family photo album to choose three separate photos, I simply took one negative to the drug store and had three copies developed. I also mailed three identical hand-written letters to the three soldiers. It sure saved a lot of time.

David was in training as a paratrooper in the 101st Airborne Division in Fort Benning, Ga., Marvin was stationed with the 9th Infantry Division in Fort Bragg, N.C., and Larry was part of a regiment in North Africa. Because they were geographically situated so far apart, it seemed to be the reasonable way to correspond. Mama reminded me that inasmuch as I was not "going steady" with any of them, her suggestion was ethically acceptable.

Within a few weeks I received an answer and a thank you for the photo from David, I did not hear from Marvin or Larry for some time. Finally much to my astonishment, I received a joint letter signed by both Marvin and Larry. They explained that Marvin was transferred from Fort Bragg, N.C. to a division in North Africa. When Marvin reached North Africa, he found himself in a desert area. Suddenly he saw an U.S. jeep with a single GI riding towards him. The driver of the jeep called out, "Hi soldier, you look like you are trying to find your way. Can I help you?" Marvin was glad to see the American and showed him his transfer orders. The driver of the jeep smiled and said, "You've been assigned to my unit. Hop on and I'll take you there."

They became acquainted as the jeep rolled across the desert. After a while Marvin asked Larry, "Do you have a girl friend?"

Larry replied, "I'm corresponding with a nice girl back in the States."

Marvin said, "I'm corresponding with a nice girl too. In fact I received a letter from her just before I received my transfer orders. She sent a picture too. I have it right here in my pocket. Here, take a look." Larry looked at the photo. The jeep swerved and came to a halt. He unbuttoned the pocket on his jacket and took out the identical photo. The two soldiers compared letters. At this point they decided to send a joint letter to me.

The opening sentence read, "In the interest of saving postage, we are mailing one letter to you." I was crushed with embarrassment.

When the war ended Marvin and Larry returned to the States. They called me and insisted I join them for dinner to celebrate their safe return.

Luckily they both had a great sense of humor and we spent the evening regaling the theme "It's a small world."

I confessed to them that there was a third letter and photo sent at the same time. "If my luck holds out, it wouldn't surprise me, even at this late date, if you both meet up with David who may be carrying my faded photo in his wallet."

Mama apologized for getting me into this dilemma. She said, "It only proves that the wrong advice is no advice at all. It is written: 'silence is wisdom.'"

MAMA AS A SENIOR

Keeping Up with the Times and Speaking Out

Mama's senior citizens club in New York is a dynamic, active group, and it makes every effort to be up to date on the current scene. They go to the theater and to lecture series, and visit major museums as well as the avant-garde galleries in the So-Ho district.

On a recent So-Ho tour, club members were invited to observe a work-in-progress in the loft of a way-out artist. The senior citizens take great pride in their open-mindedness; but this artist was not to be believed. With dissonant music in the background, they watched in amazement as he strung clotheslines across the length of the loft. Then he unpacked a huge carton of large rolls of steel wool and deftly hung the steel wool over the lines in ribbon fashion.

The elderly onlookers were waiting to see what he would do after these preliminaries. Instead the artist stepped back and viewed his "completed composition" with unabashed delight. His one mistake was to ask the senior citizen group what their deep inner response was. He asked for honest raw feedback.

Mrs. Markowitz didn't hesitate a minute and said, "Being that you're asking for the truth, I'm telling. My deepest feelings on viewing your art are that it would be better if you took some of the steel wool off the line and used it to clean up your loft, it sure could use it." Her eyes lingered on the many areas she had in mind.

Mr. Levine spoke up next, "You should excuse me, but by me this is not art. Beethoven was deaf, but if he saw this, he would be better off blind."

The artist thanked the group for being so candid but he did not ask for further impressions.

A few weeks after the So-Ho Art gallery trip, Mr. Heller, the group supervisor announced that plans were made for the senior citizen club to spend an evening at Studio Two, a discotheque in New York. Mama said it was only 52 numbers away from Studio 54.

The ladies wore their best dresses and the men their *yontif* (holiday) suits. Even the bus waiting to transport them looked festive and gay with colorful streamers hanging from the pull cord. The ladies and gentlemen boarded the bus, sang Yiddish songs on the way, and pretty soon they were at their destination.

For over an hour they listened to the pulsating disco beat. Two members even tried a few steps. On the bus ride back, Mr. Heller, the supervisor asked for their comments. Again this was a mistake. They bombarded him with complaints. "Such a tumult, our ears are still throbbing. Not one waltz did they play. And the worst part, why don't they get a good electrician. Something is wrong with the lights, they keep going on and off and it keeps blinking in the eyes and makes the head dizzy. If this continues, our grandchildren will grow up in a D&D generation — deaf and dizzy!"

How to Grow Old Overnight

One year our family gathered together on Chanukah. We were seated around the dining room table and I offered a toast,"With God's help, in three years, we look forward to celebrating Mama's 80th birthday."

Mama said, "I really don't want any fuss made. When you reach the mid 70s, every day is a bonus. Life is too uncertain to plan so far ahead."

Still we all found it pleasant to contemplate this future milestone. "Mama," I said, *"a-hin un a-hare* (here and there), before you know it, three years slip quickly by."

A few days later I received a phone call from Mama. I could tell immediately from the tone of her voice that something was amiss. Mama unburdened herself, "The other day when you said, 'A-hin un a-hare,' three years slip quickly by, you didn't realize how right you were. In one telephone conversation I found out that for me the three years already slipped by."

She went on to explain, "I was the youngest of nine children. In Europe the father of the family usually had to take a horse and buggy and ride to the City Hall to register the birth of a child. We lived in a *dorf* (small village) and my father was busy with his *ge-sheft* (business) and didn't always find it convenient to take time off to travel to town for the registration. She went on to explain that with a new baby born practically every year, he waited and registered the births of two or three children in one trip. As time elapsed, he could not always accurately remember the exact date of birth, or even the exact year.

He vaguely recalled that one son was born around Purim, another daughter arrived near Rosh Hashanah and Mama came into this world on the eighth *lichtel* (candle) of Chanukah. So Mama never had a definite birth date. Whenever the eighth *lichtel* of Chanukah fell, that was the day.

Mama's voice was listless as she continued, "And this morning my niece F'ritzie called me and in the middle of the conversation she mentioned that she just reached a milestone birthday. I asked Fritzie, 'Which birthday did you reach? *Bis a hundert un tzvontsig yur?*' (until 120 years). She answered, 'I celebrated just half of what you wished me, 60 years.'"

"I couldn't believe my ears and said, 'Fritzie there must be some mistake. You could not be 60 years old. I remember I was 20 years old when my sister Molkeh gave birth to you.'"

Fritzie insisted, "But *Ton-teh* (aunt), I have my birth certificate and it is *ge-schribben* (written) in black and white, I'm 60."

There was a sigh, a long pause, and then Mama asked me, "Are you listening closely? So what you were planning for me in the future, already was! This means I'm 80 years old. *Eppes,* I feel older in my bones. Somehow three years crept up on me from nowhere. To lose years is far worse than to lose money. *Nu,* so what is there to say?"

A thought occurred to me, and I answered, "But Mama, on the other hand you don't have a birth certificate to prove you are actually 80. Who knows, you may even be three years younger than you think. Your father had a hazy memory for dates and he may not have listed you as the youngest. Perhaps he reversed the order. Your sister Lena claims to be 74 and you know you are at least three years younger than she is. You were the baby in the family."

Mama's spirits brightened as she ended our chat with, "That's life, you lose three years and you gain three years, all in one day!"

Notes on A New York Blackout

The day is Tuesday, July 12, the time is 6:45 A.M. On his way to work, my dear friend and neighbor, Bill, gives me an early ride to Mama's apartment in New York. We arrive at 7:30 A.M. In order to make marketing easier for Mama, I am laden with food and Bill is kind enough to help carry the packages to Mama's apartment. We ring the bell and Mama opens the many locks on her door to admit us.

She is happy to see Bill and turns to greet me with: "Here comes my big food importer from New Jersey. I can open a grocery store with all that merchandise. Why do you bring so much? I'm not living in a wilderness. Why do you buy enough for a month?" she questions.

I put the food away. The perishables: cheese, butter, fruit and vegetables barely fit into her refrigerator; and the chicken and chopped meat squeeze tightly into her freezer. The freezer door closes with a *krechtz* (groan).

I answer Mama, "For the greatest efficiency, you should not have to go to the market so often. Make a list and write down what you need before you run out of an item. Then you will always have a good supply."

Mama waves her hand, "Efficient, schmicient, so what is so terrible if I run out of a potato or an onion and I go to the market every day? It is only a few blocks away, and picking out onions and potatoes by the vegetable department is as good a place to meet and greet friends as a fancy golf club. Instead of conversation over a golf cart, it's schmoozing over a shopping cart!"

It is pouring outdoors, but Mama and I spend a cheerful, delightful day. She cooks lentil soup and then compote made with blueberries, cherries and peaches, all fresh. Her tiny apartment is filled with familiar heavenly odors. I sit contentedly drinking it all in while feeling like I'm floating back in time.

Mama senses my mood and soon we are reminiscing. I love to listen as Mama turns back the years and asks, "Do you remember when we lived several blocks away from the ice-making plant? Can you ever forget the exciting big leak?"

I hadn't thought of it in years, but suddenly I remembered the event clearly. One evening there was a serious ammonia leak in the plant and the policemen knocked on everyone's door and instructed us to open all the windows wide to prevent the possibility of an explosion. They were concerned about the accumulation of combustible chemicals and air in close quarters. A half-hour later the policemen were back again directing us to close all windows tightly. This complete reversal hardly inspired our confidence and we were really scared.

Our next door neighbors, Mr. and Mrs. Pearlman came to stay with us. "We feel safer here," they explained. Mrs. Mindel Pearlman was a highly emotional woman and she was frightened lest the ammonia fumes seep into her lungs. The brightest immediate future she could envision was instant death. "It would be a pleasure," she said, looking like a fearful fawn, "compared to choking to death for hours." She prattled on nonstop, predicting doom and gloom, her voice getting shrill and tight.

Mama tried to calm her by saying, "I'm sure everything will soon be back to normal." Mindel didn't hear a word Mama said.

She sat down on Papa's chair, started to wring her hands, and called out loud and clear, "I'm planning to faint." Mr. Pearlman started to fan her face with a book.

Mama and I ran into the kitchen, tore off a *shmot-teh* (rag) from an old, clean sheet, and quickly dipped it in water and lots of vinegar. We ran back and tied it around Mrs. Pearlman's head. She seemed to perk up. Perhaps the vinegar was so strong, it helped her forget the ammonia.

Though her husband was unaware of it, Mrs. Pearlman was considerably older than he was. She had illusions of being the eternal coquette and fashioned herself after Clara Bow, the "It" (sex appeal) girl of the silver screen.

I can still remember how Mr. Pearlman would tease and say, "My Mindel is my *hitz* (hot) girl."

She tried to wear her hair like Clara Bow in a fashionable frizz, only on Mindel it turned out to be a maze of messy knots and snarls. Unlike most other woman of the era, she wore heavy cosmetics and dyed her hair pitch black. Yet she always modestly swore that she was a natural beauty.

Thriftiness was one of her outstanding traits, and she probably bought the cheapest hair dye. For years Papa claimed he was sure she *schmeered* (spread) black stove polish on her hair. Our family used to laugh at Papa's private joke.

However, Mama and I didn't laugh when we removed the *shmot-teh* from Mrs. Pearlman's head two hours later when the police announced the emergency was over.

We were astonished to see that the *shmot-teh* had turned black and the roots of her hair were gray. Mama instinctively pressed her fingers to her lips and motioned to me to say nothing. When we were in the kitchen Mama whispered, "We both learned a lesson today. The truth is not always black and white. There is a lot of gray in between!"

Soon, much too soon, the day is over and it is 5:30 P.M. I kiss Mama goodbye and meet Bill downstairs for the trip home to New Jersey. At 9:30 P.M., my husband and I watch the news on TV when suddenly the picture flickers and blurs.

Assuming that something is wrong with our erratic set, we turn off the TV, read, and go to sleep. The next day, Wednesday, July 13, 7:20 AM, I am preparing breakfast for my husband and turn on the radio for the early morning news. I learn about the blackout in New York and tell my husband. We are both worried about Mama. At 7:30 AM I call Mama and say, "I hope I didn't wake you. We just heard about the blackout and we're worried."

Mama answers in a cheerful voice, "What's to be worried? Sure there is a temporary emergency and I don't have electricity or water. How did I manage to get along all my young years in Europe without electricity? And believe me, I was stronger and healthier there than I am now. As for water, the ice cubes in my refrigerator melted and I saved it for drinking. So don't worry, a person finds a way."

I called Mama several times during the day to see how she was faring. She answered that she was perfectly fine and chided me for making the telephone company rich.

That evening, my husband came home from the office and was anxious to speak to Mama. He called her and asked, "Mama, how are you doing in the big dark city?"

She replied, "Another call, this blackout is going to make multi millionaires out of the telephone company. Everyone is making such a *tzimmes* (fuss). People should have more patience. Too many comforts make people soft and spoiled. And speaking about soft and spoiled, I had to throw out most of the food your wife brought yesterday. I'm reminded of a saying my own mother, may she rest in peace, often said many years ago in Russia: "*Meh ken nit far-sorgin vus s'vet zine morgan.* (One cannot provide for everything that tomorrow may bring)."

Mama Finds a Worm in the Big Apple

Mama lived alone in New York City. Her small apartment overlooked the East River Drive and she often joked about living in *Der Gray-ser Eppel* (The Big Apple). Luxuries were not part of Mama's life and she never had or longed for them. But it was always important to her to live in a place with a view.

When we were children Mama had a choice. For $12 a month rent, she could have had a steam heated apartment in the rear facing a dreary courtyard and endless clotheslines. Or she could have picked a front apartment a few blocks away with a coal stove and a view of Corlears Hook Park and the East River. She chose the view and often told Papa, "I'm a lucky woman. Making the stove everyday is a small price to pay for the joy of looking out the front windows and seeing the beautiful East River and the trees blooming in the park, and especially watching the seasons change."

All year long we witnessed an ever-changing flotilla of large and small boats passing languorously by. Whenever company came, Mama always invited them to "share my lovely view." It was one of her treasured possessions.

Mama moved to a high rise in New York with essentlially the same view. Often, when I visited her we would sit by her front window and talk. We felt close to the gentle rhythms and strong currents of the river. It remained a familiar, deeply etched part of our lives.

I was always concerned about her safety for there were several incidents and robberies in her neighborhood and some of the senior citizens had been the innocent victims. Mama knew I worried and she tried to reassure me, "Life itself is a great risk. There is no such place as a safe area. Sure, a person should try to be careful, but it helps if a person has *mazel*."

I'll always remember this story Mama told me that day. "I'll tell you something now I wasn't going to tell you, but my neighbor was with me when it happened, and she is blabbing the story to everyone. I didn't want you should hear it from someone else and get scared."

"What happened?" I asked, trying to appear calm.

Mama cleared her throat. "I went with Fanny Pincus to hear a concert given by the retired members of the New York Philharmonic. On the way home we were waiting for the Clinton Street bus when a big man ran over to me and grabbed my purse from my arm and started to run away.

"Fanny was so upset, she nearly fainted. I told her I was grateful he didn't hurt me. The man started to run across the street with my purse when he realized he was right in front of the Clinton Street Police Station. Just at that moment the policemen were changing shifts and were coming out of the station.

"Oy, did my purse *gonnif* turn around fast. He didn't want to get caught with the evidence. Fanny and I were still waiting for the bus. Like a flash, he came quickly towards me and he slipped my purse back on my arm."

I sat glued to the chair listening to Mama relate this frightening experience in a cool, calm voice. "Mama, what did you do then?" I asked, alarmed.

She replied with a wry smile, "*Nu*, I'm asking you, what would any *mensh* do in a similar situation? I simply said, 'Thank you,' and you'll never believe it, he answered 'You're welcome!'"

My concern for Mama's safety did not leave me for a minute. The following day I called her very early in the morning. There was no answer.

I called her every hour and still could not get her on the phone. The purse-snatching incident triggered many frightening thoughts that I tried to repress. Noontime I decided to take a bus into New York. I had *shpil-kehs* (anxiety) and I simply had to see Mama to convince myself that she was well.

I reached Mama's apartment and rang the bell. There was no answer. I have a duplicate set of her keys and I opened the door half-fearing to find foul play. My imagination was running rampant and I tried hard to quiet my pounding heart. I found Mama's sewing machine open and several embroidery and crocheting projects carefully layed out. A book of Yiddish poetry with a worn bookmark was resting on a chair nearby. Everything seemed serene but Mama was nowhere in sight.

I knocked on a neighbor's door and asked Mrs. Singer if she had seen Mama. Mrs. Singer fastened her loose fitting chenille robe over her ample bosom and said, "What's today? Today is Tuesday. It's Mama's busy day. I'm sure you'll find her at the Senior Center."

I hastened to the Center and asked the lady in the office where I could find Mama. She pointed to an activity room.

My eyes focused on a large sign over the door, "Senior Exercise Class," and underneath in bold capital letters: STRETCH AND KVETCH!

I entered quietly and stood to the side. In the second row I spotted Mama, face aglow, rotating her arms like an airplane propeller. She was so engrossed she didn't notice me. A professional leader demonstrated and instructed in rhyme:

"If arthritis lingers. Shake your fingers.

"Loosen your fists. Limber your wrists.

"Elbows tight? Pull them upright!

"Higher, Higher, it's a *mechaieh.*

"Shoulders ache? Roll them awake.

"Stretch today. Throw your liniment away.

"*Pah-mel-ech* (No Haste). Bend at the waist.

"Be my guest. Breathe in. Fill your chest.

"Your knees crack? Lift each one up and back.

"Flex your hips, side to side. Feel alive.

"Do it well. We'll all *qvell.*

"Wear a smile, a happy face.

"Give the world a warm embrace.

"Remember to relax. Let it all hang loose."

Mama was surprised and happy to see me. She asked what I was doing there. I explained I could not reach her on the phone and became *meshugge* worrying about her safety.

She introduced me to the exercise instructor and said, "Tell my daughter not to be so afraid. When we are through with our exercise program we will be in such good shape, the muggers will not bother us."

Mama took me under the arm, "Now let's walk back to my apartment. We'll have a bite to eat and sit by the front window and share the view!"

Lillian and Mama

The Search for a Poem for Mama

Several years ago, Drew University in Madison, New Jersey held a conference that lasted all day. It was titled, "The Holocaust and the Book: Destruction and Preservation." It was a memorable event. The keynote speaker was Dina Abramowicz, the extraordinary research librarian at the YIVO Institute for Jewish Research in New York City.

At the time, Abramowicz was 88 and still actively working. She practically held the entire contents of the YIVO library in her head and was a walking encyclopedia. Scholars called her "the source" because of the help she rendered with historical and biographical information.

As I listened to this remarkable woman speak, I felt privileged and connected to her on a personal level. She had helped me bring pleasure to my Mama.

The year was 1974. I was sitting with Mama on her favorite bench in Corlears Hook Park on New York City's Lower East Side. It was a lovely day, made even lovelier by Mama reminiscing about her life as a young girl newly arrived in America. She lived with her sister Mollkeh and family.

Several weeks later, her other sister, Lena who lived nearby, treated Mama to her first Yiddish stage-show. Mama fell madly in love with the Yiddish Theater. As soon as she landed her first job, Mama scrimped and saved a little from each paycheck until she could afford to buy the least expensive ticket for a seat in the top balcony. Sitting way up high did not diminish her enjoyment.

Joseph Buloff became one of her favorite actors. He was a star of the famous Vilna troupe before he reached America, where he became a giant on the Yiddish stage. (There is a Joseph Buloff Yiddish archive at Harvard University's Judaica library in Cambridge, Ma.).

Mama was particularly impressed with a poem Buloff recited at a benefit performance. It was titled "Times Square" and told of a new immigrant being overwhelmed by New York City's frenzied hustle and bustle. The poem's measured staccato beat echoed a ticking clock. "Times Square, Times Square, people rushing *a hin un a hare* (here and there)."

Mama loved the poem because it truly reflected her feelings. Although many years had gone by, she still remembered how special this poem was to her.

Mama told me she tried to find it in the poetry section of the Seward Park Library. She asked the librarian for help and told her she knew only the title of the poem, "Times Square." The librarian shook her head and told Mama she could not trace the poem without the author's name.

Mama looked at me and said, "It would give me such pleasure to read it"

I blithely replied, "Mama, I'm going to find it for you." Little did I realize that this was more easily said than done.

During the next few days I called every Jewish publishing house in New York and Philadelphia. Each time I was told that it was like looking for a needle in a haystack. One young man said he knew Joseph Buloff's New York home address and suggested I write to him and ask for a copy.

I immediately wrote the letter. Much to my delight, within a week I received a handwritten reply from the noted actor. He wrote: "Dear Mrs. Bressman, 'Times Square' is a poem by Mr. David Krivitzki. It isn't any more in my program of readings, nor do I know whether it was published. If you ever get hold of it, please let me know where. I'd like to have a copy of it myself. Years back I carried the thing in my memory together with the other 482 pieces of my repertoire and was not in the mood of saving the original or the adaptations. It really is a pity, and then again, who if not your mother would ever remember that. Blessed be your mother. Sincerely, Joseph Buloff."

After reading his letter I was more determined than ever to find the poem. Suddenly a thought came to me. Why not contact YIVO?

I called and asked for the librarian and was connected to Dina Abramowicz. She answered in a gentle voice, colored by an Eastern European accent: "May I help you?" she asked.

I started to tell her about my search. Before I could say another word, she said, "Please hold on just a minute." In less than a minute she was back on the phone. "Hello, hello, I have it right here. If you would be kind enough to send me 10 cents for a Xerox copy in a stamped self-addressed envelope, I'll mail it to you."

I replied, "Thank you, thank you. I'll send 20 cents. Can you mail two copies to me?"

"Of course, of course," she replied.

Both copies arrived in a few days. I gave one to Mama and she was delighted.

I mailed the other copy to Joseph Buloff, who wrote and thanked me for my successful search. At the conclusion of the letter he wrote, "Most of all, I was deeply touched by the efforts a daughter made simply to bring pleasure to her mother."

Dina Abramowicz made it possible.

Linking the Past and the Present Together

My mother was taken to the hospital for some tests. At the time my grandson was six years old and he asked me, "Is the 'other *Bubbeh*' (a name he gave to my mother, his great-grandmother) going to die?"

I answered, "She is 94 years old and very frail and has lived a long life."

"And then, will she just disappear—just not be here anymore?" His questioning eyes sought mine. "How are we going to remember her?" he beseeched.

I told him, "We shall always remember her special kindness. She was a person who cared deeply for the less fortunate, whether it was a poor child or a coal-miner stricken with black lung disease. Although times were bad, she somehow managed to scrape together some money to give to the needy.

"We have so many loving memories," I continued. "We can always think of the many beautiful things she made especially for us, the handmade bedspreads, the pillows, mittens, socks, the clothes for your sister's dolls. She put love into every stitch and we can think of her each day when we see and touch the things she made for us with her own hands. We can treasure the wealth of wonderful stories she told us."

"I know," he answered in an unsure wavering voice. I sensed he still did not hear the explanation he needed to help him accept the eventual loss. We sat silently for a while.

"David," I said, taking his hand in mine. "The other *Bubbeh* will simply not disappear into thin air."

His expression brightened for the first time. "That's what I want to hear—that's what I want to hear—tell me how she will never disappear."

I explained to him, "I am part of the other *Bubbeh*, your mom is part of me, you are part of your mom, and your children will be part of you. A part of the other *Bubbeh* lives on through all of us and will live on in generations to come."

David smiled, squeezed my hand and said, "I feel so much better."

Mama died Oct. 23. Six years had gone by. She was 100 years old. Oh, how we'll miss her gentle sweetness, her total selflessness and love of song and poetry. Her presence will live within us.

My grandchildren and my daughter loved my mother deeply. At her funeral they honored her with the following eulogies:

"What I knew about other *Bubbeh* were all the wonderful stories about when she was a girl. My favorite story was about the pumpkins.

When she was about 4 years old, she wanted a baby brother or sister. Her father had been killed in a pogrom, she was the youngest child in her family. Her Mom told her babies grew in pumpkins and she went out into the pumpkin patch, and opened every one of them! I also was very lucky to have the other *Bubbeh* make such wonderful clothes for my dolls when I was little. She made me beautiful socks and mittens and hats. I know from my *Bubbeh* and my mother that the other *Bubbeh* was really a kind and special person. Each time I went to visit her, I felt lucky because it was like a little bit of her seeped into my heart—and now I'll carry a piece of her forever."

Marianna Rose Sackler, Age 9

"Each of us has a special memory of my great grand mother, the other *Bubbeh*. My favorite was the story of her arrival in New York City, moving in with her sister's family. The other *Bubbeh* was very eager to learn to speak, read and write English. She applied to go to school the first week that she was here. She was able to read and write in Russian, which is a phonetic language, where everything is spelled as it sounds. Her sister came with her and they both waited in line for registration. Her sister translated for her. When she gave her name, which was Rose Pinchik, to the lady at the desk, the woman asked her, "And how do you spell Pinchik?" My great grandmother was very upset when her sister asked her for the correct spelling. She said, "Maybe we should go to another school.

If the people here don't know how to spell, how can they teach me any-thing?"

The other *Bubbeh* went to school until she was in her seventies, taking courses to improve her English and to learn new things. Though very bright, she always had difficulty with spelling, because it was not like her first language, Russian. She never could understand why a word like "knife" was spelled with a "k". I guess my love of spelling comes from my other *Bubbeh*. I also know that in addition to the trouble with spelling we shared, I carry inside of me many of the wonderful qualities she possessed. I will miss her very much."

David Alex Sackler, Age 12

"She was 'Mama' to everyone who read the hundreds of stories written about her. She was indeed that kind, wise, warm woman whose abounding sense of humor helped all of us view our lives with the proper perspective. She was that woman, and she was more. She was *Bubbeh* to me and the other *Bubbeh* to my children. As a child I spent some of my school vacations with her. I watched curiously as we made our way from the butcher to the vegetable store, from the fish market to the fabric store (her very favorite). We went to her "club", she took me to her school (she was always taking courses) and we spent hours in her apartment. It was not filled with toys or games, but I was never bored there. In that apartment were stories which spoke of times long ago, her times; she was a child who had a keen awareness of family ties and love. She went to school with the boys—why shouldn't a girl learn how to read? Those 16 years in Grodna Gubernia provided a wealth of stories that became an integral part of my life and the lives of my children. How would she want us to remember her? She was a woman who loved poetry and music and was sensitive to the plight of the poor and the downtrodden. Throughout her life, she helped in nursing homes and hospitals. She could be found in protest marches throughout New York City, helping fight a variety of injustices.

Proud of her citzenship in this country, she marched, she always voted, and she even wrote letters to presidents.

What we have left are the extraordinary riches of the times shared with her, her wisdom, her love and her kindness. We also have the remarkable collection of Afghans, mittens, socks, pillows, and dolls' clothing, which she knitted and crocheted. They are filled with beautiful, vibrant colors— a symbol of how she viewed life. They are also filled with the love she infused in each stitch. They are the tangible gifts from one generation to the next. Her spirit is in them. As a grandchild wears a pair of gloves or a great-grandchild a pair of mittens, or when my grandchildren will wear the hand-made socks I have saved for them, *Bubbeh* will be there—a part of us always."

Beth B. Sackler

REMINISCENCES OF CHILDHOOD

Don't Bank at a Savings and Loan

When a scandal revealing the shady and deplorable dealings of the savings and loan associations and the subsequent closing of some banks became public knowledge, I recalled another era when public confidence in our banking system was badly shaken. In 1933, our country was in the throes of the Depression and our economy still had not recovered from the 1929 stock market crash. Newspaper headlines read, "Banks going broke!" Depositors hearing and reading these threatening predictions flocked to the banks to withdraw their money, thus creating a run on the banks.

Mama and Papa also decided to take their total life savings out of the local branch of the U.S. Savings Bank on the Lower East Side of New York. I was a little girl and I found myself standing on a long line outside the bank clinging to Mama and Papa's hands as they stood flanking me on either side. Never will I forget the look of panic on my parents' faces as an officer of the bank came to the heavy front entrance door and solemnly announced, "President Franklin Delano Roosevelt has just declared a bank holiday. All banks are officially closed, there will be no withdrawals."

We walked home in total silence. When we reached our little apartment Papa blinked hard to hold back the tears. Mama looked straight into Papa's moist eyes and told him, "Better to lose the money to the bank than to use it for doctors. There is nothing we can do about the bank and *oyss essen de kishkehs* (eating our guts out) will not help."

229

They were resigned to never seeing their savings again. Their faith in the American banking system was completely shattered.

Approximately five days later, President Roosevelt declared the bank holiday over; banks were reopened and deposits were safe. Mama and Papa figured it was *gefunen-eh gelt* (found money) and their confidence in American institutions was restored.

Papa's joy was unrestrained. "Let's celebrate our good fortune by going to the Yiddish Theater," he exclaimed with a big smile all over his face.

His favorite humorist, Michel Rosenberg, was appearing at the Second Avenue Theater in New York. Rosenberg was also a fine actor and his greatest gift was his ability to transmit to the audience the inner feelings and insecurities of the immigrant trying to adjust to the vast and mysterious land of America.

Rosenberg came onstage and was greeted with warm applause. Quite by coincidence, he started to regale the audience with a topical monologue on the plight of an immigrant's unfortunate experience with a bank in America. Michel assumed the role of a poor put-upon husband named Getzel. "My whole life I kept my money safe under my mattress," Getzel lamented. "I could lay my hands on it whenever I wanted. I could count it over and over and over. Suddenly my wife started to nag without a stop. 'Getzel,' she warned, 'in America it's dangerous to keep money in the house hidden under the mattress. Yesterday I read in the paper that just a few blocks from us there was a robbery in an apartment house and the burglars took $1,000 in cash from under the mattress. The lady of the house barely escaped with her life. Listen to me, Getzel, take our money out from under the mattress and put it in the bank.'

"My missus did not stop nagging for a minute and I weakened. I took my whole savings, $65 cash, and brought it to the bank. And instead of money, real live money, I got in return *eppes a* green little book inside a yellow envelope—and that's all.

"When I saw this, my heart fell. First I was suspicious of the young snip of a cashier behind the window who took my money. A thought flashed through my mind. What will I do if he takes my money and runs away? I was unhappy with the whole situation. I panicked and ran to the window and yelled to the young cashier. 'Hey, I just gave you $65.'

"He answered, 'So what do you want?'

"'I don't want you to be such a wise guy,' I said.

"He answered, 'Mister, I gave you a book, that's all'

"'That's all,' I screamed. I could see I was in the hands of a bloodsucker. 'Give me back my money,' I begged.

"He answered, 'Mister, it's impossible.'

"I hollered, 'I'll give you an impossible. *A schvartz yur,* (a black year) you should have. Give me back my money before I call the police, before I scream.' When he heard the racket I made in the bank, his manner got a little softer. He explained to me that he could not give me back my money right away. I must wait two weeks and that's the rule that was written in the book. I'm shocked that in such a short time I could turn over to a total stranger such a large sum of money, my entire savings. I went home with the little book and a heavy heart.

"The whole night I had nightmares that the bank was robbed and emptied of every cent. When daylight came I ran to the bank and waited for the bank to open. I rushed in and demanded to see the president of the bank. I told him Mr. President, things are shaky, I dreamed all night that our bank was robbed.

"He replied, 'don't worry, my bank will not be robbed.'

"I asked him, 'How can you be so sure. Frankly, this bank does not seem to be built strong enough and the bars on the windows are so thin and weak looking. As a depositor, I'm telling you right now, if you will not rebuild this bank and make it more secure by putting in heavier and wider bars at the window, you will have to give me back my money.' The president saw he was dealing with no fool and he arranged for the cashier to give me back my money. And as luck would have it, on my way home on the trolley, a pickpocket stole it all. Now do you know why I say 'never, never again will I trust a bank in America!'"

Mama, Papa, my sister and I laughed all through the monologue. We had just gone through a narrow escape with the bank closing and the fact that our money was safe added to our joy and appreciation.

A number of collapsed savings and loan associations held auctions to liquidate their outrageous expenditures. The defunct banks were hoping to realize some revenue from the sale of these objects to reduce their overall debt. The president of a bank in Texas had a huge antique French bed installed in a hidden suite behind the executive conference room. It was for his private use only. He often meditated and took catnaps there before important meetings.

Now the depositors in this bank who lost their money would have welcomed Getzel's advice. If only the Texas bank President had put the bank's money under the huge antique French mattress, the money would be secure, the deposits safe and the bank solvent!

Written Treasures from a Childhood Long Ago

After living in the same house for 38 years, my husband and I moved to an apartment. I am a sentimental saver by nature, and I valiantly tried to unclutter the myriad books, journals, old love letters, theater programs, photo albums, etc.

Tucked way back in a bottom drawer I found two of my school autograph books, one from sixth grade and one from ninth grade. I started to leaf through the small 4" x 6" sixth grade album. It is a small book with a faded "Autographs" printed on the cover above an illustration of a quill pen. The first page depicted the quill dipped in an inkwell under the following saying: "To keep my friends is my delight, so in this book I pray you'll write."

My heart warmed when I turned the page and saw my mother's and father's beloved handwriting. They inscribed their good wishes in Yiddish, although they could both read and write English. I remember Mama telling me, "In Yiddish, feelings flow right out of the heart and do not have to be sifted through a strainer to come out in another language."

The next page was pale pink and inscribed with best wishes from my sister Pearl. She wrote, "I love you a lot. Please forget me not." I haven't.

I was a skinny 11 year-old. I was unaware of boys and they were not even remotely aware of me. The next entry on a yellow page puzzled me. 'Lillian is a buttercup, Lillian is a daisy, Lillian is a girl who drives the boys crazy! In the parlor there were three: Lillian, the Lights and He. Two are company. Three is a crowd. That is why the lights went out."

At that period in my life I knew the lights went out only when you didn't pay your bill to the Consolidated Electric Company.

The following page offered some strange advice from my friend Esther Tessler, a meek girl who hardly spoke above a whisper. She wrote: "When you are in the kitchen drinking tea, burn your lips and think of me."

Yetta Gottlieb, the class snob, wrote, "Bonheure" and signed in script, "Yvette." Overnight, from Yetta she became Yvette. Yetta eventually married a French artist. She later discovered he had been born and raised in Brooklyn and had acquired his beret and accent from a French cousin who lived with his family. I last heard that Yvette changed her name back to Yetta.

My cousin Lillie Ritz wrote: "Open the door, Open the gate. Here comes my cousin to graduate. Take the local, Take the express. Don't get off 'til you come to success." She signed it: "your sis gradu-8".

Another friend wrote: "May your happiness be as deep as the ocean, and light as the foam. May your life be as bright as the candles on Friday night."

I was amused to read the next entry, written way before women's liberation. "When you are married and your husband is cross, grab the broomstick and say 'I'm the Boss!'" Miriam Singer, the writer of the above, became a lawyer and later a judge. I feel sorry for any cross husbands who appeared before her bench.

In the ninth grade, I remember saving my pennies all term in order to buy the beautiful genuine leather autograph book displayed in Perlman's stationery store window. As I held it in my hand, I responded once again to the beauty and texture of the smooth padded leather with the gilt edges that glistened in the light. Embossed gold leaf flowers gave the book a luminous glow. On the inside cover I had written my graduation song.

Printed on the next page was the heading, "My Teachers." It listed all my teachers from the first through ninth grade. "Skipped" was written in for the second and fourth grades. I recalled bringing home a slip of paper from school telling Mama and Papa that I would be skipping a grade for the third time. Mama went to school and begged my teacher not to do so. "Please," Mama implored, "she is so small and skinny. I don't want her to be in the same class with all the older big and husky children. A few of them are real tough." The teacher respected Mama's concern and I was delighted to be promoted along with my friends.

The next page was sprinkled with silver glitter outlining "Mother and Father" in two entwined hearts. Again, Mama and Papa wrote their good wishes in Yiddish.

A special page was reserved for my music teacher, Mr. Walter Pheiffer. He signed: "To our little lady Lillian who brought joy to our class." Reading it now, I realized he didn't predict any great musical future for me or my violin playing. He was right.

On a happy note, Jennie Stein wrote: "Work a little, sing a little, whistle and be gay. Read a little, play a little and be busy every day. Talk a little, laugh a little and don't forget to pray. Be a bit of merry sunshine all the blessed day." Then she added. "I wish you a pushcart full of mazel," and concluded with "2 Sweet 2 B 4 Got 10" (Too sweet to be forgotten).

A shy boy who sat in the next row wrote: "Flowers may wither, flowers may die. Friends may forget you, but never will I. May you always be in a happy mood. May your life be like spaghetti, long and smooth."

A prophetic entry by Sol Gorden reads: "Roses are Red, Violets are Blue, Always remain a Kosher Jew. Be honest and kind, proud and true. This is the essence of being a Jew. As the ripples in the ocean follow the sea, so may God's blessings follow thee!" Sol became a rabbi.

When I turned the last leaf, a paper yellowed with age fell out of the album. I picked it up, unfolded it carefully, and found a message that Mama had slipped inside. She often clipped articles, sayings and poems and put them under my pillow, in my lunch bag, in my pockets or in my books to surprise and delight me. I read the note she tucked into the album. "Always remember, as you go through life, you cannot do a kindness too soon—for you never know how soon it will be too late!"

Uncle Itzhak

Looking for My Uncle Itzhak*'s* Picture

My mother's brother, Itzhak, was a handsome, distinguished looking man with perfect features, high cheekbones and a full white heard. Our grandparents never came to America, and my sister and I dearly loved our uncle who also served as our grandfather figure.

Uncle Itzhak visited our family frequently and always brought chocolate kisses wrapped in silver foil. He carried the kisses in his jacket pocket. They were often soft but always delicious. After having lunch with us one summer day, he decided to sit on a bench in the park across the street from our apartment. He loved fresh air and did not want to spend any time indoors while we helped Mama clear the dishes.

Later when we joined him in the park, Uncle Itzhak told us that he was taking a delicious *drimmel* (nap) while sitting on the bench. He was known for his ability to take instant naps at the drop of a hat.

When he awakened, he found a man next to him on the bench observing him intently. The man introduced himself. "My name is Abbo Ostrowsky and I am the head of the art school at the Educational Alliance. We use live models for our students and I've been looking for a handsome Jew with an interesting face. You would be absolutely perfect. Do you think you'd like the job of posing for our class of student artists?"

Uncle Itzhak was retired and had plenty of time. He was flattered to be offered this opportunity. "You don't have to do anything but relax and sit exactly as you did on the bench," Mr. Ostrowsky said. And he gave my uncle a slip of paper with the address of the Educational Alliance on East Broadway in New York with the date and time of day to report to the art studio.

Uncle Itzhak told us of this stroke of good fortune. We congratulated him and wished him well in his new career. Papa teased, "Hoo ha, a professional model in our *mishpocheh* (family). Maybe it wi1 1 lead to a *moom pick-cheh* (moving picture) contract in Hollywood."

Itzhak had second thoughts, *"Efsher* (maybe) I shouldn't have told you anything about this whole business."

"No, no," we assured him. "We are so excited."

We made him promise to keep us informed of his new career. He promised.

Itzhak reported to the art studio as directed. Abbo Ostrowsky introduced him to the class and directed him to sit in a chair placed in the middle of the room. The students sat at their easels encircling him. My uncle liked the strong smell of paint and turpentine and in no time he was blissfully enjoying a *drimmel* (nap). He drifted in and out of sleep throughout the session. At the end of the afternoon, Abbo Ostrowsky put his hand on Itzhak's shoulder and gently awakened him.

"Just as I thought," he said, "you were perfect, here is your pay. We pay by the hour."

Itzhak was an Orthodox Jew and he shook his head. "I cannot accept any pay. I know I fell asleep on the job."

Ostrowsky pushed the little yellow envelope into my uncle's pocket. "That is exactly what we want, a relaxed model, asleep in a chair." Itzhak posed, and slept, for the next few years. Meanwhile the budding artists were capturing his likeness on their canvases.

I came across an article in the *New Jersey Jewish News* entitled, "Painting a Place in America: Jewish Artists in New York 1900-1945." The subtitle was, "Exhibit Chronicles Work of 50 Jewish American Artists." The article, a tribute to the Educational Alliance Art School described an exhibit to be held at the New York Historical Society and traced the experiences of Jewish American artists. This exhibit was organized to honor to the 100th anniversary of the Educational Alliance.

Ostrowsky's class of young struggling artists included such famous names as: Peter Blume, Ilya Bolotowsky, Adolph Gottlieb, William Gropper, Chaim Gross, Louise Nevelson, Mark Rothko, Ben Shahn, Moses and Raphael Soyer, Abraham Walkowitz and Max Weber.

After I read the article, I could not rest. I knew my uncle was the subject of many of their paintings. How wonderful it would be to find his portrait hanging in a museum. My husband and I went to The New York Historical Society. I searched each painting and read every word of the letters and memorabilia, and carefully examined the photographs exhibited in a special case.

They did have a photograph of a bearded man sitting and posing, but alas it was not my uncle Itzhak. I was crestfallen and told the docent at the museum of my futile search.

She told me, "Don't be discouraged. Just because you did not find him in this exhibit does not mean there are not countless paintings of him in private collections and in museums here and abroad. We have only a smattering of the body of work these artists produced."

I haven't given up. Every time I visit a museum I search for my uncle Itzhak.

In my wildest dream I think of him in the Louvre looking so relaxed while *khopping a drimmel* (taking a nap) next to a Rembrandt.

Mama, Lillian and Pearl

Surprises Deemed Hazardous to Health

I was discussing with Mama the elaborate birthday parties that are in fashion today. We had just witnessed a TV news segment showing an elegant birthday party (catered and with all the trimmings) given in honor of a five-year-old girl.

I told Mama about a father who rented the Orange Bowl Football Stadium and invited hundreds of guests to celebrate his young son's birthday.

Mama was aghast and asked, "What do these young people have to look forward to?"

She turned to me and seriously said, "When you were growing up, we made very little *tsim-mes* (fuss) with birthdays. We hoped, with God's help, you were growing older and wiser each year and that was enough celebration."

I asked, "Mama, do you remember the first birthday party I had?" Mama smiled and replied, "How could I forget?"

We both recalled that special day. My sister Pearl was secretly planning to make a surprise sweet-sixteen party for me.

She managed to obtain two free tickets from the Henry Street Settlement to an all-Russian concert at Carnegie Hall and gave them to me as my birthday present. Knowing how Mama loved Russian music, I invited Mama to the concert.

This was exactly what Pearl had planned, as she wanted us both out of the house so she could orchestrate the whole party herself. Mama was in on the secret and Pearl instructed her to get me back home immediately after the concert.

As soon as we left for Carnegie Hall, Pearl whipped out the decorations she had carefully hidden and started to hang the crepe paper across the ceiling of the whole apartment allowing for graceful loops anchored with thumb tacks.

Then she blew up the balloons, tied them with strings and attached them to the crepe paper. Pearl was skilled in creating a festive background with a lot of imagination and little money. She buzzed around setting up the party refreshments.

Years ago, party refreshments consisted of pretzels, potato chips, Indian nuts, silver wrapped chocolate kisses, Dixie cups, a few bottles of soda, and Mama's home made cookies. A cup cake and candle served as a birthday cake.

Of course, an elaborate party with no budgetary restrictions might also have included Tootsie rolls, Mary Janes, twists, Milky Ways, jelly beans and jelly fishes (assorted colors and flavors), chocolate covered raisins and chocolate covered peanuts. However, Pearl's budget did not allow for these gourmet items.

Pearl didn't have to be concerned about the guests parking their cars in front of our tenement, thus arousing my suspicion and spoiling my surprise. The guests never had dreams of owning a car nor did any of their parents. All the guests, five boys and four girls, lived on our block and they were sworn to keep the surprise a secret.

Meanwhile, Mama and I reached Carnegie Hall in plenty of time to climb the steps to the top balcony. We sat down, breathless, and started to fan ourselves with our programs.

At the end of the first part of the presentation the curtain came down to enthusiastic applause and it was time for intermission.

Mama usually liked to stretch her legs and mill around observing the other concertgoers. She always searched and sometimes found a friend or relative. That invariably led to a happy exchange of hugging and kissing.

As soon as the curtain was lowered and the house lights turned on, I started to get up from my seat. Mama quickly pulled me back into my seat and said, "Sit, don't get up."

She had a strained expression on her face and I had no idea what was to follow. She reached into her pocket and pulled out a carefully folded page from the Jewish Daily Forward, the Bintel Brief page, and started to read to me a sad letter sent to the editor.

It told of a 16-year-old-girl and her older sister. The older sister wanted to plan an unusual surprise for her younger sister and she took her to an airport and onto an airplane on the pretext of showing her what the inside of an airplane looked like. Years ago hardly anybody flew or saw the inside of an airplane.

The letter further said that the big sister had purchased an airplane ride for her younger sister as a birthday surprise. It was a short ride from LaGuardia Airport to Philadelphia. An aunt and uncle were to meet her at the Philadelphia airport. She did not have enough money to pay the fare for two airplane rides, so she sneaked out and left her younger sister sitting strapped in the seat and the plane took off. What started out as a prank became a tragedy.

As the plane started to ascend, the younger sister was panic-stricken and felt the earth leaving her. Instead of being surprised, she went into a severe state of shock and lost her speech and remained completely mute.

The older sister was the writer of the letter to the Bintel Brief and she implored the readers to benefit from her unfortunate experience and never, but never, plan a surprise for anyone.

Mama finished reading, folded the paper and put it back in her pocket. I was puzzled, but just then the lights were dimmed and the curtain went up on the second and final presentation.

At the end of the concert we trudged down the many flights of steps. As soon as we were outside, Mama took my both hands in hers, looked in my face and said, "Think about the story I read to you at intermission." The words seemed to tumble out, "I don't want the same thing to happen to you. Pearl is making a sweet sixteen party for you when we get home. I really didn't want to spoil your surprise, but even more I didn't want to take the slightest risk that you might become *schtum* (mute). Please forgive me, try to understand my concern, and please try at least to act surprised."

I found Mama's worries amusing and I told her I understood how she felt and I would try to do my best to act surprised.

"Don't overdo it," she warned. She hugged me right outside of Carnegie Hall and said, "Oy, you can't imagine how relieved I am."

When we returned to the apartment, everything was very quiet. Knowing what I knew, it sounded to me like a loud quietness. Mama was at my side as I unlocked the door. Before I finished with the key, Pearl opened the door and a resounding "Happy Birthday" filled the hall.

I acted as I thought a surprised person should act and went on to thoroughly enjoy the party.

Pearl was flushed with excitement and said, "It sure went smoothly, without a hitch and nobody spilled the beans."

My friend Tillie jumped up and down happily and exclaimed, "Boy, you should know how many times I almost said something to give it away. For the past few days I've been going around repeating to myself, 'Tillie, don't let your lip slip.' But nobody could fool me, I know you were really surprised!" I could not look Tillie in the eye. Somehow my glance landed below the bridge of her nose and I tried to smile reassuringly.

Pearl never knew that I knew. When she reads this article, she'll truly be surprised. On the other hand, that letter to the Bintel Brief still lingers with me and I think it best to take Pearl to a concert at Carnegie Hall beforehand and prepare her gently at intermission time!

Games Children Played

"Mommy, I have nothing to do. I'm bored." That's a social condition that has flowered and come into full bloom within the past 20 years. Young, unsure mothers over-react to this syndrome by signing their kids up for everything in sight in order to fill the empty hours with meaningful play.

Professional structured play and instruction has become a thriving, lucrative business. Children are chauffeured from one frenzied activity to another, like products on a conveyor belt. It is not unusual for one child to be enrolled in "Creative Movement," "The Art of Self-Defense," "Expressive Dramatics" and "Do Your Thing with String—Macrame."

I am seriously thinking of offering a crash course in "Just Daydreaming," a retreat for battle fatigued, weary, over-structured children.

A few months ago I came across a classified ad in the newspaper under "Instruction — Young Girls," which offered a three-week, intensive workshop on how to beat your friends at jacks and ball. It was taught by "professionals." My eyes were glued to the ad as my mind went back to my youth

I consider myself a professional jacks player, as I won the New York City Inter-Borough Jacks Contest for two successive years. I used to spend my summers practicing for the tournament. Mama frowned upon this and said if I spent as much effort and time practicing my violin, Jascha Heifetz would have cause for concern.

The first year I became jacks champ, Parks Commissioner Robert Moses ceremoniously fastened the winner's medal around my neck. I wore it constantly, slept in it and never took it off. One day I was in the bathtub and Mama came in to wash my back. The jacks medal slipped to one side of the chain and Mama was horrified to see a big greenish circle on my skin where the medal always rested. Soap and water could not remove it. Finally, Mama took out the Rokeach scouring powder and vigorously scrubbed it off.

From that day on, the medal stayed in the dresser drawer. The following year I once again prepared to go to the final elimination of the jacks contest. Mama remembered and said, "If you win again and Parks commissioner Moses places a moldy medal on you, politely tell him that not only does he keep the parks green, but your skin, too!"

We needed no lessons in the art of self-defense—it came naturally. If someone hit you, you hit back. This could also be classified under "Creative Movement."

If you wanted to learn how to embroider or sew, you simply watched Mama. She would bite off a piece of thread with her teeth and hand it to you with a strip of *schmattah* (rag) to practice on.

As for doing our thing with string, we spent lots of time playing cat's cradle. All you needed was a piece of string and a partner. Now, with private macrame lessons, youngsters learn how to create with string at $10 a lesson.

The younger children were busy jumping rope. The more advanced jumped double dutch, two ropes going at once.

We also enjoyed playing hopscotch, a game which required a good potsy made out of a piece of flattened tin can, or an old rubber heel from a shoe.

We utilized our natural resources, mainly the street. We played boxball; no waiting for tennis courts, no expensive equipment necessary. You needed a good ball, a sidewalk with a crack in the middle, and the palm of your hand. If you learned to slice the ball with the side of your hand, you were a pro. "Hit the Penny with the Ball" was another game that could be played by two kids on the same sidewalk court. We'd put the penny on the middle crack, stand behind the box line and try to bounce the ball on the penny; one point for every hit; five points for a turnover; 21 points to win. It wasn't very complicated; however, extra pennies were not always available, so the game depended on the financial solvency of the players.

Usually someone had a popular song sheet and we'd sing for many happy hours until our voices were hoarse. If our singing disturbed Mrs.

Rosen, she would matter-of-factly throw a brown paper bag filled with water out of her fifth-floor window. Her aim was deadly accurate.

Somehow, rumor got around that silver paper peeled from chewing gum wrappers and Hershey kisses and shaped into a tight ball would eventually be worth a lot of money. We diligently saved and shaped every scrap, yet I never met anyone who became rich this way. We also hoarded rubber bands and made balls out of them. It took a long time, but the result was a lively, high bouncing ball.

Membership cards were not required for our exclusive swim club. One of the older boys had a wrench, and on hot, sunny days he would simply open the cap of a fire hydrant. All the kids on the block seemed to crawl out of every crevice to romp and enjoy the refreshing coolness of the surging water.

When we were not playing games, we could be found at the candy store. It was not easy to make a decision. Just when you felt you couldn't live without the licorice, you spotted the sugar babies and the colored candy buttons on paper sitting next to the icing candy on the little fluted tin dish. You learned to spend your penny wisely.

An exciting afternoon and a very special treat was watching the moving men hoist a blanket-wrapped piano up on ropes to the top floor of an apartment house. We were wide-eyed with excitement each time the piano teetered and was laboriously pulled up another floor. Mama warned us not to stand too close by and to watch from across the street. "If you are too near and the piano should fall, you will be a head shorter," she'd say.

The days flew by. I haven't even mentioned ringoleevio, caddy or hide-and-seek. Just going downstairs to the front stoop offered myriad unknown unplanned pleasures.

It never occurred to us to whine, "Mommy, I have nothing to do, I'm bored." And in case someone had, the answer would have been a calm and firm *Gay klop kup in vont*! (Go hit your head against the wall.) I wouldn't be surprised at all if someone offered a training course in this skill!

New Clothes for the Holidays

Holidays are nice to anticipate and they also bring warm memories. This Passover brought me back to Pesach of yesteryear.

Weeks before the holidays began, there was a growing excitement and bustling preparation. The house was scrubbed and scoured, and the pots, dishes and utensils were changed. Mama bought special cardboard at the market and every surface in the kitchen was covered with the cardboard.

Special metal covers were placed on top of the gas range burners. The walls smelled of fresh paint and the floors sparkled with new "oilcloth" (linoleum). Even the janitor caught the *yuntif* spirit and spruced up the halls of the apartment house and shined the rows of mailboxes in the vestibule entry.

Mama sang sad Russian love songs (usually about unrequited love) while she sewed special holiday dresses for us. I can still hear the foot treadle on her Singer sewing machine rhythmically going far into the night. This was also the season we trekked to the shoe store for new shoes that were usually black patent leather and squeaky.

My mother-in-law had seven children, four boys and three girls. In between her busy preparation for the Seder, my husband recalls his beloved mother carefully going over her children's clothes and deciding who would inherit the hand-me-downs. The younger sister would suddenly grow into the older sister's spring coat and the younger brother was now just right for a suit that had grown too short in the sleeves and legs for the older brother. Not only was this economically sound, it was an economic necessity. However, this did present an insurmountable problem that was loudly protested by the younger siblings. The oldest brother and sister were the recipients of all the new clothes (which they wisely outgrew) while the younger ones were always the right size for the hand-me-downs.

Little sister Ruth often lamented, "No matter how hard I try, I'll never ever get to be the oldest!" To date, no one has figured out the solution to this problem.

Each year my mother-in-law gathered her brood of children for the annual Pesach clothes-shopping trip. If she bought a suit for the eldest son, her three younger sons eyed it approvingly or disapprovingly knowing full well that this suit would eventually be theirs. When sister Birdie was trying on a holiday outfit, sisters Sally and Ruth looked on with avid and vocal interest.

The salesman used every psychological ploy to convince the young man that the suit he was trying on (or the dress the young lady was trying on) was the most beautiful and most becoming in the world. He depended upon the children to pressure and intimidate their parents into buying, not denying. If there was a split second of indecision, the fitter would swiftly appear.

It was common practice for the store fitter to gather an ill-fitting garment in the back and exclaim, "Fits perfect in the front, look in the mirror." When the customer turned around to see how it looked in the back the fitter deftly gathered the garment in the front, again exclaiming, "See, it fits perfect in the back too—like it was made to order!

My wise mother-in-law was very aware of the salesman's techniques. The more a child became enamored with an outfit he tried on, the higher the price. Money was tight and she instructed the children before taking them en masse to Mr. Chapkowitz's store on Prince Street. "Remember, if you try on something you like, never ever say you like it—try to keep quiet."

Of course, this was easier said than done. Once sister Birdie fell in love with a spring coat she was trying on. She remembered her mother's advice and jumped up and down excitedly exclaiming, "I hate it, I hate it, please buy it for me!"

However, with some unexpected *hondlen* (bargaining) by the purchaser and a compromise by the salesman who invariably said, "I swear I'm losing money on this sale, I'm giving it to you below cost because my heart won't let this child walk out of this store without this suit. He looks so handsome in it so I'm willing to sacrifice my whole profit. He should *trug gezunter hait* (wear it in good health)." Thus the sale was consummated and the lucky child greeted the holiday with *yuntif* clothes.

Nitpicking Not Always Simple

I was listening to the news recently and heard the newscaster say in a solemn voice: "There is an epidemic of" nits in the New York City schools." He advised parents to pay careful attention to their children's hair hygiene. All these years I thought nits were wiped out. I didn't even consider them an endangered species. I firmly believed they were extinct!

When I heard the newscast, my mind flashed back to my first day at Girl's Junior High School. I was eleven years old and the youngest girl in my class. Somehow I felt that junior high school was the entrance to the adult world.

The upper classmen directed us newcomers to our classrooms. They all offered one bit of advice, "Just pray you don't get Miss Colt for gym. We warn you, she is the meanest, strictest teacher alive."

I started to pray in my desk chair. We were handed our period schedule and when I got to the gym, my worst fears were confirmed. I was assigned to her class for a whole year.

Miss Colt was a masculine looking lady with a clipped boy's bob. She did not walk, she strode, and she issued orders from the side of her mouth. She informed us that she was aware of her reputation in the school and she planned to live up to it.

"First order of business," she barked, "line up in alphabetical order for hair inspection. If there is one thing I detest, it's long hair, and should I find any nits in a girl's hair, that student will have to get a short, short haircut."

My maiden name was Bernstein, and I was second in line. The girl in front of me had short hair and Miss Colt gave her a cursory inspection and an O.K.

She looked at my long curls and I saw a mean gleam in her eyes. From her gym suit pocket she took out a wooden tongue depressor and used it to go through every strand of hair on my head. Looking straight at me, she snarled, "Before I get through with you, you'll have to get a crewcut."

I could feel my heart throbbing with fright. Then I thought, just my luck, my name had to start with a "B", and the whole class lined up behind me will be a witness if she finds something. What a humiliating way to enter the adult world. How I longed to be Zelda Zimmerman and last on line!

Usually the entire class was done with hair inspection in one period. Forty-five minutes later the bell rang and Miss Colt was still examining my hair. She said, "I'm not through yet; tomorrow I will resume with you."

I ran all the way home from school and told Mama my fate. This cruel teacher was determined to scalp me and she threatened me with a crewcut. Mama listened carefully and said, "Meanwhile, stop *shuckling* (shaking). She didn't say she'd chop off your head, only your hair."

She took my hand and gently led me to the bedroom. The sun was shining brightly on the bed. She sat down on the bed and put my head on her lap, carefully looked through my hair and said, "You tell Miss Colt, in a polite way, if she finds a nit, she must pull the hair out and show it to you."

Mama felt very confident because she always washed my hair with Fels Naphtha soap and never neglected to put a few drops of kerosene in the last rinse. A thorough combing with a special fine comb followed the shampoo. She reassured me, "Your hair and scalp are perfectly clean, don't worry." I tried to follow Mama's advice, but it was hard to stop worrying.

The next day Miss Colt was waiting for me with the tongue depressor and a big flashlight. I could see the entire class watching as she started her exploration. With a sinking feeling, I took stock of my situation and realized that my fate, whether triumph or catastrophe, hung by a hair.

Again, the whole 45-minute period was taken up with my head. Finally exhausted, Miss Colt asked, "Who washes and keeps your hair so clean?" I told her. Miss Colt continued, "Tell your mother she deserves a medal. You are my first failure. Usually when I look; I find."

After school I rushed home and joyously shouted, "My hair is saved! Miss Colt got a bolt!" Mama was happy but my sister Pearl was on the verge of tears. I asked her what was the matter.

She replied, "I hate to spoil your happiness, but something terrible happened to me at Fanny's candy store today."

The neighborhood candy store used to sell 'picks.' For a penny you could pick from a box of chocolate covered candy with creme filling. It was ordinary if it had white cream inside. But if it had pink cream inside, you had picked a winner. And the winner was entitled to a prize consisting of a five-cent Baby Ruth or a five-cent Hershey Bar. My sister Pearl had the uncanny knack of picking only winners. She won the respect of many of her peers for possessing this special gift. They all agreed she was born with special perception.

Pearl didn't admit or deny this, she simply enjoyed the attention it brought her. I would implore her to tell me her secret, but she would not reveal the source of her powers.

Pearl told me that on her way home from school that afternoon she stopped to buy a "pick" and Fanny, the candy store lady, informed her she would not allow her to buy any more "picks." Fanny complained bitterly, "You win all the time, you pick every winner, and I'm left with a stale box of losers."

Pearl was inconsolable, she was in a bind. Finally, she confided in me, "All is not lost. I'll tell you the secret if you promise to share the winnings with me."

I promised and with great difficulty, Pearl plumbed her inner soul and divulged that the chocolate covering the pink winners had a tiny extra swirl that was barely discernible to the naked eye. She warned me, "Pick a loser now and then so Fanny will not excommunicate you too!"

I went downstairs to the candy store and came back with a Baby Ruth for Pearl. Her face lit up. Her magic continued to work through me.

Looking back, I can say that things worked out with the nits and the picks.

The Advantage of Being Poor

Kidnapping is a frightening word, especially to a child. When I was a young girl in elementary school, the kidnapping of the Lindbergh baby shocked the world. The newspapers printed daily articles and we all huddled around our Bosch radio listening to the latest developments.

The details of the baby being put to sleep in his crib safely at night and our visualizing a stranger placing a ladder up to the window and abducting the innocent sleeping child sent shivers down our backs. Scary beyond words was the image of terror striking in such peaceful, protective home surroundings. Our whole family felt personally involved and we prayed for the baby's safe return. When it was thought that the baby boy's body had been found, we suffered a profound sense of loss.

Mama and Papa were deeply saddened and kept repeating, "How inhuman, how heartless, what is more treasured by a parent than a child. And to have a child torn from your life is the worst tragedy that can happen."

The headlines continued for months. No one felt safe with the kidnapper at large. At long last, a man named Bruno Hauptmann was arrested and accused of the kidnapping. Finally, he came to trial, which seemed to drag on endlessly. We read every word of testimony and our lives continued to be closely entwined in this tragic event.

I remember being little, skinny and scared. In my child's mind I figured that my parents were the most precious part of my life. If the most treasured part of a parent's life, a baby, could be stolen, why could it not happen in reverse?

Sometimes I would awaken at night and look out of the window of my room to make sure there was no ladder leaning against my parent's window. Other times I would dream my parents were being held for ransom.

It was at this point that I decided to do something to help insure their safety. After saving up five pennies, I went to the local Woolworth and bought a small package of hook and eye latches for the windows and door of my parent's bedroom. I hid the package under my pillow. The following day, Saturday, my parents and sister went out to sit in the park to get some *frisheh luft* (fresh air). I invaded Papa's toolbox and proceeded (with great effort) to affix the spindly hooks and eyes to the two windows and door of Mama and Papa's bedroom.

After many attempts and numerous holes bored into the wood, I finally half succeeded in getting the hooks to almost meet the eyes. My childish plan was to secure the windows so they could not be opened and to lock the outside of my parent's door after they went to sleep. I felt these precautions would keep them safe from an abductor. In reality the tiny hooks and eyes were so fragile and shaky, a hearty sneeze could have pried them loose.

When Mama, Papa and sister Pearl came upstairs, Mama busied herself preparing supper. She went to her bedroom to get an apron from the dresser drawer. When she reached the door and saw all the holes and the spindly hook and eyes, she asked Papa, "Benny what do you make of this? Our bedroom door looks like a piece of swiss cheese with some tiny sick looking hook and eye *kaytloch* (latches). Who put them on? Wait until the landlady sees the holes in the wood. She will *plotz* (burst)."

As she walked into the bedroom, the glaring rows of holes in the window frames greeted her eyes. Mama called to Papa, "Come here, look at this mess."

Papa looked, shrugged his shoulders and replied, "We must have a woodpecker in the house!"

I stepped forward and, in an excited, high-pitched voice, I explained my mission in guarding them and protecting them from a would-be kidnapper. "Mama and Papa," I blurted out, "You are so dear to me, I cannot risk your being taken away from me."

Mama and Papa didn't laugh. They were touched by my childish concern. Papa took my hand and led me to a kitchen chair and carefully explained to me that there was no history of a poor person being kidnapped for ransom because a person without a lot of money simply did not have a ransom to pay. In a soft, gentle way, Mama and Papa convinced me that in our financial circumstances, I had absolutely nothing to fear.

Mama reassured me that there were not too many advantages to being poor, but we had just discovered one!

Family Summers on Farms

At Tante Fraydels'

I shall always remember the summer we spent on my Tante Fraydel's farm in Lakewood, N.J. It was a lovely but very rural farm. The toilet was outdoors in an outhouse, and the chicken coops were not far from the house.

Tante Fraydel had three children. They all helped with the endless farm chores. We helped, too, with whatever chores had to be done.

One of her sons, my cousin Yonkel, was ten years old as was I. Yonkel was a bright, hard working boy who had a sweet tooth for candy. His mother, Fraydel, was a health faddist who believed in feeding her family natural and fresh grown products. She was convinced that candy was unhealthy and merely ruined the appetite for nutritious food. As a result, Yonkel rarely had a piece of candy, which only made it more *geh-shmahk* (deliciously tempting) to him.

We arrived at the farm on a muggy summer day. Mama brought practical gifts for Tante Fraydel, Uncle David and family. Knowing Yonkel's longing for sweets, Mama could not resist bringing a box of Whitman's chocolate covered fruit and nut candy. Mama asked Fraydel to please make an exception to the "no candy" rule because fruits and nuts were high in food value. Right in front of our eyes, cousin Yonkel devoured half of the box of candy before his mother could make a decision. He hardly bothered to chew, he simply swallowed.

That night, before retiring, Mama took out a box of Chocolate Ex-Lax. In those days it was commonly believed that it was necessary to take a laxative (to cleanse the system) whenever a person "changed the air" from the city to the country. My sister Pearl chewed and swallowed a piece in the bedroom. I took the contents of the Ex-Lax out of the box and brought it into the kitchen. I broke off one piece, chewed it, and drank some water. Absentmindedly, I left the remaining Ex-Lax on the kitchen table. The house was very still and everyone seemed to be asleep as I tiptoed into the bedroom.

Apparently cousin Yonkel came into the kitchen a little while later and saw the nice brown chocolate sitting on the table. Thinking it was candy; he ate every bit of it. Poor Yonkel, what he went through during the next 24 hours! To this day his taste for chocolate has never been the same.

Ordinsky's Farm

One year Mama and Papa scrimped and saved so we could rent a room for the summer at Ordinsky's Farm in Spring Valley, N.Y. To get away from the crowded city and hot pavements was a luxury for my parents, my sister Pearl and me.

The sum of $50 for the whole summer entitled us to one room in a four-room bungalow. The three remaining bedrooms were rented to three other lucky families. This price also included kitchen privileges in a large communal kitchen located in the main house. Mama was allotted the use of two burners on a stove, one half of a double sink, and one half of an icebox. Another family shared the other halves.

I can still recall the excitement we felt when Mama and Papa started to pack for our summer vacation. They packed with great skill. We all pitched in and somehow managed to squeeze our clothes, sheets, dishes, silverware, and *teppels* and *fendels* (pots and pans) into two bulging suitcases that looked like they were ready to burst. Just to make sure they did-n't split open; Papa tied a rope securely around each suitcase. We had no trouble identifying our luggage.

On July 1st we took the bus to the train station and Papa helped put our stuff on the train. He then stood on the platform and waved goodbye to us as the train pulled out. I started to cry, as it didn't seem right for him to go to the shop in the city while we were breathing fresh country air. Mama understood and assured me "Papa will be bringing his nose to the country every Friday and he will fill it with *frish-eh-luft* every weekend."

Mr. Ordinsky, the farmer-owner was a nice but overworked man who had to make the most of every minute of the season. His eyeglasses were always spotted with little white dots. I wondered how they got there until I observed him milking the cows and watched the "spritz" add new dots. He never bothered to clean them and probably went through life in a white polka-dotted haze.

Once a week the *shochet* (kosher slaughterer) came and killed the chickens to be used for food. My sister and I watched horrified as he slit the chicken's neck. We were sickened to see the partially decapitated chickens run a few wild steps (like a macabre dance) and then fall to the ground. We could not eat chicken for months

In sharp contrast to the current emphasis on 'being thin,' it was then fashionable to be pleasingly plump. A summer vacation was successful only if you 'fixed' yourself and gained weight. It was the exact opposite of our present day reducing spas. My sister Pearl was beautiful, round and plump with apple-red cheeks. I was very skinny and each summer Mama tried unsuccessfully to put a few pounds on me.

Because the nation was going through the Depression, Mr. Ordinsky was left with some vacant rooms. His sons posted bold signs on roadside stands advertising, "Ordinsky's Prices are Gentle — Big Bargains— Summer Rentals." In late July, with half the summer gone, he was still determined to fill his vacancies. When prospective tenants appeared, he showed them an available room. If the viewer hesitated at all, Ordinsky desperately pulled out all the stops in an effort to assure the rental.

He swiftly dashed to find my sister Pearl and then ran to fetch me. One day as we were swinging in a hammock, he dumped us over, grabbed our hands and towed us towards the customers. In a smooth, convincing voice and with a grand flourish he pointed to me and intoned, "You see this *dareh madeleh* (skinny little girl) *far-greent un far-gelt* (with the green and yellow complexion), she just arrived today. See what she looks like, *nebech* (the poor thing). Then he gestured with pride to my sister Pearl, pausing for effect and solemnly announced "She looked just as dried out as the skinny one when she arrived at the beginning of the season. She fixed herself and gained weight right here on my farm. Milk straight from the cow and unlimited *frish-eh-luft* (fresh air). I was Exhibit A (before) and my sister was Exhibit B (after). This strong visual presentation never failed to clinch the deal. By the first week in August all the rooms were rented.

Our days on the farm were a delightful contrast to our city life. Although Ordinsky was too busy to wipe his specs, he found time to help the children set up a small fenced in "maternity clinic." This area housed expectant chickens and ducks sitting on their eggs. We cared for them tenderly, made sure they had plenty of food and water and hovered over them like anxious midwives. It was a joyous day when the first baby duck pecked through the shell and stood up on shaky legs. We had our own pet chicks and ducks and we were determined to make a better world for them safe from the sinister *shochet*.

We also picked apples from the orchard and discovered that milk did not come in bottles. The cows seemed especially gentle and we knew them by name.

When Papa came by bus to spend the weekends with us we greeted his arrival with exciting news about the new baby chicks and ducklings and the newborn calf. I hated to see Papa leave on Sundays to go back to the city to work in the shop all week. I childishly dreamed that some magical year Papa would be able to stay with us all summer.

Across the road from the farm were many acres of undeveloped land leading to a beautiful large forest. Although Mama never had any sense of direction in the city, my sister and I were amazed at the built-in compass she possessed. She had absolute confidence when she took us into the deep reaches of the seemingly endless woods.

The winding entrance was covered with a dazzling mass of daisies. Mama always stopped to gather a bunch and then deftly wove daisy chain crowns. She fastened them around our heads and we felt especially regal in our coronets. The forest was deliciously green and we loved the quiet eloquence of the old tall trees. Their leaves provided welcome shade and shelter. Countless birds flew freely from branch to branch, providing music and living in harmony with the crickets and beetles.

We took deep breaths to inhale and savor the heady profusion of smells, more beautiful than any perfume. To see the sunlight dancing on a bed of green was like viewing a ballet of gossamer gold, with the shadows and light making exquisite patterns. Each trip to the forest was a glorious adventure. But most revealing of all was our new vision of Mama. Right before our eyes she seemed transformed into a graceful, agile and nimble forest nymph. My sister and I followed close by and watched wide-eyed. She underwent a complete metamorphosis and suddenly became a young girl at one with nature, a totally free spirit. She danced. She skipped. She knew all the wild flowers by name. She transmitted her joy to us.

Many summers and decades have passed since these recollections, but the pure enchantment of the sights, smells, feelings and treasured moments enfold me to this day.

'Sneps and Hooks on Ice'

Long ago I read something that has stayed with me like a haunting refrain. I quote, "The fields of memory are like a rich archeological site." The more you dig the more treasures you find. These memories of my Mama flow from a deep well of love.

Mama's favorite places to shop were fabric and wool stores. I loved to accompany her to the fabric store to search for a piece of *vareh* (fabric), or to the wool store for a piece of *vull* (wool).

Her small palm-held purse had two compartments and snapped open on top with two intertwined twisted snaps. It was filled with more scraps of cloth and strands of wool for "matching" than with money. The saleswoman knew exactly what Mama meant when she asked for "sneps and hooks on ice" (snaps and hooks and eyes). Mama had a sharp eye for "remlets" (remnants) sold at greatly reduced prices.

When she came home and unpacked her purchases, her creative juices started to bubble. Even the Singer sewing machine must have been in awe of Mama's talent for fashioning beautiful clothes for herself, my sister Pearl and me out of bits and pieces and trimmings. Her sense of color was remarkable. She used combinations of pinks, purples, reds and greens and a vibrant palette of mixed hues before it became fashionable to put them all together. When Mama found a fabulous piece of lace, she sewed it on the underside of the hem, giving the garment a custom made, couture detail. "Nobody can see the lace underneath," she said, holding up a skirt or dress, "but you know the lace is there. Things and deeds do not always have to be seen to be appreciated," she added, never missing an opportunity for a moral lesson. Somehow my sister and I did feel special knowing the lace was there.

Mama's sewing machine stood in front of the window (to catch the natural light). Our tiny apartment faced the East River and I would sit near Mama as I looked out of the window and watched the boats. The tugboats had smokestacks with a company initial on them. I saw an old tugboat with the initial "R" on the smokestack, and I wove a story about its cargo and destination.

"Mama," I said, "just imagine that boat is coming from Russia filled with treasures, embroidered velvets, satin ribbons and toys."

Mama looked up from her sewing for a fleeting moment and saw the old tugboat puffing smoke. She quickly brought me back to reality. "From Russia—carrying *tsatskes* [toys]—this old boat will be lucky to carry itself back to the dock! Enough day dreaming already. Don't sit with *leydik-eh hent* (empty hands)."

She handed me a little wooden spool with six small horseshoe shaped prongs and some thin wool. Soon she showed me how to make a rope and stitch it round in circles to make a rug.

Evicted!

The Good Old Days Were Not So Good

As far back as I can remember, two of the most dreaded words in the English vocabulary were boss and landlord. Relatives and friends would compare notes on who had the meanest boss or the tightest landlord.

We lived in a five-story walkup apartment house on The Lower East Side and Mr. and Mrs. Epstein, friends of my parents, lived in a similar apartment house down the street. Epstein was a frail, poetic and sensitive looking man. He was a strong liberal and a progressive thinker.

Epstein worked long hard hours as a presser in a garment factory. There were rumors that he suffered from tuberculosis and that the doctor recommended lots of rest and plenty of fresh air. For 12 long hours each day the only air he breathed in the dark, dank, dusty shop was mixed with the steam coming out of the pressing machine. How could Epstein rest when he had to support his four little children, Jake, Louis, Rosie and his youngest daughter, my little friend, Ida? (Ida was exactly my age. We shared the same birthday.)

It was a sad day indeed when they carried Epstein home from the shop. He had expired at work. The shop foreman found him slumped over his pressing machine. Mama wiped a tear from her eye and hoarsely whispered, "Now poor Epstein will get plenty of rest. The bosses squeezed every ounce of life out of him."

As was the custom then, the funeral service was held in the Epstein's tiny apartment. After the home service, family and friends walked behind the casket, which was placed in a slowly driven hearse.

I was a small child and this was the first funeral I witnessed. Still fresh in my mind is the intense feeling of fright that washed over me. "Oh God," I thought, "Please don't let my Papa die in the shop." (Papa was a skilled woodturner who slaved long hours in a shop).

For weeks after the funeral I waited anxiously for Papa to come home from work. I always breathed a sigh of relief when I heard his familiar footstep. As soon as he walked through the door I would run to him and shower him with hugs and kisses. I always had a *shissel* (pan) of hot water mixed with epsom salt ready and waiting for him.

Papa would sit down on a kitchen chair and I would unlace his high special support shoes and gently take off his socks. Papa would ease his swollen feet into the pail with a deep sigh of relief, saying, "Oy, this is a *mechaieh*" (pleasure*)*. When things get unbearable in the shop, when the nasty devil of a boss, Mr. Katz, is in a terrible mood, which is always, I think of my family, my wonderful wife and children and the warm welcome I get when I come home. This helps me get through the long hard day." It made me happy to help make Papa's day more tolerable.

Epstein's death made my Papa even dearer to me. I identified strongly with my little friend Ida, and felt truly sorry for her mother and bereaved family. Two weeks after Epstein died, I looked out of the front window and was shocked to see Mrs. Epstein and her four frightened children in the street. They were surrounded by a few old pieces of furniture: some spindly beds, an old dresser, a kitchen table and chairs, dishes piled high, scattered pots and pans and a broom and a mop leaning on the table.

Mrs. Epstein and her children, scared and bewildered, were huddling together. In those days there was no financial aid, Social Security or widows' pension available to needy families. The Epsteins were left penniless, and the ruthless landlady, Mrs. Mishkin had evicted the family because they could not pay the rent. The total for the month's rent amounted to $12.

1 called Mama to the window. Mama's normally rosy cheeks paled. She was astounded and said, "That landlady has a stone for a heart." Mama ran downstairs to see what she could do to help. Within a short time she organized a captain in each apartment house. By knocking on doors and explaining the great need to the tenants, they collected the necessary $12. The contributions were mostly nickels, a few dimes and one quarter. Mama contacted the landlady, gave her the money, and returned with the key to the Epstein apartment.

In no time at all the neighbors *schlepped* the stuff piled on the sidewalk up the stairs and into the tiny apartment. I helped by carrying small pots and pans. It felt good to see the family settled back in their apartment.

Many years later, by chance I met Louie Epstein. He was now a financially successful man. We talked about the "good old days" and he told me he still has nightmares about landladies and bosses.

Can't Find Your Way? You're in Good Company

If I were granted three wishes, I would wish for good health, peace for all mankind and a sense of direction. Secretly I yearn to wake up one morning and know East from West and North from South. Just let me loose, or simply let me turn a corner, and I'm sure to get lost. While I like to think I have a few of Mama's and Papa's better genes, I know for sure that I inherited this *far-blund-jet* (getting lost) factor from Mama. How she ever found her way to America is a miracle!

When I was a child, during school vacations and in the summertime Mama would take me to visit relatives in Brooklyn or to Coney Island for the day. My sister Pearl wisely begged off going on these wandering excursions.

Papa would give Mama directions. He had an instinctive and uncanny ability to find his way. I never remember Papa getting lost. He would go off to work and Mama and I would start brightly on the day's trip.

Invariably we would take the wrong trolley or make a wrong turn. Once we followed a large noisy crowd getting on a BMT train and we wound up in Times Square instead of Coney Island. Mama defended her reasoning, "After all, isn't it logical to think that they would all be going to Coney Island on such a hot summer day instead of Times Square?"

It was just like Mama to find a bright side to a situation as she commented "Think of all the interesting places we stumbled onto that were never near where we were heading." It reached a point where Mama would exclaim, "Oh, we are lost again, it's a shame for Papa to know.

We kept few secrets in our house, but I somehow was most discreet when Papa asked at suppertime, "Nu, did you and Mama have a nice trip to Coney Island?" I didn't see any point in giving details on how we took the wrong trains. We considered ourselves lucky to be able to retrace our steps (and trains) and find our way back home.

I was quite young when I realized that although I had the best Mama in the world, alas, she was born without a sense of direction. Not too long afterwards, I discovered I was afflicted as well. Once I asked Mama, "Why did God punish us so that we are always lost?"

A bemused smile crossed Mama's face as she replied, "Don't question God: He may say, "If you're so anxious for answers, come up here." She quickly added that this was a quote from the Talmud and had many interpretations.

As I grew older the condition did not change. For years I kept this dark secret to myself. When I married and moved to New Jersey, I took driving lessons. I had no problem in learning the physical aspects of driving.

At the start of the third lesson the instructor told me to drive Northeast. I looked at him blankly and begged him, "Please, do you mind saying left, right, or forwards or backwards?" He could see immediately what a hopelessly confused customer he had sitting beside him. I passed my driver's test, got my license-and then I was really in trouble. No longer was I lost on foot, by trolley or train, but in the driver's seat of a car! I found myself visiting places I never knew existed and rarely reaching the places I set out to find.

Such was my lot in life until two years ago when my eyes fell upon an article in the New York Times. I was convinced that fate was signaling help to me.

A lengthy article detailed the important research that was being done at Cornell University. They were extensively monitoring homing pigeons and migratory birds to determine what special gene they possessed that enabled them to have an exact sense of space and place. The research team banded the birds at their northern habitat. The birds flew south for the winter and always returned to their precise point of departure when spring came. After carefully checking the bandings, the researchers came to the conclusion that these birds had some form of built-in radar, a phenomenon they should try to isolate.

My excitement mounted as I read the article. I ran to get a pen and paper and wrote what was on my heavy heart for years. I wrote to the head of the program and asked him whether any similar research was being done on human beings. I gladly volunteered as a human guinea pig with visions of my legs being banded. I asked in the letter, "Did you ever consider creating a serum extracted from a homing bird to inject into constantly lost humans?" I mailed the letter with an expectant heart.

I was then co-chairman of the UJA Telethon and told my co-chairman, Charlotte, about the letter I just mailed. Charlotte is a biology professor. As I related the details of the letter, she· looked at me in utter disbelief.

"Do you know that the professor to whom you wrote is one of the world's leading scientists, a Nobel Prize winner?" She asked. "How do you ever have the *chutzpah* to write to this important man about your petty problem? You'll never get a reply. His secretary will throw your letter into·the wastebasket."

Frankly, I didn't know he was such a renowned man. Then again, I thought, aren't humans as important as pigeons? He could also spend some time on us. I didn't dare tell Charlotte my thoughts.

A few weeks later I received a lovely long letter from the professor. He wrote that he deeply sympathized with my problem and that I struck a responsive chord in his heart, as he too was the victim of this same syndrome. His letter continued: "Believe me, you have my empathy, but there is no research being done on human beings in this area. May I offer a suggestion that helps me and may help you? Whenever I am lost, I think of Albert Einstein who had absolutely no sense of direction and often had to be helped to find the way to his lab. This gives me great comfort."

Now when I am lost, I simply think of the great professor and Albert Einstein, and I know that I am in good company!

Recalling the Magical Moments of Movies

Years ago we didn't use the arty word "film" for a movie. We never heard anyone say they were going to the "cinema" or to see a "film." A movie was simply called a movie.

Most of our young friends usually went to the neighborhood Windsor Theatre on Saturday morning every week. Admission was ten cents. Our friends frequently took their lunch along and sat through two or three consecutive showings.

In addition to the movies, a new serial was shown each week. Often, the last scene showed the heroine tied to the railroad tracks by the villain. The tension reached unbearable heights when the sign "continued next week" flashed on the screen. All through the week our best friends talked about the last serial and counted the days until they would see the next week's episode.

Mama discouraged us from going to the movies. That only made my sister Pearl and me more eager to go. When we begged Mama to relent, she had a ready reply. "On a bright sunny day, to go sit in the dark and watch a movie, *meshugge* (crazy). With the beauty of nature all around us (pointing to the small public park across the street), the blue sky, the sun shining, it's a shame to waste such natural gifts." And, referring to the popular cowboy movies, she added, "What can you learn from a horse?"

Pearl and I waited for a rainy Saturday morning. We reminded Mama, "It's raining, can we go to the movies? Why don't you come with us?" we urged, hoping it would help.

Mama thought for a moment. "On such a miserable day, why *shlep* to the movies? It is pouring out, and even with an umbrella, we'll get drenched walking to the Windsor Theatre. Then we will have to sit in that dark movie with wet clothes clinging to our skin. For sure, we'll all wind up with 'pin-eh-moan-yeh' (pneumonia). It doesn't make sense to go out in such a heavy rain. Better yet, it is perfect weather to climb into my bed, under the soft fluffy *peh-reh-neh* and I will read Yente Telebende stories by B. Kovner to you and also some beautiful Yiddish poems. What a treat for all of us." Pearl and I didn't fully appreciate the "treat," but I remember we did enjoy listening to Mama read the Yente Telebende stories and the poetry. Of course, we would never admit this to Mama or to ourselves. But Mama did promise, "Maybe another day, when it's only drizzling lightly; not pouring."

We prayed hard for just such a day. Our prayers were answered one Saturday morning. We could not believe our good fortune when Mama looked out of the window and announced, "Today we are all going to the *moom pick-chehs* (moving pictures)." We were ready in a flash. Mama took a small bag along with fruit and home-baked cookies. While it drizzled, we walked happily to the Windsor Theatre hoping the weather would not clear. Pearl and I were afraid that if the sun peeked out we would have to turn back. Mama paid the admission and, much to our delight, she bought us a box of Jujubes and a chocolate Hershey candy bar. She was giving us the full treatment.

Once inside the movie, we tried to adjust our eyes to the black velvet darkness. All the seats appeared occupied. The usher's flashlight signaled us to three seats in the second row. We sat down and had to crane our necks. The screen looming close above us seemed enormous. We opened the box of Jujubes and the Hershey bar wrapper, trying to keep the crackling paper noise to a minimum.

I looked up and, suddenly, there on the screen, I saw a train rounding the bend of a track. The engineer was giving it full throttle and steam poured out of the engine. I was sure it was headed for the second row. I quickly grabbed Mama and Pearl's heads and pushed them down while I shouted, "Stop the train, stop the train!" I closed my eyes expecting the worst.

When I opened my eyes, I heard people all around us shushing me. One lady called out, "Little girl, be quiet, the train doesn't stop here." The opened box of Jujubes scattered all over the floor and the Hershey bar rested somewhere under some seat. I heard laughter and giggles.

Mama and Pearl were very kind. They sensed my embarrassment, straightened their tousled hair and whispered to me, "It's okay, the train looked like it was coming right over us from this close up. We were both scared too. If you didn't push us down, we would have pushed you down."

We all held hands and enjoyed the rest of the movie. It was great except we had three stiff necks the following day.

I asked Mama why I could not go to the movies every week with my friend Tillie Goldner. Mama frowned, "I suppose Tillie's mother didn't read the article in the Jewish Daily Forward written by Dr. Aigelmann, the famous eye specialist."

"What did he write, Mama?" I foolishly asked.

She answered, speaking very slowly to emphasize the point. "He wrote that children can go blind from looking at too many movies. And it can harm the vision of adults too! In fact, I saved the article and I must show it to Tillie's mother. She'll thank me."

I felt like a traitor and hoped Tillie never found out the source of this information.

To increase attendance, movie houses offered a bingo game in between the evening showings. One evening Tillie's mother won a "fortune" playing bingo. She held the "lucky winner" card and was called to the stage to collect twenty-five dollars in cash. She became a celebrity on our block, the only person we knew who was fleetingly "on stage."

I excitedly told Mama about Tillie's mother and suggested, "Why don't you go and play bingo. Maybe you'll be lucky too."

Mama's reply was quick and to the point. "Although twenty-five dollars is a nice sum of money, Mrs. Goldner will not wind up a winner. I showed her the article written by Dr. Aigelmann. She didn't take his advice so she'll probably end up spending all her winnings on the eye doctor. As a matter of fact, I met her in the kosher butcher store last Friday and I noticed her squinting. She couldn't tell a chicken from a turkey."

This was the era when movie houses offered a free dish with each admission. If you went every week for 52 weeks, you could collect a whole set of matched pressed glass dishes free. Pearl and I started our campaign, "Mama, just think, we could get a whole set of matched dishes free: 12 dinner plates, 12 salad plates, 12 soup bowls, 12 dessert plates, two serving platters and two serving bowls. Wouldn't it be beautiful if we opened our kitchen cupboard and saw a complete matched set just like it is displayed in the lobby of the Windsor Theatre? We could use the set only for company. Mama, we counted, it adds up to 52 pieces!"

Mama replied, "It's a high price to pay to sit in the dark for 52 straight weeks, a whole year. Who needs a matched set? I like to mix colors and designs."

Pearl looked at me and shrugged. Mama didn't buy this plan either.

If the weather is overcast and it is slightly drizzling, a Pavlovian response is triggered and I automatically think, "What a perfect day for the movies!" To this day, going to the movies has remained a treat. But childhood indoctrination has a deep, strong and lasting effect and in my whole life I have never been in a darkened movie on a sunny day.

The Power of a Cherished Memory

In Dr. Robert Coles' book *The Call of Stories,* the Harvard professor of psychiatry and medical humanities shows that parents, teachers and students learn some of their most lasting moral lessons from stories. This begins with stories read aloud in the family circle and continues through formal education and beyond.

In one chapter, "Looking Back," Coles states, "I'll see someone or I'll hear something and 'click' I'll have some personal memory come to mind, and I can't let go of it all and it all becomes part of me."

He continues, "A memory is an aspect of experience that lives in a particular mind. A recollected moment is a moment forceful enough, charged enough to survive other moments. Without such compelling memories, we are not ourselves, but rather anyone."

As I read Coles' words, so many memories came back to me. I recalled Mama urging us to treasure each moment. She frequently reminded us, "Today is a gift, that is why they call it the present."

Buying new shoes for the Jewish holidays is a memory I fondly recall. Our entire family went to the shoe store together. Mama may have scrimped and saved on other things, but she told the shoe salesman, "Only the very best for my two girls, only Dr. Posner's shoes you should show them."

I don't know where Dr. Posner got his doctor's degree, but by Mama he was a shoe specialist. Mama bought her own shoes in a bargain basement store, and only when they were on sale. This lesson was not lost on my sister Pearl and me.

Another special memory still evokes the love and joy I felt when I came home from school each day and was met by Mama's beautiful, smiling face. She welcomed me with a tender hug and a glass of milk. Two home-baked cookies were on the kitchen table waiting for me. Even the cookies looked happy. On each cookie Mama placed two raisins for the eyes, one for the nose and several raisins curved into a smiling mouth. I knew even then that no child in the world was as lucky as I was.

A friend recently asked me, "What memory do you especially cherish?"

The following memory washed over me like a soothing balm. I was about six years old at the time when I asked Mama, "Where do babies come from?"

She replied, "Babies grow in their mother's stomach and are part of her body."

When there was no school, and especially on rainy days, my sister Pearl and I snuggled with Mama under the *peh-reh-neh* as she read to us. She filled us with Sholom Aleichem stories, poetry and tales of Yenta Tellebendeh. Somehow, in my child's mind, I thought that if I came from my mother's body, I should be breathing in when she breathed in and breathing out when she did. As I snuggled close to Mama, I synchronized my breathing with hers. Many years later when I married, I found I instinctively adjusted my breathing to my husband's, for now we were one.

When my daughter was born, each day and every night I held her close and softly sang Yiddish lullabies to her. When she fell asleep on my shoulder, I lingered long before I put her in the crib. I was reluctant to relinquish the sheer deliciousness of her petal-soft cheek against mine. At such close moments, I found myself breathing in unison with my child. Again I thought, "I know I am the luckiest mother in the world."

When my granddaughter, Annie, was born, I slept in the same room with her for the first week of her life. I found myself synchronizing my breathing with hers. Although Annie was far removed from Mama's stomach, this gesture somehow forged a closer link with my precious granddaughter, my beloved daughter and my wonderful Mama.

Without cherishing and sharing these special moments that linger on as memories, we are as Coles says, "not ourselves, but rather anyone."